An Invitation

LUNCH
DINE
STAY
& VISIT

THE HEART OF ENGLAND

INNS, PUBS, HOTELS, RESTAURANTS

*Potted History of Areas, Exciting Attractions,
and places to Visit
Great Venues, Great Food and Comfort, Great Value*

By
JOY DAVID

'The book as a whole will not date: National Trust concur that
with their knowledge of a substantial proportion of the
hostelries, they rank the contents very highly
National Trust 'Oakleaves'

THE PERFECT COMPANION FOR LOCALS
& VISITORS, YOU CANNOT AFFORD TO BE
WITHOUT

The Editor, Joy David, wishes to thank the team for their enthusiasm, humour and hard work in helping to compile this book: Sue Dymock, Hilary Kent, Philomena Mclaughlin, Adrian Carey, Ann Naughton and Michelle Tebb. Particular thanks are given to Andrew 'Spud' Spedding.

Thanks are also given to
Emma Macleod-Johnstone, Andrea Rowe, Rose Kennedy and Graham Scott for all the drawings.

William Shakespeare

ISBN 1 873491-30-1
First published in 1992
Copyright Joy David
All rights reserved

Typeset, printed and bound in Great Britain by Troutbeck Press a subsidiary of R. Booth (Bookbinder) Ltd. Cornwall. Tel: (0326) 373226

CONTENTS

INCLUDES:

Guide Map   p.   4
Introduction   p.   6

WARWICKSHIRE & SHAKESPEARE COUNTRY
Chapter 1   Sights to see and places to visit   p. 10
            Venues in which to lunch, dine and stay   p. 40

THE WEST MIDLANDS AND BIRMINGHAM
Chapter 2   Sights to see and places to visit   p. 56
            Venues in which to lunch, dine and stay   p. 76

WORCESTERSHIRE
Chapter 3   Sights to see and places to visit   p. 100
            Venues in which to lunch, dine and stay   p. 121

HEREFORDSHIRE
Chapter 4   Sights to see and places to visit   p. 136
            Venues in which to lunch, dine and stay   p. 176

SOUTH SHROPSHIRE
Chapter 5   Sights to see and places to visit   p. 204
            Venues in which to lunch, dine and stay   p 235

NORTH SHROPSHIRE
Chapter 6   Sights to see and places to visit   p. 262
            Venues in which to lunch, dine and stay   p. 282

STAFFORDSHIRE AND THE POTTERIES
Chapter 7   Sights to see and places to visit   p. 298
            Venues in which to lunch, dine and stay   p. 324

Index of Place Names   p. 344

God made the wicked Grocer
For a mystery and a sign
That men might shun the awful shops
and go to inns to dine.

G.K. Chesterton

HEART OF ENGLAND

1. Warwickshire
2. West Midlands
3. Worcestershire
4. Herefordshire
5. South Shropshire
6. North Shropshire
7. Staffordshire

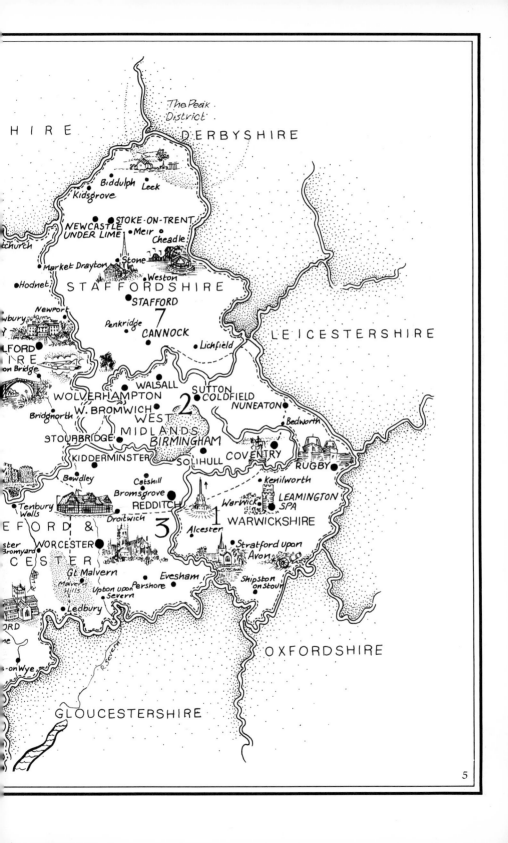

The Peak District

HIRE   DERBYSHIRE

Biddulph Leek
Kidsgrove

STOKE-ON-TRENT
NEWCASTLE Meir
UNDER LIME Cheadle

tchurch

Market Drayton Stone

Hodnet   Weston

STAFFORDSHIRE

Newport

bury   STAFFORD

y   Penkridge **7**

LFORD   CANNOCK

IRE   Lichfield   LEICESTERSHIRE

on Bridge

WALSALL   SUTTON
WOLVERHAMPTON   COLDFIELD   NUNEATON
W. BROMWICH   **2**
WEST   Bedworth
Bridgnorth   MIDLANDS
STOURBRIDGE   BIRMINGHAM
KIDDERMINSTER   SOLIHULL   COVENTRY
RUGBY
Bewdley   Catshill   Kenilworth
Bromsgrove   LEAMINGTON
Tenbury   REDDITCH   Warwick   SPA
Wells   **1**
Droitwich   **3**   WARWICKSHIRE
Alcester
ster   WORCESTER
Bromyard   Stratford upon
CESTER   Avon

Gt. Malvern   Evesham
Malvern   Shipston
Hills   Upton upon   Pershore   on Stour
Severn
Ledbury

RD

ne   OXFORDSHIRE
-on Wye

GLOUCESTERSHIRE

5

AN INVITATION TO
LUNCH, DINE, STAY & VISIT IN
THE HEART OF ENGLAND

INTRODUCTION

It was a family discussion about where we should go for lunch on the Sunday before Christmas that prompted the writing of this series of books. I thought we knew the local area well enough to make it a fairly simple choice but when it came down to brass tacks this was definitely not the case.

We did not mind whether it was an hotel, a restaurant or a good pub but with the gathering of the clan for the festive season, the group's demands were somewhat exacting. It had to be somewhere that children were welcome and grannies would not be out of place; the men wanted a decent pint of Real Ale and to be well fed. Log fires, old beams, and a good malt Scotch were added to the List with the request for provision of some kind of activity after lunch to help one's system limber up for the annual Christmas gorge. Either a scenic walk near the venue if the weather was kind or an indoor entertainment if it were not, and to add to this ever growing list of requirements, one of our number was a vegetarian!

Having got together all the ingredients that were required to make a successful outing the question still remained unanswered, Where?

We dug out old newspapers, looked through Yellow Pages but not once did we discover, listed, the information that we sought. Finally we did find a super pub, had an excellent lunch and walked along the banks of the river enjoying a matchless December day; but what an effort!

This book has been designed to help you find easily a suitable establishment to answer your needs, whether it be for lunch, dinner, a stay or a visit. Some are simple down to earth pubs, others are more sophisticated but every venue has its own dedicated page which tells you exactly what you can expect in the way of food, the sort of establishment it is, the opening hours, if they take credit cards, have access for the disabled, if children are welcome, if there are letting rooms and finally if there is a garden.

The beginning of every chapter is devoted to what there is to do and see around the pubs, restaurants and hotels. Some places you will know, others may be new.

This is an all the year round book, as pertinent in summer as in winter. Useful to couples looking for somewhere different, for families and perhaps, a secretary wanting to find somewhere for her boss to take a visiting client.

I have tried to make sure there is something for everyone which is almost an impossibility but hope that readers will be kind enough to write to me and tell me about their favourite spots so that they can be included in the next edition.

Warwick Castle from Mill Lane

INCLUDES:

The Friendly Inn	*Frankton*	p. 40
The Gaydon Inn	*Gaydon*	p. 41
The Boars Head	*Hampton Lucy*	p. 42
The Gamecock	*Harbury*	p. 43
The Two Boats	*Long Itchington*	p. 44
The Sheaf and Sickle	*Long Lawford*	p. 45
The College Arms	*Lower Quinton*	p. 46
The Hollybush Inn	*Priors Marston*	p. 47
Jephson's Restaurant	*Royal Leamington Spa*	p. 48
The Leamington Rendezvous	*Royal Leamington Spa*	p. 49
The Oddfellows Restaurant	*Stratford upon Avon*	p. 50
Sorrento Restaurant	*Stratford upon Avon*	p. 51
The Cape of Good Hope	*Warwick*	p. 52
The Golden Cross Inn	*Wooten Wawen*	p. 53

'And must I wholly banish hence
These red and golden juices,
And pay my vows to Abstinence,
That pallidest of Muses?'
William Watson

WARWICKSHIRE AND SHAKESPEARE COUNTRY

'This other Eden, demi-paradise,
This fortress built by Nature for herself...'

Those lines from Richard II conjure up images of a rural idyll and doubtless the beautiful countryside around Stratford-Upon-Avon did much to inspire Warwickshire's most famous son. More than two centuries later, Shakespeare's affection for his native county was to be echoed in the words of the eminent novelist, Henry James, who described Warwickshire as 'The core and centre of the English world; midmost England, unmitigated England... the genius of pastoral Britain.' James was an American and his words have done much to encourage his fellow countrymen and women to visit this quintessentially English region. Although the late twentieth century has left it's mark with evidence of industrialisation, the construction of motorways and some of the less appealing manifestations of the intensive tourist industry, there is still much of the gentle grace and beauty beloved by both men; turn off the coach-laden main roads and one can enjoy pastoral scenery little changed since the Bard's day or, turning away from a modern shopping precinct, one can delight in architectural gems that would have been equally familiar to the great playwright and his contempories.

Many facets of the history and culture of our 'sceptr'd isle' are inextricably bound with that of Warwickshire; great houses and estates bear witness to political power and wealth whilst enterprise and ingenuity are reflected in the industrial bases that were created within the old county boundaries in towns such as Birmingham and Coventry. At the height of the British Empire it can fairly be said that this area at the heart of England exerted an influence out of all proportion to it's size. The Empire has gone and the boundaries have been re-drawn to exclude the largest of the commercial conurbations (now part of the newly created West Midlands) but dramatic change is not new to this gently undulating countryside which rose to greatness through war and peace yet whose humble beginnings are reflected in it's earliest recorded name of Waeinewiscsr meaning 'the dairy farm by a river dam'.

When exploring Warwickshire for the purposes of this book I deliberately chose to start my travels at the southern border of the county at a point that provided beautiful scenery and historical interest - and it is only fair to mention that there are a great many such places in this most attractive of counties.! I took the A422 which leads north-west from Banbury to Stratford-Upon-Avon and as I crossed over from Oxfordshire into Warwickshire I turned right towards Ratley. I found myself on a wooded escarpment which is, in fact, part of the easternmost spur of the Cotswolds. Tall beeches lined the road and I pulled off into a car-park in order to stretch my legs along one of a number of well marked trails. Before long, I found myself gazing northwards from a vantage point that gave a panoramic view over well-ordered countryside. In the foreground was a small village partially hidden by mature trees, then a large house built of honey-coloured stone surrounded by parkland whilst beyond lay rich agricultural land laid out in the gently haphazard manner that is so essentially English. Broad flat acres interspersed with copse, stream and hedgerow, marking out the irregular patchwork of fields - predominantly the lush greens of pasture and crop but occasionally adulterated with the alien yellow brightness of rape. It was a peaceful, bucolic scene interrupted only by the squabbling of rooks in the lofty beeches and the drone of a far-off tractor. Michael Drayton, a poet and contemporary of William Shakespeare's and also a Warwickshire man was moved to describe his native county as 'That shire which we the Heart of England well may call,' and, gazing at the tranquil countryside below, I could well understand his sentiments.

Serenity and a feeling of permanence are illusory, for on the plains below me was fought one of the bloodiest battles of the Civil War. The slope upon whose crest I stood is called Edge Hill and it was down these inclines that the Royalist cavalry charged on the afternoon of Sunday, October 23rd, 1642. In a little over three- and-a- half hours the Battle of Edgehill was over and some five thousand men lay dead or wounded. The battle was hard-fought yet indecisive but it can be argued that it eventually led to the military defeat of the Royalist cause since the confusion, disorganisation and lack of discipline, particularly amongst the Parliamentarian forces, led Cromwell to create the effective and efficient New Model Army.

The village below me, Radway, was inevitably caught up in the battle and it must have been a sad evensong that took place in the little parish church on that tragic Sunday long ago. The church was rebuilt in 1866, using much of the original material and contains a monument to a Royalist officer, Captain Henry Kingsmill, 'slaine by a cannon bullet', and local legend has it that every year on the anniversary of the battle, flowers are to be found on or by the soldier's effigy - although no-one knows who puts them there ! On the same day, it is also said, the great grey charger that he rode into battle can be seen wandering across the battlefield searching for it's master. More concrete evidence of the battle can be found in the shape of three memorials; one a simple stone cylinder with a bronze plaque which records that 'Between Here and the Village the Battle of Edgehill the First of the Civil War, Was Fought on Sunday, 23rd October, 1642. Many of Those Who Lost Their Lives in the Battle Are Buried Three-quarters of a Mile to the South of This Stone.' The second memorial is rather more obvious and certainly more cheerful; a castellated octagonal tower on the hillside built to mark the spot where King Charles raised his banner and which is now part of a local pub, THE CASTLE INN, whilst the third memorial is perhaps the nicest of all and can be seen all along the ridge. Some hundred years after the Battle, William Pitt, later to become first Lord Chatham and referred to in history books as Pitt the Elder, was responsible for the planting of many fine trees to mark the site. Oak, ash, elm and beech - although sadly, the elms are gone; noble trees, once known as the 'Worcestershire Weeds' and prolific throughout the county. Dutch Elm Disease has much to answer for.

The builder of the tower was also once the owner of the large house that lay below my vantage point. One of those rich multi-talented eccentrics that the English seem to take a delight in, Sanderson Miller was the son of a wealthy businessman from Banbury who acquired the Radway estate in 1712. Miller took a keen interest in agriculture and the arts and Henry Fielding, a close friend, wrote Tom Jones whilst staying at RADWAY GRANGE. Miller reserved his greatest enthusiasm for architecture and eventually earned for himself the soubriquet 'Master of the Gothick'. An early example of his work was the re-modelling of the Grange and it's outbuildings. From Radway and Edgehill there are some delightful drives along winding lanes that run south-west to north-east along the foot of the higher ground that runs in from the Cotswolds. To the north-east lie the hamlet of **Arlescote** and the village of **Warmington**, both worth visiting and both with interesting connections with the Battle of Edgehill. Arlescote's Tudor manor-house was the refuge of the King's two sons, the princes Charles and James and their tutor, William Harvey the distinguished physician best-known for his discovery of the circulation of blood within the human body. It is said that there is a window within the house whereon the young Prince Charles, bored and frustrated at being kept from the battle, scratched his name and date into the glass with a diamond ring. I wonder if the graffiti of today will have the same appeal in three centuries time !

Warmington is one of the most picturesque villages in the county but sadly sandwiched between the A41 and the new M40 extension. Nevertheless, it is well worth a visit to see the attractive cottages grouped around the village green (complete with duckpond and some extremely friendly ducks who obviously know a tourist when they see one !). The principal construction material is Hornton stone which has that wonderful mellowed-honey look that seems the perfect background to a well-tended garden. The CHURCH OF ST MICHAEL is built of the same stone and stands above and apart from the village on a rocky outcrop and has a memorial to a Scot who fought at Edgehill, one Alexander Gourdin. The parish records tell of other soldiers buried in the graveyard, mostly unknown, and still more, equally anonymous, who lie buried somewhere 'within the fields and windes of Warmington aforesaid...'. One of the horrors of the Civil War lay in the fact that the last resting-place of so many was unknown and unmarked and yet they died in their own country, often close to where they were born and bred...

The church is 14th century, and apart from it's position, has the unusual added attraction of an anchorite's or hermit's cell, later converted to living accommodation for a caretaker-priest. Legend has it that this room is haunted by the spirit of it's original inhabitant who was reputedly a woman. Another local legend concerns the reason for the church being built on the outcrop. Apparently, it was originally intended to build the church down in the village but, after a start had been made, the stonework was discovered on the following morning to have been dismantled. This strange state of affairs continued until the alternative site was chosen and construction then proceeded without further interruption. Fairies were alleged to be the culprits although no-one seems to know the reason for their mischievous behaviour. The story particularly interested me since there is a similar tale concerning a church built high on a rock overlooking my own part of the world at Brentor on Dartmoor. Naturally, being Dartmoor, the culprit was altogether more unpleasant; it was the Devil himself and it is said that his motive for encouraging the construction of a church on top of such a sheer rock was that he reckoned that no-one would then bother to climb the rough tor to worship God ! An interesting co-incidence and particularly in the light of both churches being dedicated to St Michael...

A mile or so to the east of the M40 lies **Farnborough,** a slightly larger village which also has a church set above the community containing a number of memorials to the Holbech family who owned neighbouring FARNBOROUGH HALL from 1684 until it was given to the National Trust just after World War II. Famed for it's magnificent 18th century rococo interior plasterwork, it is still tenanted by members of the same family and is open to the public between April and September. There is a wonderful terraced walk amongst the landscaped gardens which was designed by the talented neighbouring squire of Radway, Sanderson Miller.

A couple of miles to the north-west of Farnborough one comes across a further reminder of the Battle of Edgehill and of far earlier conflicts that took place in this now most peaceful of counties. Winding lanes bring you once again to that edge of the Cotswolds known as the Dasset Hills from where, once again you can gaze over the rich agricultural lands of South Worcestershire, known locally as the Worcestershire Feldon. At **Burton Dasset** there was once a thriving mediaeval village but plague followed by evictions left the area de- populated and now there is little more than a farm, a most attractive Norman church with a well and well-house, and a stone tower or beacon.

This was built by the landowner responsible for the evictions, Sir Edward Belknap, who cleared the land to improve the grazing at the end of the 15th century. Since he was also a Commissioner for Warwickshire and Keeper for Warwick Castle, the building of a beacon for the purposes of signalling the alarm by means of a fire, would have been a natural responsibility of his. Edgehill comes into the story because legend has it that a Parliamentary Officer, one Oliver Cromwell, climbed up the Beacon at the height of the battle in order to discover what was going on amidst the smoke and confusion. What is certain though, is that after the engagement was over, a party of Parliamentarians ascended the hill and set fire to the pitch-soaked faggots laid in a brazier at the top of the stone tower. However, this was not the first time that men had warred over these pleasant hills for in 1908 a Saxon burial ground was discovered nearby which contained the remains and effects of over thirty men killed in battle at about the time of the 7th century.

The majority of the area once enclosed is now designated as a country park with some most attractive views and with the only threat to peace and tranquillity coming from the nearby motorway.

Down on the Feldon, some two-and-a-half miles northwest of Burton Dasset is the village of **Gaydon** which lies on the intersection of the A41 and the B4451. Now it is a pleasant rural community of no seeming distinction but things were very different some two hundred and fifty years ago. The A41 was then little more than a pot-holed and muddy track but, by the standards of those times, it was as busy and as important as the modern motorway that runs nearby; the reason being that it connected the two important centres of Warwick and Banbury and, for highwaymen, the robbing of coaches and carts made for rich pickings. The village pub, THE GAYDON INN, was the headquarters of the most notorious thieves and cut-throats that operated at that time. Known as the Culworth Gang, after the village they came from in Northamptonshire, they terrorised a large area along the borders of Warwickshire, Northamptonshire and Oxfordshire for nearly twenty years before being caught. Imprisonment for the rank-and-file with execution for the ring-leaders followed, but even then, the story was not over for the eldest son of the principal robber served a gaol sentence then returned to his old ways. Eventually, he was captured and sentenced to the gallows, but not before he had spent his last night of freedom in the original gang's headquarters where he carved his name into a beam. Today, the Gaydon Inn is a warmly hospitable pub with a strong family following - highwaymen are no longer welcome!

If you wish to double-back and explore to the west of Edgehill then a visit to another National Trust property, that of UPTON HOUSE, is an excellent way to begin. It lies not far from the villages of **Tysoe** and **Ratley** within an eccentric bight of the county boundary with Oxfordshire and near the top of the delightfully named Sunrising Hill . The area of South Warwickshire that the house overlooks is the Feldon, and it is still sometimes referred to as the 'Vale of the Red Horses' after a figure that was once carved into the neighbouring downland exposing the red soil beneath.

Upton House dates back to the 15th century although the facades that we see today were completed in the 1700's and later, with some of the alterations being designed by our old friend, Sanderson Miller, together with much of the landscaping.Previously the property of the Jersey family since the latter part of the 18th century, the house was presented to the National Trust by Viscount Bearsted in 1948 and contains the most wonderful collection of English and Continental Old Masters, tapestries, porcelain and furniture. It is an interesting reflection on times past that when the then Earl of Jersey inherited the house through marriage there was considerable family debate as to whether they should live there or not. In the end, it was decided not, since the roads were too poor and the situation too remote!

Upton House - Edgehill

Remoteness and romanticism go hand-in-hand with the neighbouring stately home of COMPTON WYNYATES which lies in a small valley some three miles to the south-west of Upton House. To my mind this is the most English of stately homes, a true family house that reflects the continuity and care that generations have lavished upon it. It is not beautiful in the classical sense for it is a house that has evolved over the centuries. The home of the Comptons since 1204, the house has grown to match the social rank of the family as service to the Crown raised them from knighthood to barony, from earldom to marquisate (that of Northampton). The Civil War saw the most dramatic events in the history of Compton Wynyates beginning with the Earl of Northampton and his three eldest sons fighting the Parliamentarians at nearby Edgehill to siege and capture of the house by the Roundheads in 1644. Counter-attacks failed and the War ended with the Earl's death on the battlefield and the family fleeing into exile. They were soon to return and it was to be a further hundred years before the great house was once again under threat; the family fortunes had declined and Lord Northampton ordered the contents sold and the house pulled down. That the house survived and is still the family home is due entirely to the obduracy of the then steward, one John Berrill, who bricked up the windows, patched up the roof and patiently waited for better times. His loyalty and optimism were rewarded, for the family returned in 1812 and promptly set about a process of repair and restoration. Although the house is not regularly open to the public it is well worth a trip to look down from the road in order to gaze upon this extraordinary house that has offered hospitality to the likes of Henry VIII, Elizabeth I and James I. It seems to glow with an inner radiance even on the dullest of days, it embodies those most English of virtues of continuity and tradition.

Compton Wynyates

*A few miles to the west along the winding country roads is the immaculately preserved little village of **Honington**, a mile or so to* *the north of Shipston on Stour. The church has a Norman tower but is otherwise a 17th century re-construction in the Wren style containing a rather grandiose memorial to Sir Henry Parker, owner of nearby HONINGTON HALL, and his son Hugh. Another resident of the Hall, also remembered in the church is one Joseph Townsend whose macabre memorial bears a skull and an evil-looking deformed cherub. The bridge over the River Stour possesses decorative stonework surmounted by 22 stone balls. Motorist's mis-judgements over recent years has apparently provided a local group of sub-aqua enthusiasts with considerable expertise in the specialised art of stone ball recovery !*

*Both Drayton and Shakespeare used the next area that I visited in their works; the poet in his poem 'Polyolbion' and the playwright in 'Macbeth'. **Meon Hill** stands on the border with Gloucestershire and is the northernmost spur of that part of the Cotswolds that stretches up into south-west Warwickshire. Shakespeare was reputedly inspired to write the three witches' scene in Macbeth after a visit to the area, then renowned for associations with early pagan religions. There is some basis for fact in this, since the area has yielded up archeological evidence of Neolithic and later Iron Age settlements. The Romans were also acquainted with Meon Hill since it was mentioned by the historian Tacitus (circa 55-120 AD) as the site of a legionary camp. Undoubtedly it would have had considerable strategic importance with it's prominent position looking over the Vale of Evesham and the Feldon.*

Later settlements on the northern slopes established the communities of Lower and Upper Quinton where there was once a Benedictine nunnery, for the name Quinton in Saxon means 'Manor of Women'. Little physical evidence remains, but there is a fine brass memorial to one of the inhabitants of the nunnery, Lady Joan Clopton, in the church of St Swithin, Lower Quinton.

Although the villages now lie comfortably within the county boundary, they were originally enclosed by that of Worcestershire and the chief complaint of the inhabitants, on being informed of the alteration, was that they objected to such changes on the grounds that the weather in Warwickshire was much colder !

*The hospitable and attractive inn at **Lower Quinton** is worthy of mention not only for it's unique sign-board which bears the arms of*

Magdalene College, Oxford, to which it once belonged, but also for it's comfortable accommodation and excellent food. Naturally, it is called THE COLLEGE ARMS.

Moving north from the mellow lime-stone buildings that predominate in proximity to the Cotswold Hills, one soon comes across that form of construction that typifies Warwickshire to the first-time visitor ; that of the timber-frame infilled with brick or wattle-and-daub, the wooden framing of oak blackened with pitch and the infill often painted white to give a 'magpie' effect. These most attractive buildings are, I think, seen at their best in proximity to water where the dramatic inverted reflections set off the complex geometry of their shapes.

Water, in Warwickshire means, above all, the River Avon, meandering gently through five counties but perhaps to be seen at it's best here as it wanders through the rich countryside, its banks frequently strewn with rushes and overhung by willows. The hamlets and villages on the course of the river to the west of Stratford-Upon-Avon show this scenery to perfection; such places as **Luddington** *(where Shakespeare is reputed to have married Anne Hathaway),* **Weston-on-Avon** *and* **Welford-on-Avon** *(which still has a maypole on the village green). The fertile soil of this region lends itself to market-gardens, orchards and nurseries as well as intensive arable farming, and it is fascinating to reflect that this area, and indeed , nearly the whole of the low-lying West Midlands was, many millenia ago, covered by a vast lake whose sediment did much to enhance the richness of the land. Agricultural wealth is reflected in the handsome farm-houses, barns and cottages and the power of rivers and their tributaries was harnessed by mills in order to grind corn.*

If Warwickshire can be described as the Heartland of England then the Avon must be it's principal artery in that it's waters have provided the means of irrigation, transport and power. Just upstream of the area described one comes to the central tourist attraction of the county - perhaps of the entire country - **Stratford- Upon-Avon**. *Shakespeare may be synonymous with Stratford, but the town was of importance long before his birth (reputedly on St George's Day, 23rd April 1564)and had it's beginnings as a Roman camp and a Saxon monastic settlement. The name Stratford simply means 'a ford where the street crosses the river' and a market was first recorded in 1196, King John granted the right to hold a three- day fair in 1214 and in*

1553 the town was incorporated as a borough and, regardless of Shakespeareana, Stratford is still an attractive and prosperous market town.

The central part of the town which contains it's chief attractions is arranged along the north bank of the Avon with three streets running parallel to the river and three at right angles, the names being unchanged since before Shakespeare's time. The predominant style of architecture is Tudor/Jacobean half-timbering, much of it genuine but with more than the occasional false facade; nevertheless the overall effect is pleasing and the town is an attraction in it's own right.

HOLY TRINITY CHURCH, lying beside the banks of the Avon, is an excellent place to start exploring the town for it is a dignified and graceful building that reflects both the early importance and history of the town as well as being the last resting-place of England's greatest dramatist. It is probable that there was a Norman church upon the site but the present building is essentially Early English (1189-1272) with later additions, the most important being the late-fifteenth century chancel and the spire, built in 1763 to replace an earlier wooden structure. The proportions and spaciousness are almost cathedral-like and the church was granted collegiate status by Henry V in the year of Agincourt (1415) and remained as an important theological centre until the Reformation in the sixteenth century. Throughout the building there are numerous memorials to many local worthies and associations and the former Lady Chapel is almost entirely given over to the Cloptons who contributed much to the growth and development of Warwickshire and to Stratford- Upon-Avon in particular. They, like many of their mediaeval neighbours, made their fortune from the wool-trade and Sir Hugh Clopton is doubly remembered for having built the multi-arched bridge upstream from Holy Trinity and for being a Lord Mayor of London in 1492.

William Shakespeare died at the age of fifty-two on St. George's Day, April 23rd 1616 and is buried, along with his wife Anne and other members of his family, in the chancel and every year, on the anniversary of his death, the whole area around the tomb is covered in floral tributes from all over the world. We sometimes forget how great a man he was and just how much his works are appreciated throughout the world; he would not be forgotten even if he had been

buried in an unmarked grave and perhaps this is best summed up by
the epitaph written by his friend and contemporary, Ben Jonson :-

'Thou art a monument without a tomb,
And art alive still, while thy book doth live,
And we have wits to read, and praise to give.'

There is something comforting about the fact that such a
towering talent came from such an intrinsically English country
town - although we must be careful not to dismiss Stratford-Upon-
Avon as a minor county market-town; in Shakespeare's time the
population was around 1500 which compared favourably with that of
London at 200,000 .

The eldest son of a glover and sometime Bailiff or Mayor of
Stratford, he was born in Henley Street and SHAKESPEARE'S
BIRTHPLACE must be the most visited house in the town.
Restoration and refurbishment began in 1891 under the aegis of the
Birthplace Trust, who also own and manage five other relevant

Shakespeare's Birthplace

properties. Although no contemporary records survive, we can be
certain that the young William would have attended the GRAMMAR
SCHOOL which was famed throughout the country and continues as
a school to this day. The earliest records of a school date back to 1295

21

and the main block facing Church Street was built around 1416. Here he would have learned his 'little Latin and less Greek' and may possibly have first been exposed to the magic of the theatre in the GUILD HALL below, where dramatic performances were given by groups of travelling players.

At the age of eighteen he married Anne Hathaway and it is believed that he earned his living at this time as a schoolmaster although a year or so later after his marriage he left for London. However, he was to return to Stratford at regular intervals and, with the prospering of his fortunes, he purchased NEW PLACE in 1597 and twelve years later settled there permanently with his family. That the house no longer exists is ascribed to the fact that a later owner, the Reverend Francis Gaskell, irritated by rating assessments and constant pestering by Shakespearean enthusiasts, was moved to pull down the entire house ! That there is nothing new about the pressures that can be caused by tourism is evidenced by the fact that the demolition took place in 1759. The foundations have been preserved, together with a beautifully re-created Elizabethan garden. The entrance is by way of NASH'S HOUSE, once the home of Thomas Nash who married Shakespeare's grand-daughter, and now containing what is effectively the town museum.

Halls Croft - Old town, Stratford

HALL'S CROFT belonged to the physician, Dr John Hall, who married the playwright's daughter Susanna and contains his dispensary complete with instruments and apothecaries' jars; situated in Old Town, it is a large timber-framed house with an attractive walled garden.

Quite rightly, Stratford-Upon-Avon is home to the Royal Shakespeare Company who are housed in the ROYAL SHAKESPEARE THEATRE. Originally known as the Memorial Theatre, it was designed by Miss Elizabeth Scott, a niece of the great Victorian architect Sir Gilbert Scott, and was opened by the Prince of Wales in 1932. Considered controversial and innovative when first built, it stands massively beside the river and is a wonderful place to spend an evening being entertained by one of the finest theatrical companies in the world. In the BANCROFT GARDENS, adjacent to the theatre is the impressive SHAKESPEARE MONUMENT, cast from sixty-five tons of bronze which shows the dramatist seated on a plinth surrounded by four of his principal characters (Hamlet, Lady Macbeth, Falstaff and Prince Hal). Also in close proximity to the Theatre are the OTHER PLACE, a small and intimate theatre which presents a wide range of drama, and the BLACK SWAN INN, a favourite theatrical haunt that is better known as the Dirty Duck.

The town and surrounding area is naturally well-provided with pubs, hotels, restaurants and guest-houses, ranging from the cheap-and- cheerful to the plush-and-expensive. During my last visit, I had an extremely good Italian meal at the SORRENTO restaurant which is housed in an old timber-framed building in Meer Street, close to Shakespeare's Birthplace. Good service and value make the Sorrento a popular before or after the theatre venue. Numerous inns and pubs attract attention, but it was while investigating some of the other attractions of Stratford that I discovered the cheerful Victorian ambience of the ODD FELLOWS ARMS in Windsor Street, deservedly popular with both locals and visitors alike. Just around the corner can be found the splendid TEDDY BEAR MUSEUM which presents the history of this most favourite of toys and is filled with valuable and much-loved exhibits - including Rupert, Paddington and Winnie-the-Pooh.

Other 'alternative' attractions well worth a visit include the BRASS RUBBING CENTRE, situated in the Royal Shakespeare Theatre Summerhouse, Avonbank Gardens. Many of the memorial *brasses in our churches have become worn through time and a centre such as this contains a large collection of replica brasses that can be used without damage to the originals. Instruction and materials are provided. Perhaps the unlikeliest attraction is to be found south of the river in the BUTTERFLY AND JUNGLE SAFARI, where one steps off the street... and into a jungle ! Exotic butterflies, insects and plants all exist within a carefully controlled environment in a most attractive and fascinating display.*

On the whole, the town copes well with it's immense number of visitors and has developed an infrastructure that operates extremely efficiently but it should be appreciated that Stratford - Upon-Avon is perhaps the country's premier tourist attraction. A little planning will pay dividends in enabling you to enjoy your visit and the TOURIST INFORMATION CENTRE at Bridgefoot, Stratford-Upon-Avon (Tel: Stratford 293127) can provide considerable help and advice including details of guided tours.

Anne Hathaways Cottage - Shottery

West Warwickshire is often referred to as Shakespeare country, providing numerous literary and historical connections , some true and some apocryphal , but one does not have to travel far from the centre of Stratford to find one of the most famous sites associated with the Bard of the Avon . His wife , Anne, came from the picturesque little village of **Shottery** *, now part of the modern Borough of Stratford , and her family home , once called Hewland's Farm and now known as ANNE HATHAWAY'S COTTAGE , still exists . With it's thatched roof , tall brick chimneys , latticed windows , and half-timbered construction , it stands in a most attractive old-fashioned garden complete with a mass of traditional flowers including fox-gloves , hollyhocks , violets , primroses and traditional roses . The cottage (really a sizeable house) belonged to the Hathaways until 1892.*

Shakespeare's mother came from a well-to-do farming family who lived at **Wilmcote**, *three miles to the north-west of Stratford and, to my mind , MARY ARDEN'S HOUSE is the most fascinating of the properties managed by the Birthplace Trust and the farmhouse and it's outbuildings contain much of interest including a fascinating collection of agricultural and rural implements .*

Charlecote Park - Wellesbourne

It is only natural that stories and legends should abound with a man of Shakespeare's stature , and one of the best-known concerns the stately home of the Lucy family since 1118 , CHARLECOTE PARK . Now in the hands of the National Trust , it was in the grounds surrounding the magnificent house that Shakespeare was reputedly caught poaching deer . The story tells that in consequence of this disgrace he was obliged to leave the neighbourhood and make his way to London , and thus to fortune . There is no evidence to support this tale although some cite the following lines from Titus Andronicus for proof of the Bard's youthful misdemeanors :

> *'What , hast thou not full often struck a doe ,*
> *And borne her cleanly by the keeper's nose ?'*

In 1769 , the grounds were landscaped by Capability Brown and are still home to herds of red and fallow deer who peacefully graze amongst the oaks and chestnuts . Close-by lies the village of **Hampton Lucy** *with it's handsome Gothic Revival church and cast-iron bridge over the River Avon . The associations with Charlecote Park and the Lucy family seem to have been particularly close with the family providing not only the re-built church , school and many of the houses but also a number of the clergy . The hospitable BOARS HEAD public house was also once attached to the living and it is rumoured that in those days entrance could only be gained on a Sunday with permission of the Vicar !*

If the connection of Shakespeare with Charlecote is doubtful , then it is certain with **Snitterfield,** *some three miles to the north of Stratford. Richard Shakespeare and Henry Shakespeare, grandfather and uncle , both farmed here and worshipped at the 13th-century church of St James the Great . The vicar from 1751 to 1784 was another literary figure , the poet Richard Jago , and there is a slab to his memory in the vestry . The KING'S LANE , which runs nearby is so- called in memory of the time when Charles II escaped from the Parliamentarians disguised as a maid-servant .*

Feeling that I had neglected the extreme west of the country , I made for the attractive small town of **Alcester,** *eight miles due west of Stratford . The light industries of needle-making and cabinet-making still continue here , although a long time ago industry must have been considerably heavier since it is recorded that the mediaeval Abbot Ecgwin , unable to make his sermon heard over the hammering of local blacksmiths , invoked God's wrath upon the town ! The Almighty must have been in a benign mood that day for Alcester appears to have prospered over the years ; witness to that fact is the handsome 17th-century Town Hall which contains a list of the Bailiffs elected , in unbroken sequence , for nearly 700 years .*

*Close by are two intriguing , and contrasting , National Trust properties . Tucked away in the little village of **Kinwarton** there is the 14th century KINWARTON DOVECOTE which was built to provide meat for the Abbot of Evesham and his guests . This is a cylindrical building of surprising size , entered through a small arched doorway . The real fascination of the building becomes apparent when your eyes have become accustomed to the gloom and it is then possible to see exactly how the dovecote worked : a central vertical beam has projecting horizontal beams attached supporting a ladder which could be swivelled around to enable the monk in charge to reach any of the 500 nesting boxes . The Abbot's hospitality would have undoubtedly been enjoyed by the Throckmorton family , staunch Catholics who lived at nearby COUGHTON COURT for over five hundred years . Originally built around a quadrangle , the east wing was demolished after damage incurred during the Civil War . I was particularly impressed by the superb early Tudor gatehouse with it's octagonal towers and the double oriel windows ; the coats of arms are those of Henry VIII and those of the Throckmortons and there is a touching story that the family shield fell and was broken on the same day in 1916 that Colonel Courtenay Throckmorton was killed in battle . It was in the gatehouse that some of the wives whose husbands were involved in the Gunpowder Plot waited for news of their husbands actions .*

South of Alcester lies another stately home and estate , open to the public but still in private hands ; RAGLEY HALL , belonging to the Marquess of Hartford . The Hall is a handsome 17th-century Palladian mansion with a beautiful park by Capability Brown and an impressive aspect , but it's real attraction lies in the fact that it is quite evidently still a family home with modern works alongside those of the Old Masters and contemporary items amongst the classical furnishings . There is entertainment to be had in the grounds which include a maze , children's amusements , woodland trails and a boating lake . Incidentally , 'Capability' Brown was given his nickname (his real name was Lancelot) because of his habit of saying to clients that an area had 'capabilities of improvement' - I am surprised our generation has not produced an estate-agent called Potential Smith ...

Whenever time permits I try to travel through an area by means of minor highways and byways since it often reveals far more of the true character of the region than can be gained by simply visiting the

Ragley Hall

more notable attractions via the most direct routes. Heading north-east from Alcester , I came across the oddly-named village of **Wooton Wawen** *(pronounced Wooton Warn) . The name reveals it's origins to be Saxon , meaning 'farm by the wood and the handsome church incorporates a sanctuary from that period together with a number of fascinating tombs and memorials to local worthies. One of these was a true Shakespearean character although belonging to a later period : William Somerville , the Squire of neighbouring Edstone, of whom it could be fairly said that 'he conducted his life to his entire satisfaction'. A popular and much-loved character , he devoted his life to hunting , fishing and shooting yet nevertheless found time to attend to his public duties and responsibilities , entertain his many friends and write poetry and prose to such a standard that even that most grudging of critics , Dr Johnson , was moved to remark that he wrote well for a gentleman'.- He died in 1742 , much lamented and is buried in the church together with two of his huntsmen and his epitaph , composed by himself , reads :-*

'If thou in me has found ought of good -imitate it ,
If aught of evil - avoid it with all thy strength ,
Trust in Christ and know that thou art also frail
and mortal.'

*Doubtless he would have been a welcomed visitor at the many local hostelries and I had a drink to his memory in the cheerful surrounds of the GOLDEN CROSS INN at **Bearley Cross**, a splendid period establishment with massive oak beams , open fires and hospitality to match . From here I continued my cross-country ramble via **Henley-In-Arden** (with its mile-long High St and delightful Tudor architecture) and through the smaller fields and patches of woodland that were once the Forest of Arden and on to one of the most famous ruins in all England, KENILWORTH CASTLE . Sir Walter Scott used it as the setting for much of his novel, Kenilworth, but it's real story is far more dramatic than any fiction . Standing on a gentle grass slope a short distance from the small town of the same name , Kenilworth was first begun around 1120 by the Chamberlain to Henry I, William de Clinton . Building and improvements continued well into the 16th century under various owners, including the Crown, the Dudleys, the de Montforts and John of Gaunt . It was besieged by Henry III in 1266 after de Montfort's defeat at the Battle of Evesham, and in 1327 was the scene of Edward II's enforced renunciation of the Crown . In the Elizabethan era , magnificent extravaganzas and feasts were held as Robert Dudley tried in vain for the Queen's hand . The castle was taken by the Parliamentarians shortly after Edgehill and was slighted or destroyed by them at the end of the Civil War .*

Kenilworth Castle

Five miles to the south lies another great castle in a far better state of preservation . The county town of **Warwick** *surrounds the northern approach to WARWICK CASTLE , guarded to the south by the River Avon . Successive owners of this most impressive fortification did much to form and influence the nation's history , none more so than Richard Neville , Earl of Warwick (1428-71) known as 'The Kingmaker' because of his power and influence during the Wars of the Roses.*

The site of the town and castle is elevated and it undoubtedly contributed to the area's strategic importance . This was recognised as early as 914 when Ethelfleda , daughter of King Alfred , fortified the Saxon settlement against the Danes . William the Conqueror provided the first purpose-built fortification in 1068 . Two centuries later this had grown into a castle which was sacked by Simon de Montfort . The Beauchamp family then embarked on a programme of re- building which was continued by the Grevilles who owned the castle for 375 years before selling it to Madame Tussauds in 1978 . Splendidly restored and furnished with many works of art , displays of armour and exhibitions, Warwick Castle and it's beautiful grounds should not be missed .

The town is as great an attraction as the castle for it escaped the industrialisation that affected so much of the Midlands and it's architecture is of historic interest because of a fire that destroyed much of the centre of Warwick in 1694 . Reconstruction began immediately and over the years resulted in a happy blend of Georgian with the earlier Tudor . The principal church is that of ST MARY'S , a building of almost cathedral size whose principal glory , the BEAUCHAMP CHAPEL , miraculously survived the fire. Built at a cost of £2,481 4s 7½d between the years 1442 and 1462 it is as much a monument to the craftsmen of those times as to those it commemorates. It is a true architectural gem and is considered by many to be the equal of Henry VII's chapel at Westminster or King's College Cambridge. It was originally built to house the superb monument to Richard Beauchamp , Earl of Warwick and father of 'the Kingmaker' who died at Rouen in 1439 .

Also spared from the flames were the picturesque half-timbered group of buildings known as LORD LEYCESTER'S HOSPITAL . Originally Guild Halls , they were turned into a hospice for old soldiers in 1571. The tradition continues to this day and so does the

Warwick Castle

practice of the inhabitants wearing Elizabethan hats and cloaks with silver badges (all except one being original) for church and ceremonies. The principal reception rooms are open to the public and include the Regimental museum of the Queen's Own Hussars . Note the many heraldic devices , mottoes and carvings including a bear with a ragged staff , which is now also found on the County Arms , and a most engaging blue porcupine , a device used by the Stanley family.

For all it's splendid history and tradition , the town is very much a living entity and possesses an air of engaging eccentricity that reveals itself in such unusual items as SALTISFORD GASWORKS. Lying close by the famous race-course , this appears to be a smart , white- painted mansion in the Regency style with octagonal towers at either end . These towers enclose the gasholders but at first sight you would never think so since they are complete with windows ! A fine example of civic pride circa 1822 and reputedly the oldest in the country.

Although industrialisation missed the town , it did not miss by far as the busy network of roads around the area bear witness although the earliest exploitation of the region's wealth by transport utilised water - first using the rivers and then , in the eighteenth century , canals . The Grand Union Canal passes through the outskirts of Warwick on it's way to Birmingham and a visit to the splendidly-named CAPE OF GOOD HOPE public house beside the towpath is highly recommended . The pub was once a bargees' rest where they refreshed themselves and their horses before tackling the arduous passage of 21 locks that makes up the Hatton Flight .

The canal and the Avon also make their way through and around Warwick's close neighbour , **Royal Leamington Spa** , whose tree-lined avenues , river-side walks and wealth of handsomely-proportioned architecture laid out in a grid pattern are in happy contrast to it's mediaeval companion . Named after the River Leam , a tributary of the Avon , Leamington (or Leamington Priors as it was then known) was little more than a hamlet until the beginning of the 19th century when the fame of the curative powers of the local spring-water became more widely known . Speculators and developers created the town we see today at the most astonishing speed ; some idea of the rapid development that took place may be gained from the fact that in 1801 there were 315 inhabitants and yet by 1841 there were 13,000 ! As the town rapidly expanded , the rich and fashionable flocked in to see and be seen , to promenade , to take the waters and indulge in entertainments'. One writer declared the town to be the 'King of Spas' and Queen Victoria , shortly after coming to the throne in 1837 , granted the prefix 'Royal'. The locals must have been somewhat bemused since the original use for the salty waters was for seasoning meat and curing rabid dogs ! Although the town has expanded further since the 19th century , much of architectural interest has been retained around the centre and the original source of prosperity , the spring water , can still be sampled at the ROYAL PUMP ROOM AND BATHS . This elegant building , designed in the Classical style with a colonnade , was first opened in 1814 ; the waters are described as being a mild aperient (a polite word for laxative) and 'particularly recommended in cases of gout , chronic and muscular rheumatism, lumbago , sciatica , inactivity of the liver and the digestive system , anaemia , chlorosis and certain skin disorders' . The town is blessed with many parks and gardens , perhaps the best-known being THE JEPHSON GARDENS whose entrance lodge faces the Pump Room . Originally planned as an arboretum , these spacious gardens contain mature specimens of many unusual trees together with magnificent floral displays , a lake , and two fountains modelled on those at Hampton Court . The gardens were named after one Dr Henry Jephson who did much to promote the curative effects of the waters as well as much charitable work . His *consulting rooms were in the main thoroughfare , the Parade , and in the adjacent REGENCY ARCADE his name, together with his sensible emphasis on the importance of good dietary principles , are further remembered in the excellent and deservedly popular JEPHSON'S RESTAURANT , which is open throughout the day . The Arcade is one of a number of modern shopping developments to attract visitors to Leamington , another being the very handsome ROYAL PRIORS SHOPPING CENTRE . The dignified yet cosmopolitan atmosphere of the town is evidently appreciated by both tourists and residents alike and facilities in terms of accommodation , catering and entertainment are of a very high standard and variety ; qualities I enjoyed at David Wong's Chinese restaurant , THE LEAMINGTON RENDEZVOUS ..*

*Just to the East of grand Royal Leamington Spa is the small village of **Offchurch** and well over a thousand years ago the roles of the two communities were reversed for whilst Leamington cannot have been any more than a hamlet , Offchurch was a residence of Offa, King of the Mercians (757-796) . It is thought that he was buried in the CHURCH OF ST GREGORY that he founded in honour of his son , Prince Fremund . Although there is no real proof of this , the church , which is essentially a happy blend of Early English and Norman , was built on the site of a far earlier building and during restoration in the 1850's stone coffin-lids of Saxon design were found built into the chancel and nave together with skeletons , weapons and jewellry .*

*Fremund was murdered close to neighbouring **Long Itchington** which lies the other side of the dividing Fosse Way , the old Roman road which ran from Topsham in Devon to Lincoln , and throughout the area numerous Saxon relics have been found . Long Itchington lies by the River Itchen and the Grand Union Canal and was the birthplace of another famous Saxon , St Wulfstan (1009-1095) who became Bishop of Worcester , was a friend of King Harold and Lady Godiva , and by his preaching , good works and example probably did more than any man of his period to promote peace between Norman and Saxon .*

The ancient and attractive village was also the site of a famous 'picnic' in July 1575 when a tented palace was erected on the village green and Robert Dudley , Earl of Leicester , threw a splendid party for Good Queen Bess . It says much for the iron constitutions of those days that the party , which featured hunting , feasting , juggling and jesters was simply a warm-up to an immense extravaganza at Kenilworth which went on for seventeen days ! Simpler pleasures can be enjoyed in the village today and I recommend a visit to the TWO BOATS , a delightful and very professionally-run pub by the canalside; where you can enjoy good food and watch the passing waterborn traffic .

*Although my intended route was to the north-east I decided to take a diversion in the opposition direction to visit the extraordinary windmill at **Chesterton,** close to the Fosse Way and about 4 miles south of Leamington . The CHESTERTON WINDMILL is a noted landmark for miles around and is like no other windmill in the country , being a cylindrical stone building raised on piers with moulded arches and a domed roof . The reason for this eccentric yet aesthetically pleasing building is that it was designed by Inigo Jones as an observatory .It was built in 1632 for Sir Edward Peyto whose house at Chesterton was also designed by the great architect but was demolished in 1802 . Exactly when the observatory became a windmill , no-one quite knows - but a clue exists in that the only other mill similar in construction is in Rhode Island USA and was thought to have been built in 1675 , complete with sails .*

*A more conventional windmill is to be found above nearby **Harbury,** a pretty village of Cotswold stone popular with the many walkers and cyclists who enjoy the area , and where they can enjoy the warm and happy atmosphere of the 400-year old GAMECOCK pub - not that you have to walk or cycle to appreciate the excellent food and drink .*

*Shakespeare and the Civil War are brought back to mind at **Southam**, a small market town nestling by the River Itchen overlooked by the 15th century church with it's 120 foot high spire . Henry IV , Part III , makes mention of the town and the first engagement of the Civil War took place a short distance away at **Bascote** . Charles I also stayed here the night before the Battle of Edgehill .*

*From Southam to **Rugby** is only about ten miles but it is well worth taking a diversion via DRAYCOTE WATER COUNTRY PARK with it's picnic areas and adventure playground and if you are interested in the crafts and skills of the countryside , such as* *thatching wheelwrighting , saddlery and shepherding , the MARTON MUSEUM OF COUNTRY BYGONES is not far away . Like so much of Warwickshire , this is pleasant and welcoming countryside that seems very much at peace with itself . The main roads and motorways may bustle with transport and tourist traffic and the principal industrial centres may sprawl nearby , yet it is ridiculously easy to turn aside and find oneself in a pocket of rural calm . The village of* **Frankton** *, just south of the Leamington to Rugby road , with it's appropriately-named FRIENDLY INN seems to typify the tranquil charm that is to be found in so much of the county . This is not to imply that it is some preserved tourist attraction existing in a time-warp ; simply that , on the whole , Warwickshire and it's inhabitants appear to have achieved a happy balance between the enormously heavy demands of tourism , industry and commerce without endangering too much of it's precious heritage of landscape and vernacular architecture . The Friendly Inn typifies this and is popular with both visitor and local .*

In the area I have been describing , the largest industrial area is that of Rugby and its surrounds which lies to the east and it's importance as a commercial centre can be deduced from the fact that it is surrounded on three sides by motorways (M1 , M45 , M6) , is a major rail junction and is riven by both canal and river . The town is referred to in the Domesday Book as Rocheberie and had a population of about one hundred ; a far cry from today's busy industrial and market town . It's name is synonymous with the game of Rugby Football , invented at RUGBY SCHOOL by one William Ellis who , according to a plaque at the school ,'with a fine disregard for the rules of football as played in his time , first took the ball in his arms and ran with it , thus originating the distinctive feature of the Rugby game . AD 1823 .' One suspects that , in accordance with the disciplinary standards of the day , Ellis's pioneering initiative was probably first acknowledged with a beating rather than a plaque ! The origins of the game are also remembered at the JAMES GILBERT RUGBY FOOTBALL MUSEUM in St Matthews Street and by the fact that the distinctive oval shape of a rugby ball can be found on numerous local business logos - including that of the local Tourism Association . Rugby School is also famous as the setting for 'Tom Brown's Schooldays' by Thomas Hughes , which did much to promote the educational reforms and philosophies introduced by Dr Thomas Arnold (1795-1842) .

The bustling modern town still retains much of the friendly and informal parochial air of a market town and I much enjoyed investigating the numerous antique shops .

*The county still retains it's agricultural roots and the headquarters of the Royal Agricultural Society is at THE NATIONAL AGRICULTURAL CENTRE , **Stoneleigh** , some ten miles or so to the west of Rugby , whilst the NATIONAL CENTRE FOR ORGANIC GARDENING is at near- by **Ryton-on-Dunsmore** , an absolute must for those interested in gardening and also headquarters of the HENRY DOUBLEDAY RESEARCH ASSOCIATION .*

*Mention of matters rural brings to mind our national summer game and on the way to visit these important agricultural centres I spent a very pleasant hour watching cricket at **Long Lawford** from the vantage point of the SHEAF AND SICKLE ; where the pitch is conveniently situated at the back of the pub , known for the excellence of it's beer and as popular with supporters of the Campaign for Real Ale as with those of the local cricket team.*

At the time of my visit to Stoneleigh the ROYAL AGRICULTURAL SHOW was in full swing and there can be no doubt that this enormous exhibition with it's myriad stands and exhibits offers an incomparable day out - and to judge from the crowds , the farming community seemed to be in the minority ! Families from all over the country could be seen thoroughly enjoying themselves watching the many varied demonstrations and displays . Particularly fascinating was the number of delegations being shown around from ex- Iron Curtain countries . One can only hope that our agricultural industry can play a major part in helping them solve their present problems .

STONELEIGH ABBEY is a fine Georgian house , set by the banks of the Avon and was built on the remains of a Cistercian abbey founded in 1154 . In 1365 , monastic discipline was evidently not all that it should have been for it is recorded that the monks made a formal complaint about the conduct of their abbot . Apparently he had been selling off abbey property in order to maintain his mistress - even worse , their illicit union had produced more offspring than there were monks in the abbey !

The Abbey was home for centuries to the Leigh family and there is a fine tomb in the village's Norman church to Alice Leigh , the first and only woman in England to be created a Duchess in her own right in acknowledgement of her many good works . The family were obviously of a generous disposition - and so were their retainers - for the church also has a touching memorial to one Humphrey How , a servant of the Leigh's and who died in the 17th century. The inscription reads

> *'Here lyes a faithful friend unto the poor ,*
> *Who dealt large almes out of his Lordship's store ,*
> *Weepe not poore people tho' ye servant's dead ,*
> *The lord himselfe will give you dailye breade ,*
> *If markets rise , raile not against their rates ,*
> *The price is still the same at Stoneleigh gates .'*

The village has a fine 16th century manor house and the Almshouses were the gift of Alice Leigh . There are also six 'cruck' houses ; an early form of timber construction that means that the gable ends are created by splitting the bole and main branch of an oak tree down the middle to create an inverted 'V'-shape.

*Heading back in a south-easterly direction across the Feldon I made one final diversion to explore the rising countryside that borders with that of Northamptonshire. **Shuckburgh**, named after the family that has lived there since the 11th century, has, like so many other places in the area, a connection with the Battle of Edgehill. The village was very isolated in those days and news from from the outside world would have been fragmentary to say the least. Richard Shuckburgh, who lived the quiet country life of a squire, was out with his hounds when he was seen by Charles I. The King, who was making his dispositions for the battle, asked who the gentleman was who could enjoy himself while his Monarch was preparing himself for the opening round of the Civil War. Shuckburgh, of course , knew little or nothing of all this, but, after receiving the King's compliments on the condition of his hounds, he rode home and collected a small force of his servants and tenants. The following day he was knighted for his valour on the field. He died in 1656, after being wounded defending his own home and having been imprisoned in Kenilworth Castle. In the CHURCH OF ST JOHN IN THE WILDERNESS, in Shuckburgh Park, he is buried amongst many others of his family and his memorial bust is that of a true Cavalier.*

The Shuckburgh's tradition of service to their Sovereign is also reflected in the exotic names given to four of their estate cottages - Joaki, Cabul, Gundamuck and Nowshera - reflecting the Afghan War campaigns of a later member of the family.

My final visit before leaving Warwickshire was to **Priors Marston**, a few miles to the south, a quiet and attractive village on the slopes of Marston Hill. Little of note seems to have occurred here since the monks of Coventry established a church in Edward the Confessor's day ; the great events and personalities that shaped the county and the nation seem to have passed it By yet it's charm and situation make it well worth a visit . Sitting in the warm comfort of the HOLLYBUSH INN , having had a stroll around the village and feeling pleasantly full of excellent food , I felt I had truly discovered. "This other Eden . . . ."

Shakespeare Countryside Museum at Mary Arden's House
- Wilmote

Warwick Castle from Mill Lane

THE FRIENDLY INN

Inn

. Main Street, Frankton,
Rugby, Warwickshire.

Tel: (0926) 632430

Frankton is a charming, sleepy Warwickshire village where life is taken at a leisurely pace. It is situated between Leamington Spa and Rugby, and at the heart of the village is The Friendly Inn, which lives up to its name.

The pub was originally a farm house and a barn dating back to the 16th century. A farmer, Richard Fosterd, left it to the village in a trust to support the upkeep of the bridges over the river in Rugby and Newbold which still exist today. It was not until the 19th century that it became a pub, but in so doing the part timber framed and heavily beamed structure of the front and older part of the building were retained giving the whole pub a wonderful atmosphere.

It is one of those comfortable places in which it is easy to relax with a drink or enjoy eating a meal. The lounge has highbacked settles and a roaring open fire in an inglenook fireplace - a super place to be on a cold winter's day. There is also a games room and a small snug bar. 'Ruddles Best Bitter' is kept in perfect condition by the landlord, Richard Levitt. He is a genial host and runs his pub in what appears to be an effortless manner. It is only a true professional who can do that. He has no delusions of grandeur and it is a true country pub. The food is traditional and wholesome with all the time honoured favourites on the menu including some good daily specials. There is no food here on Sundays.

USEFUL INFORMATION

OPEN: Mon-Sat: 12-3pm & 6-11.30pm
Sun: Normal hours. No food
CHILDREN: In eating area
CREDIT CARDS: None taken
LICENSED: Full Licence
ACCOMMODATION: Not applicable

RESTAURANT: Not applicable
BAR FOOD: Traditional Pub Fare
VEGETARIAN: 3 dishes
ACCESS FOR THE DISABLED: Yes
GARDEN: No

THE GAYDON INN
Public House

Banbury Road,
Gaydon, Warwickshire.

Tel: (0926) 640388

This lovely old pub, warmed by open log fires, is at least 400 years old. It has charm both inside and out. The landlords, John and Joan Taylor, are warm-hearted people and full of life. Situated on the B4100, halfway between Banbury and Warwick, ½ mile from J12 on the M40, it is a busy place but the atmosphere is totally relaxing. Inside it is warm and comfortable, furnished in a manner which compliments the age of the building. Outside, the large garden and grounds are the home of hens, geese and White Faced Woodland sheep. Children love it.

The Taylors have been here since 1985 and run the place with the help of their daughter, Beverley. Joan is the cook and prides herself on producing good, home-made food. Her ham, cooked on the premises and cut off the bone, is definitely the speciality of the house. People come from miles around for meals. The restaurant seats 22 and meals are served in the bar and lounge too. Breakfasts are served everyday. Eating here is a simple affair, it is inexpensive but always generous and excellent value for money. The choice is wide and includes everything from sirloin steaks, gammon steaks and chilli con carne to steak and kidney pie and fish. If you only want a snack you can choose from freshly cut sandwiches in white or wholemeal bread, jacket potatoes with fillings and a salad garnish or a variety of ploughman's lunches. On Sundays there is a traditional roast Topside of beef, Yorkshire pudding, roast and boiled potatoes plus 3 other vegetables, followed by a home-made fruit pie and custard. You will not go hungry!

USEFUL INFORMATION

OPEN: Mon-Fri: 8am-11pm
  Sat: 8-3pm 6.30-11pm
  Sun: 8-3pm 7-10.30pm
CHILDREN: Yes
CREDIT CARDS: None taken
LICENSED: Full Licence
ACCOMMODATION: Not applicable

RESTAURANT: Good, home-made fare
BAR FOOD: Wide range, wholesome food
VEGETARIAN: 2 or 3 dishes daily
ACCESS FOR DISABLED: Yes
GARDEN: Large grounds with animal

THE BOARS HEAD

Public House

Church Street,
Hampton Lucy,
Warwickshire.

Tel: (0789) 840533

The Boars Head has belonged to St Peter ad Vincula, Hampton Lucy, since it was erected over 450 years ago. The pub stands within 50 yards of the church which is known widely, as the 'Cathedral in the country'. It is a delightful spot, less than four miles from Stratford and half a mile from Charlecote House and Park. It is also within a mile or so of the well known Wellesbourne air base used in World War II.

The Boar is much as it was a century ago, the oak beams and open fire places give it a timeless beauty. There is nothing fussy or elaborate about its character; it is unashamedly a pub enjoyed and amply supported by the locals, although many travellers throughout the world have, at one time or another, partaken and thoroughly enjoyed, its hospitality. Sally Fairfield Steele became the landlady after her mother, Thelma retired. It was Thelma who first produced the recipe for steak and kidney pies which Sally makes today but are still known as 'Thelma's Pies'. The name Hampton Lucy, conjures up something of beauty and this is so true of this pretty and unspoilt village. The Boar has its own darts team and two quiz teams, they hold regular quiz nights, open to the casual visitor, with impromptu barbecues through the summer. The wide and varied menu, caters for all tastes including vegetarians.

Everything is freshly cooked and local produce is used wherever possible. It is very busy from Easter through the summer months but a visit during other periods will undoubtedly reward any hungry visitor with excellent personal service and a quiet tranquillity, so rare in these days of hustle and bustle.

USEFUL INFORMATION

OPEN: 11-3pm 5.30-11pm
   Sun: 12-3pm 7.30-10.30pm
CHILDREN: Within reason
CREDIT CARDS: None taken
LICENSED: Full Licence
ACCOMMODATION: Not applicable

RESTAURANT: Not applicable
BAR FOOD: Home made
  specialities
VEGETARIAN: 6 dishes minimum
ACCESS FOR THE DISABLED:
  Easy access
GARDEN: Yes

THE GAMECOCK
Public House

Chapel Street, Harbury,
Warwickshire.

Tel: (0926) 612374

Four hundred years have allowed The Gamecock to grow old gracefully and still keep most of its orginal features, including the Coach House stables at the rear. When you see what a pretty village this is, with many of its houses built in mellow Cotswold stone, you will be pleased that you chose this venue. It is an ideal haunt for hikers and walkers. The Fosse Way, the old Roman road from Lincoln to Bath, is closeby and so are Stratford-upon-Avon, Leamington and Warwick Castle. Chesterton Windmill built in the 1600s is another favourite place to visit.

New plans are afoot for The Gamecock, but David Mason and Mandi Wood who recently took over have promised that the very special atmosphere will not be affected. The locals would be horrified if it were. They use the bars regularly and the darts teams play home and away, competing with other pub teams. The patio and beer garden with a pets corner are very popular in summer. The food is sensibly priced, good pub grub with a range that has something for everybody. You can eat here either at lunchtime or in the evenings, seven days a week. Daily specials are always available and these home-cooked dishes are extremely popular. Sunday traditional roast lunch attracts people from many miles around and you are advised to book in advance. In addition to full meals there are the usual bar snacks which include some very tasty quiches and a super ploughman's. If you are a lover of malt whisky you will find a good selection here.

USEFUL INFORMATION

OPEN: 11-3pm & 6-11pm
Sun: 12-3pm 7-10.30pm
CHILDREN: Welcome
CREDIT CARDS: None taken
LICENSED: Full Licence
ACCOMMODATION: Not
applicable

RESTAURANT: Not applicable
BAR FOOD: Good range, lunch &
evenings
VEGETARIAN: Yes, varied
ACCESS FOR THE DISABLED:
Yes, easily
GARDEN: Patio, beer garden,
pet's corner

THE TWO BOATS

Free House

Southam Road,
Long Itchington,
Nr. Rugby, Warwickshire.

Tel: (0926) 812640

Canals have a great deal of fascination for most people and to find a pub where you can sit outside in the summertime watching all the waterway activity is most people's idea of heaven. The Two Boats, a Free House, at Southam Road, Long Itchington is just such a pub. Owned by Alex McKerlie and Richard Wormell, two very professional men, this is one of the nicest pubs in Warwickshire. They have not been at the Two Boats for very long but their friendly dispositions and the warmth of their welcome has ensured that people who visit once are keen to return.

The pub is on split levels with a comfortable lounge and a nice public bar. A new bar, The Forge Bar, opened in May, has enhanced the pub and given more room. It is needed because of the increasing number of people who use the canal from Stratford to Rugby and can tie up alongside the pub, and for all those who are discovering how delightful the pub is. For those who come by road there is ample car parking.

The menu has many interesting dishes on offer as well as the tried and tested favourites. You can choose from a simple basket meal, fish, succulent steaks, an enormous mixed grill or two dishes in Crockpots, Lasagne Verdi and Chicken Curry. Fresh Batches and Steakwich's are made to order and there is a daily selection of specials. Vegetarians will enjoy the excellent Broccoli and Mushroom Mornay or the Courgette and Mushroom Lasagne.

USEFUL INFORMATION

OPEN: Mon-Sat: 11-11pm
Sun: 12-3pm & 7-10.30pm
CHILDREN: Yes & in garden
CREDIT CARDS: None taken
LICENSED: Full Licence
ACCOMMODATION: Not applicable

RESTAURANT: Not applicable
BAR FOOD: Good pub fare & specials
VEGETARIAN: 4 dishes daily
ACCESS FOR THE DISABLED: Yes
GARDEN: Yes & Childrens area

THE SHEAF AND SICKLE

Coventry Road,
Long Lawford, Rugby
Warwickshire

Public House

Tel: (0788) 544622

What better way to enjoy a pint than doing so whilst watching a cricket match from the gardens of a pub. This you can do at The Sheaf and Sickle on the edge of Long Lawford village. The pub is blessed with a cricket pitch at the rear, and three or four matches are played there every week in the season.

Talking to the contented regulars, who have been coming here for years, they will tell you that not only does The Sheaf and Sickle have the bonus of cricket, it has a remarkable couple as mine hosts. Shan and Steve Jones, they tell me, are specialists in a friendly atmosphere, good beer, good food and good fun. You certainly get this impression from the moment you enter the pub. Somehow everyone makes you feel 'special'. The pub is included in the CAMRA Good Beer Guide for 1992/93 and has a good reputation for traditional beers. It is regularly awarded certificates by local CAMRA drinkers. There is a large bar with a darts area, a cosy cottage style lounge, which is home to Shan Jones' ever increasing collection of pottery ducks, and a family room has a skittle table, pool, darts and video games.

The traditional home-cooked dishes on the menu, and the Daily Specials are super with the emphasis on quality and value for money. Vegetarian dishes are always available and so are children's portions. There are freshly made sandwiches and batches with a variety of fillings, and a generous Ploughman's lunch with either Cheddar, Stilton or Ham.

USEFUL INFORMATION

OPEN: Mon-Fri: 12-3 & 6.30-11pm
  Sat: 12-11pm Sun: 12-3 & 7-10.30pm
CHILDREN: Family Room. Play area
CREDIT CARDS: None taken
LICENSED: Full Licence
ACCOMMODATION: Not applicable

RESTAURANT: Not applicable
BAR FOOD: Home-cooked. Quality
  & value
VEGETARIAN: 3 always & Specials
ACCESS FOR THE DISABLED: Yes
GARDEN: 2 Beer Gardens. Play area

THE COLLEGE ARMS

Inn/Restaurant

Lower Quinton,
Stratford-upon-Avon,
Warwickshire.

Tel: (0789) 720342

Lower Quinton is a delightful village between Cheltenham and Stratford-upon-Avon, on the very edge of the Cotswolds. Chipping Camden is closeby and Warwick too, so it is a wonderful place to use as a base for exploring this magical countryside.

The place to stay is The College Arms, where not only do you get comfortable accommodation but great food and hospitality as well, in an establishment that reeks of history. The inn was owned originally by Henry VIII who gave it to one of his wives as a gift. Sometime later it was purchased by Magdalene College, Oxford and remained under its ownership for 400 years. Because of this connection The College Arms is the only public house in England permitted legally to display the Colleges Coat of Arms.

Accommodation is limited and booking is advisable. There is a new dining area just off the lounge and an attractive bar with inglenook fireplaces; but it is the restaurant on the first floor which will delight architectural buffs. The College Arms has a darts team, pool team and, during the winter when barbecues are not possible, quiz nights. Lynn and Tony Smith, the proprietors, are a popular couple who have an excellent relationship with their regulars and visitors. Most of the food which is varied and traditional, is home-cooked. Whether it is a snack or a full restaurant meal, the quality is outstanding. Specialities are Gammon and eggs, Game in season. Sunday lunch is very popular and it is advisable to book in advance.

USEFUL INFORMATION

OPEN: Mon-Fri: 12-2.30pm & 7-11pm
Sat & Sun: 12-3pm & 7-11pm
CHILDREN: Yes with diners
CREDIT CARDS: Access\Visa
LICENSED: Full Licence
ACCOMMODATION: Limited ensuite
GARDEN: No. Outside seating,
enclosed terrace

RESTAURANT: Home-cooked,
varied, traditional
BAR FOOD: Delicious & very
reasonable
VEGETARIAN: Several & well
presented
ACCESS FOR THE DISABLED:
Yes, easily

THE HOLLYBUSH INN

Hollybush Lane,
Priors Marston,
Rugby,Warwickshire.

Pub & Restaurant

Tel: (0327) 60934

Once upon a time The Hollybush Inn was a 'Bake House' as well as an Inn. You can imagine sitting there supping a pint, whilst waiting for the fresh bread. The Bake House is there no more, but the pub is. It is still a place that tempts you to linger. Every now and again tempting smells waft from the kitchen and tickle the taste buds. Steve and Liz Newby the proprietors are local people and have gathered around them a strong local trade but it is a welcoming, friendly establishment making the first time visitor equally at home. The warm stone walls, exposed timbers and two large fireplaces, ablaze during the winter months, make one feel immediately relaxed.

You are deep in beautiful countryside here which will encourage you to take a walk after the good food you will eat. In the large garden, where you can eat during the summer, there is also a splendid play area for children. Plenty of parking space too. In the comfortable restaurant, . the menu covers a variety of good, home-cooked dishes with plenty of local produce being used. If you enjoy steak, cooked exactly as you order it, or a handsome mixed grill you will be totally happy here. In the bar you can choose from a host of bar snacks plus daily specials. The sandwiches are always freshly cut, jacket potatoes are served with a number of different fillings and the ploughman's are as good as you will find anywhere. The good news is that it is all reasonably priced and children are welcome.

USEFUL INFORMATION

OPEN: Mon-Thurs: 12-3pm 6-11pm
Fri, Sat: 12-4pm 6-11pm
Sun: 12-3pm 7-10pm
CHILDREN: Welcome to eat
CREDIT CARDS: Visa\Access
LICENSED: Full Licence
ACCESS FOR THE DISABLED: No
ACCOMMODATION: Not applicable

RESTAURANT: Fresh home-cooked traditional
BAR FOOD: Wide range. Daily specials
VEGETARIAN: 3 standard & 2 specials
GARDEN: Full eating & playing area

JEPHSONS RESTAURANT

Restaurant

Regency Arcade,
154-156, The Parade,
Royal Leamington Spa.
Warwickshire.

Tel: (0926) 330449

Henry Jephson was a doctor who believed that a healthy diet was better than conventional medicines for preventing or curing illness. His claim to fame is tied to the promotion of the mineral spring waters of Leamington Spa. His memory has been resurrected in the delightful Jephson's Restaurant where delicious but healthy eating is the prime consideration of the Manager, Sue Gallagher. Oddly enough, although the restaurant is part of the new Regency Arcade development, it is only yards from Dr Johnson's first consulting rooms in the Parade.

For two years running, Jephson's has won the 'Heartbeat Award' presented to restaurants who offer healthy choices on their menu. There are some 'No Smoking' tables and a very high standard of hygiene; in fact 100% of the staff have Food Hygiene Certificates. So you can see how very important this is to the restaurant, enabling them to give the customer the best of all worlds. Fresh foods are always in season. Every dish is prepared on the premises which means that the menu changes daily, offering a wide range of dishes, all of which are low in fat, salt and sugar, high in fibre and nothing is ever fried. Vegetarian meals are always available and hot food is served between 11.30am-2pm. At other times there is a cold buffet, home-made soups and a tempting variety of home baked cakes.

USEFUL INFORMATION

OPEN: 8.30-5.30pm
CHILDREN: Yes, highchairs
CREDIT CARDS: None taken
LICENSED: Restaurant Licence
ACCOMMODATION: Not applicable
ACCESS FOR THE DISABLED:
  Level entrance, lifts

RESTAURANT: Delicious, home-
  cooked, fresh ingredients,
  healthy eating
BAR FOOD: Not applicable
VEGETARIAN: Several dishes daily
GARDEN: No but charming
  balcony

THE LEAMINGTON RENDEZVOUS

Chinese Restaurant

97 Warwick Street,
Royal Leamington Spa,
Warwickshire.

Tel: (0926) 428880

Within the welcoming doors of The Leamington Rendezvous you find an immediate sense of the Orient and a certainty that you will enjoy a memorable meal. Nothing is hurried yet, there is a quiet air of efficiency in this expertly run establishment. Cantonese cuisines are the speciality of the house and it is especially famous for Cantonese Crispy Aromatic Duck and various Hors D'oeuvres.

If you are a connoisseur of Cantonese food you may decide that you wish to select the dishes yourself from the extensive menu but for those of us not quite so experienced it is more than sensible to let the waiters decide for you. You can indulge in what is known as the 'Leave it to us dinner' for a minimum of two persons. It will be a feast of selected dishes depending on the number of people in your party and according to the Chef's favourite - a choice which might not necessarily appear on the menu. You are asked to indicate to the staff if there are any dishes which you particularly wish to be included or excluded from the feast! There are other set dinners too which are excellent if slightly less exotic. Strangely enough there are no other Chinese restaurants in Warwickshire but even if there were it would be hard to compete with the Leamington Rendezvous. There is an excellent 'Take Away' service as well.

USEFUL INFORMATION

OPEN: Mon-Thurs & Sun: 6-11.30pm
   Fri-Sat: 12-2pm 6-11.30pm
CHILDREN: Welcome
CREDIT CARDS: Visa/Access/
   Diners/Amex
LICENSED: Full Restaurant Licence
ACCOMMODATION: Not applicable

RESTAURANT: Delicious
   Cantonese dishes
BAR FOOD: Not applicable
VEGETARIAN: Several dishes
ACCESS FOR THE DISABLED: Yes
GARDEN: No

THE ODD FELLOWS ARMS

Public House

Windsor Street,
Stratford-upon-Avon,
Warwickshire.

Tel: (0789) 204022

This interesting pub was the last public house in Stratford to brew its own beers and make its own wine. There is a fascinating publication called 'Victorian Stratford-upon-Avon' which is well worth reading if you can get a copy. It tells the whole story of The Odd Fellows Arms. It is run by Paul and Maureen Carter who have made quite sure that its Victorian image remains unchanged and unspoilt by modern decor. There is a comforting open fire in the bar and you will not be disturbed by the noise of juke boxes or fruit machines.

It is a regular haunt of local people who enjoy its warm, friendly atmosphere as do all the visitors who seek it out. Two minutes from the centre of the town and five minutes from Shakespeare's birthplace, Paul keeps his Flowers Best Bitter in excellent condition and if you want something a little different ask him for a pint of Scrumpy Jack - beware though, it is very potent. The food offered is good pub fare. It does not pretend to be sophisticated. Maureen produces her own homemade steak and kidney pies which have pastry that melts in the mouth. Every day there are 'Specials' on the blackboard, all of which are made on the premises. Wherever possible Maureen uses fresh produce. If you want a snack, the jacket potatoes with various fillings are popular. Maureen has a special recipe for making coleslaw for which she is known, and this she serves with a plentiful ploughman's. Sandwiches are always freshly made and more than generously filled. This is a value for money pub and one that is a pleasure to visit.

USEFUL INFORMATION

OPEN: 10.30-11pm
   Meals: 12-2.30pm inc Sunday
CHILDREN: Over 14 only
CREDIT CARDS: None taken
LICENSED: Full on Licence
ACCOMMODATION: Not applicable

RESTAURANT: Not applicable
BAR FOOD: Wholesome pub food
VEGETARIAN: Yes. Quiches etc.
ACCESS FOR THE DISABLED:
   Easy access
GARDEN: Seating outside in
   summer

THE SORRENTO RESTAURANT

Restaurant

1st Floor,
13-14, Meer St.,
Stratford-upon-Avon,
Warwickshire.

Tel: (0789) 269304

In the midst of Stratford, just 200 yards from Shakespeare's birthplace, The Sorrento Restaurant offers a taste of Italy; in a building which is at least 450 years old with wonderful black and white exposed timbers. Inside it is equally beautiful with a wealth of oak beams, white walls and attractively set tables. It has an air of old fashioned graciousness. It is a very busy place and so popular that bookings are advisable although, Jackie and Antonino, who have been there since 1984, will make every effort to accommodate people who have not booked.

Situated on the first floor, which a view of the Rother Market place, this is an ideal venue at any time, but it is especially good for people who want to eat before or after going to the theatre. An A La Carte menu is available and if you are in need of a quick meal, all you have to do is ask. The service is friendly and helpful, the food is produced by Antonino, who not only has a creative flair but also has a love for his task. Like all good chefs, Antonino has his favourite dishes and one of his specialities is Chicken a la Romana, a mouthwatering recipe with a brandy, pepper, mushroom and cream sauce. Every day he produces similar favourites and a set lunch is available. You will find it difficult to select something from the main menu because it all looks - and tastes - so good. The range is wide and includes something for vegetarians. Everything is freshly prepared and cooked to order so it is important to allow enough time, it is also good value for money.

USEFUL INFORMATION

OPEN: 7 Days Mon-Sun: 6-11.30pm
Lunch: Mon-Sat: 12-2pm
CHILDREN: Yes
CREDIT CARDS: Access/Visa/Amex
Diners/JCB/Switch
LICENSED: Full. Italian beer & wines
ACCOMMODATION: Not applicable

RESTAURANT: Authentic Italian
BAR FOOD: Not applicable
VEGETARIAN: Very wide choice
ACCESS FOR THE DISABLED:
No-as stairs
GARDEN: No

THE CAPE OF GOOD HOPE

Public House

66, Lower Cape,
Warwick,

Tel: (0926) 498138

The Cape of Good Hope has a patio alongside the canal and there can be no pleasanter place to sit, enjoying a drink in the summer, whilst you watch the narrow boats go by. A short walk after that along the towpath enables you to enjoy the varied wild life and especially the ducks and two families of swans who have made it their home.

It is difficult to believe in this very pleasant setting on the Grand Union Canal, that you are really in the heart of Warwick within 1 mile of Warwick Castle and just ½ mile from the town centre. Only ¾ mile away are the 21 locks known as the 'Hatton Flight'. Originally The Cape was a boatmans' rest where the barges would tie up. It dates back to about 1800 and for 150 years was in the hands of the same family. Paul Farley and Sue Hillage are the partners who are the proud owners today. They have built up the trade since they arrived and whilst the long suffering locals find themselves having to take a back seat during the summer season, they enjoy the fun as much as Paul and Sue. Sue's children also help in the hectic period. Inside the pub there is a small lounge. The hub is the large but cosy bar with a dartboard and everywhere is decorated with canalside memorabilia. There is a car park at the rear. Paul and Sue have plans for extending the lounge area to make more room for eating but they have promised not to destroy the atmosphere of this super pub. There is a wide range of hot and cold food, rolls and sandwiches. The blackboard shows the daily specials which change regularly. Vegetarian meals are always available.

USEFUL INFORMATION

OPEN: 12-2.30pm 6-11pm
Sun: 12-3pm 7-10.30pm
CHILDREN: Welcome
CREDIT CARDS: None taken
LICENSED: Full Licence
ACCOMMODATION: Not applicable
GARDEN: Patio, Canalside beer garden

RESTAURANT: Eating area in
Lounge
BAR FOOD: Wide range. Daily
Specials
VEGETARIAN: 4 dishes daily
ACCESS FOR THE DISABLED:
Sadly, No

THE GOLDEN CROSS INN

Bearley Cross, Wooton Wawen,
Stratford-upon-Avon
Warwickshire.

Inn/Restaurant

Tel: (0789) 731250

On the main A3400 midway from Stratford and Henley in Arden, is the Golden Cross Inn, a delightful hostelry, thought to be well over 250 years old. It has all the charm of its age; vast open fires and heavy oak beams. Many people stop for lunch or dinner here, having been to see the home of Mary Arden, Shakespeare's mother, which is open to the public and just three miles away. In fact it is close to several popular venues including the famous Iron Bridge over the Viaduct, the new golf driving range at Snitterfield and the local Gliding Club.

Wayne and Wendy Kerr have been at the Golden Cross since 1986 and have established a well deserved reputation for their hospitality and food. The intimate restaurant seats 30 people and it is here that Wendy produces her delectable meals which accompany the wines from the limited but well chosen list; she cooks for private dinners and luncheon parties too. You can eat simply, choosing from sandwiches, salads and cold platters from fare which includes steak and kidney pie, grills, fish dishes, vegetarian meals or what is called 'A Bit More Posh' perhaps Roast Duckling with Grand Marnier sauce. Children have their own section on the menu. Reservations are needed for the three course Sunday Lunch but a simpler version is served in the bars from 12 noon until 2pm. Sunday Supper is very popular offering a hot 'Platter of the Day' or mixed meat salad with jacket potato plus a choice of sweets and coffee, the choice is yours, but whether it is a meal in the restaurant or a snack in the bar, it is excellent food and good value.

USEFUL INFORMATION

OPEN: 11-2pm 6-9.30pm
Sun: 12-2pm 7-9.15pm
CHILDREN: Well behaved very welcome
CREDIT CARDS: Access/Visa/Amex
LICENSED: Full, 24 wines
ACCOMMODATION: Not applicable

RESTAURANT: Excellent menu. Wide choice
BAR FOOD: As above
VEGETARIAN: 6 dishes daily
ACCESS FOR THE DISABLED: Easy access
GARDEN: Yes

St Phillips - Birmingham Cathedral

INCLUDES:

The White Lion	*Aldergate*	p. 76
The Rainbow Inn	*Allesley Village*	p. 77
The New Inn	*Arley*	p. 78
The Gate Inn	*Atherstone*	p. 79
The White Lion	*Atherstone*	p. 80
The Mount Pleasant Inn	*Bedworth*	p. 81
The Great Western	*Bewdley*	p. 82
The Terrace Restaurant	*Brownhills*	p. 83
The Eagle and Spur	*Cookley*	p. 84
The Red Lion	*Corley Moor*	p. 85
The Prince William Henry	*Coventry*	p. 86
The Forest Hotel	*Dorridge*	p. 87
The Eagle and Sun	*Droitwich*	p. 88
The Why Not Inn	*Halesowen*	p. 89
The Little Tumbling Sailor	*Kidderminster*	p. 90
The Whittington Inn	*Kinver*	p. 91
Badgers Wine Bar	*Nuneaton*	p. 92
The Hotel Montville	*Redditch*	p. 93
The Red Lion	*Shatterford*	p. 94
The Black Star	*Stourport on Severn*	p. 95
The Oak Inn	*Walsall*	p. 96
The Gate Hangs Well	*Woodgate*	p. 97

'Seeing is deceiving,
It's eating that's believing.'
James Thurber

THE WEST MIDLANDS

"Forward" - motto of the City of Birmingham.

It seems only fitting that the West Midlands, like so many of its products, should be of modern invention, being an amalgamation of the most heavily industrialised areas of Staffordshire, Warwickshire and Worcestershire. Created in 1974, the region covers an area of 347 square miles and incorporates the cities of Birmingham and Coventry and has a population in the millions.

It is an area preoccupied with production, effectively created by the Industrial Revolution and vastly expanded by the insatiable demands of Empire. It has been touched by the dread hands of War and Recession, yet continues to thrive, producing goods and providing services that are in demand all over the world. Thousands of its acres have disappeared under industrial and suburban sprawl and it is soil scarred and riven by roads, motorways, canals, mines and railways, yet there is still much of beauty and a great deal of value. It can be both depressing and inspiring but if the poet's vision of the 'Heart of England' referred to the rural charm and historical assets of neighbouring Warwickshire then the West Midlands is where the pulse can be felt.

It is hard to imagine this immense area of urbanisation as being 'remote and heavily wooded countryside with but the occasional settlement' yet that was how the early Saxons viewed it; but even then there was a dawning realisation of its rich potential. One of the first commodities to be exploited was that most useful of common minerals, salt, which was vital for the preservation and spicing of foods. **Droitwich,** in the south-west of the region, was probably a Roman centre for the trade which was well-developed by the time of the Domesday Book. The town lies in the south on the western side of the M5 and production of salt continued until comparatively recently. It also made a bid for spa status, following the lead of Leamington and the town achieved some measure of popularity from the 1830's onwards - apparently the saline solution was some 40%

stronger than that of the Red Sea! At around the same period, John Corbett, the Droitwich Salt-King rose to prominence by modernising and developing the salt-mines and workings, particularly around **Stoke Prior** *where he achieved the astonishing feat of turning the annual output of salt from 26,000 tons to 200,000 tons. Very much a man of his period, he had started life as the son of a bargee and at the peak of his success controlled a vast empire. He built himself an ornate home, now a hotel (CHATEAU IMPNEY on the slopes of Dodderhill) but was an enlightened employer providing his workers with gardens, schools, a dispensary and cottages. Much of his product would have been taken by barge for distribution countrywide and such vessels can still be seen - although now mainly used for pleasure rather than transport - from the attractive water-side environs of the EAGLE AND SUN public house at Hanbury Rd, Droitwich.*

The town centre has a few good half-timbered buildings although the majority are Victorian fakery, erected at the time of the Spa boom. The Roman Catholic CHURCH OF THE SACRED HEART in Worcester Road has a striking mosaic depicting an earlier notable, St Richard, who rose to be Bishop of Chichester (1335-1401).

Once past the M5, travelling to the east through a pleasant rural landscape, it is worth stopping almost immediately to visit the National Trust run property at HANBURY HALL. This is a well-proportioned William and Mary brick house designed by the local architect who was obviously an admirer of Sir Christopher Wren and contains a quite outstanding mural by Thornhill, whose work can also be seen in St Paul's Cathedral, and a wonderful collection of porcelain.

The many rivers, streams and canals that vein the entire Midland region mean that angling is one of the most popular local past-times and **Redditch** *has been providing fish hooks for generations, as well as many other items of fishing tackle. The hooks are a natural adjunct to the town's chief industry and claim to fame, that of being the headquarters of the needle-making industry, indeed, THE NATIONAL NEEDLE MUSEUM is situated here. The craft is thought to have originated at now-defunct BORDESLEY ABBEY. With the Dissolution of the Monasteries the monks departed but their industry remained. At first production was by hand and numerous small mills, powered by water, were involved in the various processes* *of tempering, pointing and eyeing, but in 1828 the first steam-powered needle mill was built at Redditch and full mechanisation of the production process began.*

Despite pressure from the north, the town has retained an impressive amount of open space and the original power source of it's industry, the River Arrow, is now utilised for recreation which, at the ARROW VALLEY PARK naturally includes fishing amongst its many attractions. For those staying in the area, I can recommend the HOTEL MONTVILLE with its excellent GRANNY'S RESTAURANT, close to the city centre and once the home of a prosperous factory owner.

Counting House - Avoncroft Museum

I had decided to tour the region's less populated areas first and from Redditch I headed north-west towards **Kidderminster**, *stopping first at the fascinating AVONCROFT MUSEUM OF BUILDING,* **Stoke Heath, Bromsgrove**. *This open-air museum is full of various structures that have been saved from destruction by careful dismantling and then re-building on the Bromsgrove site. They come from as far away as North Wales and include buildings as diverse as a mediaeval merchant's house, a World War II pre-fab, an 18th century three-seater earth closet and a working windmill! The collection is steadily growing and is a lively affair with demonstrations and displays of the numerous techniques and equipment.*

Open-air museums are always a good way to work up an appetite and not far away, in the pleasant little village of **Woodgate**, *you will find a pub which specialises in catering to hungry families. The happily-named THE GATE HANGS WELL is a trenchman's paradise and excellent value for money.*

An unfortunate legacy from the late 19th and early 20th centuries is the popular idea that this part of England is covered by grim industrial buildings and monolithic factories with skies blackened by the output of thousands of chimneys. I was pleasantly surprised by the wealth of open spaces, the generally high standard of cleanliness, imaginative development and the attractiveness of the countryside around the largest towns. There are nature trails and wildlife reserves even amongst the most concentrated of urban developments and a large variety of parks, gardens and leisure centres, not forgetting innumerable golf-courses.

Between Bromsgrove and Kidderminster lies the pretty village of **Chaddesley Corbett** *with its fine timbered houses and church dedicated to St Cassian, a schoolmaster who was condemned to death by his own pupils! The building is a good example of 14th-century architecture on an earlier basis and has a handsome 12th-century carved font. Nearby are the CHADDESLEY WOODS with nature trail and reserve and HARVINGTON HALL, a late mediaeval moated manor house which has a number of ingenious priestholes.*

Weaving and carpet-making built up the wealth of Kidderminster and the industry continues to this day. I do not know whether this trade is particularly renowned for its friendly spirit but certainly the town's good-natured atmosphere is as tangible today as it was over two hundred years ago when one John Brecknall established a charity to provide every child or unmarried person living in Church Street with a plum cake every Midsummer's Eve. A still earlier reflection of this happy atmosphere can be found in St Mary's Church where most of the interesting monuments with it's walls feature both husbands and wives together on the tombs and brasses. A visit to the LITTLE TUMBLING SAILOR public house will enable you to sample this cheery environment as well as the excellent beer and food. The name alone is enough to produce a smile!

In 195 acres a mile or so west of Kidderminster is the WEST MIDLANDS SAFARI AND LEISURE PARK, providing an entertaining day out for all the family with big game reserves, an aquatic show and a number of hair-raising fairground rides. The animals are kept, as far as is possible in spacious near-natural habitats and visitors can drive through the various enclosures.

The Civil War, as we have already seen, wreaked immense damage upon the Midlands in particular and HARTLEBURY CASTLE, which was first built in 1255, was one of it's victims. Happily, a new 'castle' was rebuilt on the mediaeval site which lies just to the south of Kidderminster and in appearance resembles a large and spacious Georgian country house. It is now the Palace of the Bishop of Worcester and the WORCESTERSHIRE COUNTY MUSEUM. The ecclesiastical connection dates back to 850 AD when King Burhred of Mercia gave the manor to the Worcester diocese whilst the museum is a rather more recent innovation, and has a wide-ranging collection of items related to almost every aspect of county life.

Close-by lies the small town of **Stourport-on-Severn,** unusual in that it is almost entirely a product of the Industrial Revolution, and an attractive one at that. The canal systems of the Midlands were the fore-runners of the Victorian's railway networks and our own motorways, opening up the country's industrial centres to national and international trade and Stourport was created as a 'new town' around the point where the Staffordshire - Worcestershire canal ran into the River Severn. Neat rows of cottages were built tidily around the central basin, which is almost an inland port, and the town still has a pleasant late-Georgian feel to it, although it has grown considerably since the days when the hard-working and often hard-drinking bargees would gather to exchange cargoes, swap horses and gossip. THE BLACK STAR, built in 1750, possesses much of the flavour of those days since the canal-side pub incorporates a brewery and a non-conformist chapel! There is something very appealing about waterside pubs and this one is no exception.

A couple of miles to the north-west lies **Bewdley** which also contains many fine Georgian houses but also architecture of earlier periods. It also rose to prosperity because of water-born traffic but that of the pre-canal era utilising the natural facilities of the River Severn in the 15th and 16th centuries. It was also a centre for *weaving, manufacturing saltpeter, brass, horn goods, and cap-making (apparently this trade was so important that at one time the citizens of Bewdley were compelled to wear caps on pain of a fine!).*

It is said that the town suffered a decline in the 18th century because, unlike Stourport, it refused to become the junction of the Worcestershire - Staffordshire canal, declaring that such an innovation was but 'a mere stinking ditch'. Bewdley also produced two notable citizens, Richard Willis (1664-1734) who was bishop of Gloucester, Salisbury and Winchester, and Stanley Baldwin (1867-1947) three times Prime Minister and later created 1st Earl Baldwin of Bewdley. He was born at the corner of Lower Park Street and Lax Lane, the latter giving rise to a suspicion that there may have been a far earlier trade than those already mentioned - that of salmon fishing, since lax is Norse for salmon. The SEVERN VALLEY STEAM RAILWAY has a station and it's workshop in the town, and close by the viaduct lies a friendly little pub whose name celebrates earlier railway associations; THE GREAT WESTERN, which once dispensed hospitality to passengers and staff of the GWR and now does the same for a happy blend of locals, tourists and railway enthusiasts.

*In Load Street there is the excellent BEWDLEY MUSEUM with many displays devoted to local crafts, one of which was charcoal-burning which was of major importance to many of the Midlands industries. The craft was extensively practised throughout the region but particularly in the WYRE FOREST, of which some 6,000 acres still remain. Remains of the ancient woodland art of coppicing can still be found, where trees were cut periodically to encourage numerous new growths used for tanning, fencing, hurdle-making and charcoal-burning. The Forest lies principally to the west of the Severn and is a most attractive area although in many places there has been undue emphasis on the planting of conifers. At **Pound Green, Arley,** in the heart of the Forest you will find a splendid pub, the NEW INN, which advertises itself as particularly welcoming 'Accordionists, Pianists, Opera Singers, Ramblers and Cyclists! Sadly, I fall into none of those categories but nobody seemed to mind and the hospitality and live music was excellent. As the New Inn had no accommodation (they plan to have a least one room available by the time that this book goes to print) I moved on to the nearby village of **Shatterford** where I stayed at the extremely comfortable RED LION*

INN. Sadly, I arrived out of season and therefore missed Richard and Pam Tweedie's speciality, Romsley Lamb Pie, for there can't be too many landlords in this day and age who have their own herd! However, the many alternatives on the extensive menu more than made up for this minor disappointment.

It is not hard to find reminders of the local, if eccentric genius, James Brindley (1716-1772) who left his mark on the landscape in the shape of 365 miles of canals; the Staffordshire and Worcestershire being one of his creations. Largely self-taught, this brilliant engineer remained illiterate to the end of his days and solved his problems without recourse to pencil and paper by simply retiring to bed and thinking things out! He must have spent a day or two between the sheets figuring out how to construct the longest tunnel on the canal at Cookley which passes under the main street. Barges called here to unload coal and iron 'pigs' or billets for the foundries and doubtless this thirsty work required a visit to the unusually-named EAGLE AND SPUR which brewed it's own ale on the premises. The brewery has long gone but excellent proprietary ales and fine food make up for the loss of a beer which was described as 'mild, light, sweet and strong'.

Kinver lies by both the canal and the River Stour and is popular with the boating fraternity and those from the built-up area of the Midlands. A steep climb leads from the town up to KIMBER EDGE, the dramatic hill beside the town. From the summit one can see four ranges of hills - the Clents, the Cotswolds, the Clees and the Malverns; half-way up is HOLY AUSTIN ROCK, a large sandstone formation with caves some of which were said to have been populated by long-lost tribes and were certainly inhabited until recently. On a neighbouring hill stands ST PETER'S CHURCH which contains memorial windows to members of the Brindley family, to whom James the canal-builder is said to have been related.

The name Kinver is derived from Kine-fare meaning cattle-market and the village was once owned by the Whittington family from whom the famous Dick Whittington (1358-1423) was descended. Dick's grandfather, Sir William, built the manor house in 1310 which still exists under the guise of the WHITTINGTON INN and a splendid institution it is too. Historically, the house has many other connections: Lady Jane Grey lived here as a child (and her ghost is said to walk the corridor on the first floor), Charles II stayed a night after being defeated at Worcester in 1651 and Queen Anne left evidence of her stay here in 1711 in the shape of an iron seal on the front door. The Inn is beautifully preserved, serves excellent food and has most attractive gardens.

The image of grime, poverty and pollution in the Midlands may be out-moded now, but it has a basis in truth and particularly applied to that area known as the Black Country, bounded by Wolverhampton to the north and by Stourbridge to the south and so-called because of the region's numerous open-cast coal-mines and smoke-belching factories. Thomas Carlyle, visiting in 1824, described it as; '... a frightful scene ... a dense cloud of pestilential smoke hangs over it forever ... and at night the whole region burns like a volcano spitting fire from a thousand tubes of brick. But oh the wretched thousands of mortals who grind out there destiny there!' A later visitor, the American, Elihu Burritt, said of the region in 1868 'The Black Country, black by day, red by night'. Paradoxically, from this vision of hell on earth came skills and objects of beauty that were to be admired and coveted the world over and a tough warm-hearted people proud of their heritage. The mining has gone, along with the old-style furnaces but many of the skills, trades and industries survive albeit in cleaner more efficient, and pleasant surroundings.

Wightwick Manor - Wolverhampton

*Industry is not a modern innovation to the area for although this once heavily wooded region seems to have been generally ignored by early Britons and the Romans, 13th century monastic documents refer to coal and iron ore being mined in the region from surface outcrops - although the iron was first smelted by means of charcoal. By the 17th century the craft of iron-making had become a true mass-production industry; the ore being burnt or 'annealed' with kindling and then taken, together with charcoal, to the furnace which was fired up by means of water-powered bellows. The melted iron was then run off into moulds to form 'pigs'; these were taken to another furnace to be 'wrought' by alternately heating and beating out by means of hammers, once again powered by the motion of water-wheels. Water-power was also used in the final part of the process when the iron was rolled into sheets and then cut up into rods. These were then distributed to the thousands of smiths working in the area to fashion into objects such as buckles, knives, stirrups, needles and nails. Coal was used by the smiths but not by the iron-makers since it produced insufficient heat and was not utilised until the 18th century and the invention of coke; an innovation that was largely instigated by the Admiralty who were alarmed at the vast tracts of mature timber being cut down to feed the voracious smelting furnaces. In addition to the huge supplies of iron ore, coal and timber, other resources such as limestone and fire-clay were discovered which led to the establishment of a glass-making industry. **Stourbridge** was, and still is, a great centre for this trade and familiar names such as Royal Brierley, Stuart and Thomas Webb still produce glassware of the finest quality. To see how glass is made and the incredible standards and varieties that are available, go and visit the BROADFIELD HOUSE GLASS MUSEUM in **Kingswinford**. The factories themselves welcome visitors and I particularly enjoyed the Stuart Crystal factory with it's amazing glass cone; a brick structure like an elongated beehive which housed the furnaces and the glass-makers.*

As with so much of the region, canals played a large part in the growth of industry and the STOURBRIDGE BRANCH CANAL AND WHARF is worth visiting to see the old restored Bonded Warehouse and canal company offices and also to take a trip on one of the boats.

Further to the east, a reflection of the wealth generated by the area can be seen in the form of the fine Palladian mansion of

HAGLEY HALL which was completed in 1760 and has an outstanding collection of furniture and paintings.

*Heading north towards the heart of the Black Country I stopped in **Halesowen** once a centre of the nail-making industry, a fact commemorated in the town's coat of arms by the inclusion of an anvil. William Shenstone (1714-1763) hailed from here and it was he who wrote the well-known 'Lines Written to an Inn':-*

> *'Who'er has travell'd life's dull round,*
> *Whe'er his stages may have been,*
> *May sigh to think he still has found*
> *The warmest welcome at an inn.'*

In the charming WHY NOT INN the landlady keeps the poet's words very much to mind, serving excellent food and drink in immaculately kept premises.

*As I have already mentioned, one of the pleasantest surprises to the first-time visitor is the discovery of so much open space and often these parks and nature reserves have been created from old industrial sites, such as clay pits and quarries. In an age when we are increasingly conscious of the environment it is heartening to see how rapidly the scarred earth can be returned to nature and I greatly enjoyed stretching my legs in the SALTWELLS LOCAL NATURE RESERVE, at **Brierley Hill**.*

*Industrial, political and social history all combine at **Dudley** in the heart of the Black Country, together with varied architecture and attractions. The ruined castle, standing on a wooden rise above the busy industrial town, dates back to the 11th century although the basic structure that we can see today is principally 14th century. DUDLEY CASTLE has had a checkered history and was first destroyed in 1175 when the then owner made the tactical error of backing Prince Henry in the revolt against his father, Henry II. A century later, re-building began but proceeded slowly; one of the reasons being the unpopularity of the bullying and dishonest John de Somery, whose forcible taxations and reluctance to settle debts led to a natural dis-inclination on the part of the locals to help with construction. The Dudley family took over during the reign of Henry VIII, but John Dudley followed in the footsteps of his predecessor by backing Lady Jane Grey for the throne and paid the supreme penalty.*

The family fortunes, like those of the castle, must have declined somewhat for in 1585 a report was submitted that the castle was unfit for Mary, Queen of Scots to visit - and she was a prisoner at the time! However, the increasing value of the surrounding mineral and manufacturing wealth soon put things right and the castle survived (apart from a slight Civil War battering) as a residence until a severe fire brought about it's downfall in July 1750. Rumour has it that this was caused by counterfeit coiners working in the dungeons; but whatever the cause, the massive ruins still stand and are well worth a visit - particularly as they are now part of the well-known DUDLEY ZOO; the two being connected by a chair-lift. Nearby is PRIORY

Land Train - Dudley Zoo

PARK where mediaeval remains of a former monastery can be seen and a little further on is the WREN'S NEST NATURE RESERVE, noted for its geological formation of Wenlock limestone. Thousands of fossils have been found here during mining operations (in the last century fossil-dealing was something of a local industry) and many fine specimens can be seen in the DUDLEY CENTRAL ART GALLERY AND MUSEUM which also has a fine collection of ceramics, enamels and furniture. On the subject of museums, the BLACK COUNTRY MUSEUM at Tipton Road is a must. An open-air site, it is essentially a reconstruction of a 19th century Black Country village complete with canal, mine, houses and factories *where all the skills and crafts are demonstrated. It's authenticity can be judged from the fact that special permission had to be sought to contravene the regulations of the Clean Air Act so that the cottages could burn coal!*

Working museums are always fascinating with their emphasis on ancient skills and crafts and to the north-east of the Black Country can be found the WALSALL LEATHER CENTRE MUSEUM. Leather working developed alongside the specialist metal trades in stirrups, bits, buckles and spurs with hides being provided by the sheep and cattle of Shropshire and Warwickshire and bark for tanning coming from the surrounding oak forests. Saddlery and tack-manufacture are still local trades to this day, surviving amongst the more high-tech industries of the 20th century. Walsall is proud of its past and possesses a charter dating from the early 13th century and yet has always taken a progressive and enlightened approach to its own affairs, being one of the first towns in the country to have its own police force, library and cottage hospital. The WALSALL ARBORETUM, a private venture opened in 1874 and taken over by the Council some ten year later, has provided both entertainment and leisure facilities for it's citizens ever since and is renowned for it's splended illuminations. The progressive theme is continued in the WALSALL MUSEUM AND ART GALLERY, which apart from its collections and displays of local interest also houses a remarkable range of pictures by artists such as Van Gogh, Picasso and Jacob Epstein.

The author of 'Three Men In A Boat', Jerome K. Jerome came from Walsall and his gentle but pertinent humour typifies the welcoming friendliness of the town and to sample this, I recommend a visit to THE OAK INN, a family-run pub close to the shopping centre. Apart from the hospitality and excellent fare, it has the added advantage of plentiful parking and a garden.

We are an island race and our fortunes were founded upon the great waters of the world where the rapid expansion of international trade provided the basis for the West Midland's export market. Maybe this has something to do with the population's obsession with water for wherever you go in the region there are people walking, picnicking, fishing, boating or just simply looking at water, whether it be stream, reservoir, lake, river or canal. One of the most popular spots for aquatic activity of all kinds lies north of Walsall in the shape of CHASEWATER, a large reservoir close to **Brownhills** where a large number of top-class events are held. Alongside the water runs a fascinating light railway, the CHASEWATER STEAM RAILWAY, which was originally built to service the mining operations in **Cannock Chase** (see Chapter 7). Apart from rides on the various trains there are additional attractions such as a children's play area, displays and a wildfowl reserve.

A really good meal is always a good way to round off major family expeditions and Brownhills provides the venue in the form of THE TERRACE RESTAURANT. Comprehensive menus and excellent value ensure the popularity of the Terrace with both large and small parties, and both conference and banqueting facilities are provided.

As I drove south towards **Birmingham** I reflected that such facilities are very much part of the new industry of the area, with the building of the NATIONAL EXHIBITION CENTRE, THE INTERNATIONAL CONVENTION CENTRE and THE NATIONAL INDOOR ARENA. These impressive and still-expanding facilities are equipped to the highest standards and play host to a multitude of events as diverse as opera, international athletics and Cruft's Dog Show as well as numerous conferences and trade shows which attract several million people a year representing some 95 countries! Nevertheless, these massive centres are not alone and it is typical of Birmingham's ability to react to market demand that numerous other conference venues are available, from five-star hotels to stately homes, together with an impressive infrastructure that covers everything necessary, such as accommodation, travel, leisure facilities and marketing. Perhaps more than any other skill, it is this ability in the market-place that has brought Birmingham from being a 'vill of ten adults and valued at £1' in 1086 to today's priceless 65,000 acre metropolis of one million inhabitants. The basis of Birmingham's wealth was established with the granting of a market charter in 1166 and initial trading would have been in cattle and sheep which then led to the establishment of the first manufacturing industries of leather and cloth. Exploitation of the Black Country's mineral wealth combined with a plentiful supply of water-power attracted skilled metal-workers and men of vision who founded the first factories mass-producing goods for the nation and overseas. The adaptability of the city (declared so by Queen Victoria) *was reflected in its innovatory attitude to industry - steam and coal gas were utilised in manufacturing processes before anywhere else, and it's enlightened attitude towards city planning and provision of houses and services were far in advance of their time. Cutlery and fastenings were joined by the more sophisticated trades of gun-making and jewellery until by 1873 there were more than 745 listed trades and professions; the 20th century adding yet more with the invention of the internal combustion engine and the establishment of the motor industry. To this day, the city provides a home to both mass-production and the individual craftsman together with those of the space-age and the facilities and services already mentioned.*

Monument to Birmingham

The city is constantly changing and intensely alive and it is difficult to know where to start in order to get some idea of this vibrant place. Perhaps the best place is the BIRMINGHAM MUSEUM OF SCIENCE AND INDUSTRY in Newhall Street which amongst many other fascinating exhibits features the world's oldest working steam engine. For an insight into an early example of mass-production allied to social concern (plus a thoroughly enjoyable time) visit CADBURY WORLD at **Bournville** *- a must for every chocoholic! Old skills still relevant today can be seen in the JEWELLERY QUARTER in* **Hockley** *whilst the network of canals provide a unique opportunity to explore the many waterways that wander through the city - Brum has more miles of canals than*

Venice! The past can be seen in places like ASTON HALL, a fine Jacobean house furnished with tapestries and pictures whilst the contemporary present can be enjoyed in the many art gallerys and exhibition centres such as the IKON GALLERY in John Bright Street. Zoos, parks, gardens, sports facilities and theatres abound (one of the theatres, THE ALEXANDRA, being home of the D'Oyly Carte Company whilst THE HIPPODROME is base to the Birmingham Royal Ballet, formerly the Sadler's Wells).

Town Hall - Birmingham

With the 19th century expansion of Birmingham its residents began to look to the surrounding countryside for more congenial places to live, away from the grime and noise that accompanied industry in those days, and one of the outlying villages chosen was **Solihull**. Now a borough, the centre still has a pleasant atmosphere reminiscent of its origins as a small market town created by the 12th century Lords of the Manor Ulverlei. The 15th century MANOR HOUSE with it's attractive gardens and the 13th century CHURCH OF ST ALPHEGE do much to add to this feeling; yet the Borough is very much in the 20th century since, contained within its boundaries, are the National Exhibition Centre, Birmingham Internation Airport (the one connected to the other by an electro-magnetic railway), the M42 motorway and numerous sporting and *leisure facilities including an international ice-rink. The NATIONAL MOTORCYCLE MUSEUM, with hundreds of exhibits from over 150 companies, is at **Bickenhill** whilst the rural past is reflected in over 1000 acres of parks and open spaces. The attractions of Stratford-Upon-Avon and Warwick are only a few miles to the south while closer to hand are the two splendid and contrasting National Trust properties of BADDESLEY CLINTON (a moated mediaeval manor house) and PACKWOOD HOUSE (a Tudor mansion with an amazing yew topiary). This concentration of attractions, together with good communications and proximity to the business and industrial areas, attracts many to the borough and I found a splendid cross-section when I stayed at the FOREST HOTEL, **Dorridge**, where overseas visitors, business people and families were all happily enjoying the warm hospitality and excellent facilities.*

*The rural area lying between Birmingham and Coventry is well worth exploring containing a number of villages and small towns of interest such as **Knowle**, with it's timbered buildings, GUILD HALL and church with beautifully carved chancel screen. **Temple Balsall**, a unique and historic hamlet which owes it's origins to the Knights Templars, a religious order of knights who fought in the Crusades. They are remembered in the lovely 13th-century church which reflects much of the pageantry of those long-past times and in the village's name whilst charity and kindness of a later period is marked by the almshouses that were founded in 1670 by Lady Katherine Leveson. **Hampton-in-Arden**, a mile or so to the north, slopes down to the River Blythe, where there is a fine pack-horse bridge built for the salt-traders. The village has connections with Shakespeare, being the setting for 'As You Like It' and with the Peel family; Sir Robert Peel (1788-1850) founded the Metropolitan Police Force and was twice prime minister. I also recommend a trip to **Meriden**, the 'geographical centre of England', a cheerful and attractive village where the FOREST HALL is headquarters to the ancient and exclusive Woodmen of Arden, the oldest archery society in England. On the village green is a 500 year old cross set up to mark the geographical centre and an obelisk which commemorates cyclists killed in the two World Wars.*

*The area is rich in pubs and hostelries and two I particularly enjoyed were the RAINBOW INN at **Allesley** and the RED LION at **Corley Moor**. Both establishments have much in common - quite apart from the warmth of their welcome, their snug and historic* *interiors and the high quality of food and drink - for the landlady of the Rainbow and the landlord of the Red Lion are both native of their respective villages and both pubs have had other uses in the past; the Rainbow for cock-fighting and as a post-office, whilst the Red Lion was once the village morgue. It is considerably more cheerful today!*

The region's second city is **Coventry** *and although smaller than Birmingham it is far older, originating in the 7th century. It was the centre of the cloth-weaving industry from the 14th to the 17th centuries, was the fourth city in England in importance and from its iron-worker's skills developed the engineering expertise which led it to become the centre of the British motor industry. The city's proud past was very nearly wiped out on November 14th 1940, when German bombers destroyed 40 acres of the city centre, killing or wounding over 1500 of the inhabitants. The fire-gutted ruins of ST MICHAEL'S CATHEDRAL remains as a moving memorial and a charred cross made from the remains of two oak beams was set up in the ruined chancel with the words 'Father Forgive' inscribed on the wall behind. Immediately adjacent is the new Cathedral designed by Sir Basil Spence and consecrated in 1962. It contains works by Graham Sutherland, John Piper, Jacob Epstein and many others and the whole is a moving testimony to the faith and optimism of the people of Coventry.*

Re-building of the city centre began shortly after the war and the occasion was marked by the erection of a statue to one of Coventry's earliest notable citizens, LADY GODIVA, who is best remembered for having ridden naked through the streets in order to persuade her husband, Leofric, to reduce the heavy taxes that he had imposed upon the townsfolk. History records that Leofric relented but I doubt that today's Inland Revenue would take much notice !

Although the city centre is now a bustling modern development some notable remnants of the city's mediaeval past escaped the Blitz and are well worth a visit. The GUILD HALL contains some splendid glass, wonderful carvings, the Arras tapestry and a minstrel's gallery with a display of mediaeval armour. Mary, Queen of Scots was once incarcerated in it's tower. BOND'S HOSPITAL and FORD'S HOSPITAL are both 16th-century almshouses and are still used as such while SPON STREET is a re-constructed mediaeval cul-de-sac with ancient houses enjoying a new lease of life as shops and galleries.

The 14th-century WHITEFRIAR'S GATE is a renovated Carmelite friary housing a number of exhibitions including a charming TOY MUSEUM. The immediate past has not been forgotten and in Hales Street can be found the MUSEUM OF BRITISH ROAD TRANSPORT, which includes the Land Speed record holder, Thrust II, while at nearby **Baginton** there is the MIDLAND AIR MUSEUM.

Just north of the city centre, in Foleshill Road, is the PRINCE WILLIAM HENRY, probably Coventry's oldest pub and originally a coaching inn, which serves extremely good food of both Indian and English origin, served in historic and comfortable surroundings.

One of our greatest novelists who made much use of this area of the Midlands in her books was Marian Evans (1819-80), better known under her pen-name of George Eliot. She was born north of Coventry at **Nuneaton** when her father was steward at nearby ARBURY HALL, a fine example of Gothick Revival built onto an earlier Elizabethan house and with a porch and stables that were designed by Sir Christopher Wren. There are fine landscaped gardens and the stables are now home to THE PINKERTON COLLECTION OF CYCLES AND MOTORCYCLES.

When exploring this area there are two ideally situated establishments providing good food and drink. On the Leicester Road in **Bedworth** there is the aptly-named MOUNT PLEASANT INN, a cheerful one-time coaching establishment which offers excellent value for money, while Nuneaton has the popular BADGER'S WINE BAR in Queen's Road, where you can eat at the bar or in the restaurant. The town MUSEUM AND ART GALLERY has many personal items associated with George Eliot as well as displays and collections of local interest.

Atherstone once claimed to be the centre of the hatting trade and certainly it was known for this craft in mediaeval times. Henry of Lancaster stayed here the night before he defeated Richard III at Bosworth and received communion in ST MARY'S CHURCH. The town is some six miles to the north-west of Nuneaton, standing on the old Roman road of Watling Street, and deserves to be rather better known than it is, for it would seem that the game of football has it's origins here. Since the reign of King John, the inhabitants of the town have played their version of the game once every year, on Shrove Tuesday. It all takes place in the town's attractive Long Street, which is specially boarded-up for the occasion, and the game is held to raise money for charity - a far cry from the old days when it was played for a bag of gold and frequently lasted all day with not a few serious casualties!

The WHITE LION in Station Street is the place to repair after a game of football - or at any time for that matter - since it is a most welcoming local pub with generous helpings of good local food.

Home cooking with local produce is also very much the keynote of THE GATE, in neighbouring **Ratcliffe Culey** and the neat little white-painted pub is not difficult to find for instead of a conventional painted sign hanging outside, it has a five-barred gate!

The famous TWYCROSS ZOO, known for it's successful breeding programmes with endangered species, is just to the north in **Leicestershire** and another smaller zoo can be found at DRAYTON MANOR FAMILY LEISURE PARK AND ZOO, **Fazeley**. All manner of attractions can be found within the 160 acres of parkland from hair-raising funfair rides to a collection of slot machines. **Drayton** is close to the historic town of **Tamworth**, once capital of the ancient Saxon Kingdom of Mercia and now a pleasant town with some attractive architecture but surrounded by modern development; nevertheless, the town is well worth visiting, particularly for it's splendid castle. The predecessors of TAMWORTH CASTLE were destroyed by the Danes in 874 and 943 AD but the present structure has stood firm since Norman times and, apart from the odd ghost, has an almost homely feel about it! A Jacobean manor house was built within the circular keep and occupation has been continuous until recent times. There is now a museum in the castle and the attractive grounds are open to the public and include a garden for the blind and the disabled. Other attractions include the massive ST EDITHA'S CHURCH, re-built after a fire in 1345 but still retaining the great Norman arches that carried the original tower. There is a beautifully carved memorial to Sir John Ferrers by that master of the art, Grinling Gibbons, and glass by Burne-Jones and Morris. The TOWN HALL is also worthy of note, being set up on Tuscan columns with open arches and has a splendid cupola on top with ornate weather-vane. It was built in 1701 by Thomas Guy who later founded Guy's

Hospital, London, and contributed to St Thomas' and to several almshouses. Strangely, for a man given to such generous acts, he had a reputation for being mean and avaricious. Sir Robert Peel is reputed to have delivered his manifesto speech from the Hall and there is a statue of the great man in front. Close by, there is also another WHITE LION pub which is a lively institution of Victorian appearance in the centre of the town. Cheerful pubs like this seem to be a keynote of West Midland life, offering both good value and good fun.

Holloway Lodge Study Centre, Tamworth Castle

Tamworth is like so much of the region with modern development and ancient heritage happily co-existing; forward-looking yet concerned with the older values of a caring and friendly society. The West Midlands is continually evolving to meet the challenges of tomorrow whilst acknowledging the traditions and achievements of the past.

THE WHITE LION
Public House

Aldergate,
Tamworth, Staffordshire

Tel: (0827) 64630

This friendly establishment is in the centre of Tamworth and within walking distance of all its amenities. Formerly a Coaching Inn, the building dates back to the middle 19th century and possibly earlier. Recently refurbished for the first time in twenty years, it is an attractive and comfortable pub. Part of the new decor is a set of framed Sale Bills from 1897 when the 'Inn' was auctioned off .

Locals know The White Lion well but for visitors, Graham Smith the owner, a local man, born and bred in Tamworth, is a mine of what he describes as 'Useless and Useful' information. He is always willing to have a chat and is abetted by his friend, Karen Brown. Apart from Tamworth itself there are two Zoos within easy reach, Twycross, 7 miles away and Drayton Manor roughly 2 miles. It would be difficult not to enjoy yourself in this happy atmosphere; the staff obviously enjoy working here. There is a large Bar, a Lounge, a non-smoking Diner and a car park. On Sunday evenings there is a Disco and that is the one evening when no food is available. The able chef, who amongst his varied experience includes Concorde, produces excellent food which is fantastic value. Every day there are three or four specials at less than £3 as well as a full range of other meals and bar snacks. You can eat wherever you choose, including the non-smoking diner. The traditional Sunday lunch is a very popular feature of The White Lion with a choice of meats, poultry and Vegetarian dishes.

USEFUL INFORMATION

OPEN: Mon-Thurs 11-3 & 5-1 pm.
Fri- Sat 11-11pm.Sun. 12-3pm
& 7-10.30pm. No food Sun. eve.
CHILDREN: In Lounge & Dining Rm.
CREDIT CARDS: None taken
LICENSED: Full Licence
ACCOMMODATION: Not applicable

RESTAURANT: Excellent food.
Great value
BAR FOOD: Wide range
VEGETARIAN: Yes 2-4 daily
ACCESS FOR THE DISABLED: Yes
GARDEN: No.

THE RAINBOW INN

73, Birmingham Road,
Allesley Village, Coventry.

Public House

Tel: (0203) 402888

Allesley Village is only two miles from the historical heart of Coventry. An attractive place that has been a conservation area since 1968. In its midst is the three hundred year old pub, The Rainbow Inn. It was first used as a meeting place for sportsmen engaged in cock-fighting and over the years it served as a Coroner's court and then in 1841 became both pub and post office.

Cock-fighting, inquests and the post office are things of the past and today this friendly, unassuming pub is the busy focal point for local people and for many who have sought it, finding it has a great deal to offer. It is owned and run by Lyn and Terry Rotherham who have a love for, and a great deal of knowledge about, the village. Lyn has lived here for most of her life and her family still have a farm in the village. They have absolutely the right attitude for publicans. The Rainbow is run with great professionalism which at the same time remains informal. There are two rooms, a bar and a lounge in which bar meals are served at lunchtime and then in the evening, meals are served only in the lounge, from 6.30-8.30pm. This is an excellent arrangement because it allows you to eat in relaxed surroundings and permits the drinkers to enjoy the bonhomie of the bar. It is a fascinating pub and the menu offered is comprehensive with dishes for vegetarians and children. Saturday nights in summer are devoted to barbecues.

USEFUL INFORMATION

OPEN: Weekdays 11-11pm
Sun. Normal hours
CHILDREN: Welcome
CREDIT CARDS: None
LICENSED: Full Licence
ACCOMMODATION: Not applicable

RESTAURANT: Wide Choice
BAR FOOD: Extensive menu
VEGETARIAN: 3 Lunch & evening
ACCESS FOR THE DISABLED: Yes
GARDEN: 2 Patio areas

THE NEW INN

Inn & Restaurant

Pound Green,
Arley, Near Bewdley,
Worcestershire.

Tel: (0299) 401271

Three and a half miles outside historic riverside Bewdley, just a quarter of a mile from the river and the Arley station of the famous Severn Valley Steam Railway, in the heart of Worcestershire's beautiful, hardwood Wyre Forest, is The New Inn at Arley, a Freehouse in which you will find an old fashioned welcome from the owners Malcolm and Maddie Gee. It is a pub where a special welcome is offered to acoustic musicians such as Pianists, Accordionists, Folk and Opera Singers! Malcolm publishes the international magazine 'The Accordion News' and runs high profile accordion concerts and festivals, and hence some of the 'Pavarottis' of the accordion world often stay and play in this little corner of England. The piano lid is always up, and many other instruments adorn the walls, should visiting musicians be travelling light!

This is essentially a 'conventional' pub which has only 'middle of the road' background music, with plenty of 'music free' zones. The pub caters for an important family holiday area and so children are welcome to enjoy the use of the family room but are not allowed to roam the lounges. Families may dine in the family room and may use the 22 cover restaurant in the early evening at the Gee's discretion. The New Inn has an excellent reputation for good food with generous portions at modest prices. The service is friendly, informal yet particularly efficient. Book in advance for Sunday lunch please.

USEFUL INFORMATION

OPEN: 7-11pm & 12-3pm at weekends
CHILDREN: In family room
CREDIT CARDS: Access/Visa/ Euro/Master
LICENSED: Full Licence. Freehouse
ACCOMMODATION: Available
1993

RESTAURANT: Traditional. Good value
BAR FOOD: Wide range, generous portions
VEGETARIAN: Several dishes
ACCESS FOR THE DISABLED: Wheelchair access
GARDEN: Lawns. BBQ. Safe children's area

THE GATE INN

22 Main Road,
Ratcliffe Culey,
Atherstone, Warwickshire

Public House

Tel: (0827) 713242

Approximately 1½ miles north east of the historic hatting town of Atherstone, is the village of Ratcliffe Culey, where the focal point of community life is the comfortable Gate Inn. You get a sense of well being when you walk through the doors. It is a typical village pub and reassuring because of it. It has been a pub for the last 120 years and for 112 of those years an interesting annual event has been held, known as 'Lane Setting'. An auctioneer from a local Estate Agents comes along and all the local farmers gather. Then the grass verges in and around the village are sold off to the highest bidder. The event is held on the first Thursday after Easter and all the proceeds go to the local parish council for the well being of the village.

Colin and Eileen Bambrook are mine hosts; the sort of people for whom nothing is too much trouble. They make you welcome and no matter how busy, they make you feel special.

The small restaurant seats 18, and a back bar furnished with tables takes 32. If they are very busy then you can eat in the bar and the lounge as well. Families are very welcome. The daily menu offers some 40 home cooked choices, plus seasonal specials. On Sundays the traditional roast takes pride of place. The prices are sensible. Children love the happy atmosphere and enjoy the garden play facilities.

USEFUL INFORMATION

OPEN: Mon-Thurs: 12-3 & 7-11pm
Fri/Sat 6.30pm
Sun: 12-3 & 7-10.30pm
CHILDREN: Welcome
CREDIT CARDS: None taken
LICENSED: Full Licence
ACCOMMODATION: Not applicable

RESTAURANT: Excellent home-cooked food
BAR FOOD: Wide range. Home-cooked
VEGETARIAN: At least 5 dishes
ACCESS FOR THE DISABLED: Yes
GARDEN: Picnic tables for 50 +
Play area

THE WHITE LION

Public House

Station Street, Atherstone,
Warwickshire.

Tel: (0872) 714194

Chris and Mary Rose are the hospitable and welcoming proprietors of The White Lion in Atherstone. It is a well established pub which has been licensed for about 200 years during which time it has acquired a very definite character of its own. It is the local for many regulars who enjoy, not only the well kept, traditional beer, but the fun and banter that goes on in the bar. Sometimes outsiders can feel excluded in such circumstances but here you will find yourself included, if that is what you want.

The attractive garden provides a good setting for Saturday afternoon barbecues during the summer and occasionally if the weather is especially good on Sundays as well. These fun occasions are extremely popular with locals and visitors. In the winter darts and pool become the main activities. There are keen players here who welcome a challenge from visitors. The bar menu, which is only available at lunchtimes between 11.30 and 2pm, is wide ranging with the emphasis on good wholesome food. The portions are generous and good value for money. From the menu you can start with a home-made soup of the day served with French bread followed by a plate of home-cooked ham, served with two free range eggs and chips. One of the unusual combinations is a super ploughman's lunch which consists of a choice of cheese or ham, French bread, salad and pickle plus a hot sausage and an apple.

USEFUL INFORMATION

OPEN: 11-2.30pm 7-11pm Sat: All day
  Sun: 12-3pm & 7-10.30pm
CREDIT CARDS: None taken
LICENSED: Full Licence
ACCOMMODATION: Not applicable

RESTAURANT: Not applicable
BAR FOOD: Wholesome food using
  local produce
VEGETARIAN: Yes
ACCESS FOR THE DISABLED: Yes
GARDEN: Yes

THE MOUNT PLEASANT INN

Leicester Road,
Bedworth,
Warwickshire.

Free House & Restaurant

Tel: (0203) 640130

There are so many interesting places close to Bedworth, that it makes it more than worth while to spend a little time at The Mount Pleasant Inn, in Leicester Road, before or after exploring. The pub is quite near the site of the Battle of Bosworth and Nuneaton, famous for many things including the novelist George Elliott, who lived and wrote 'Mill on the Floss' there. The pub has been a major focal point in Bedworth since the early 1800's when it had stables and was used by the many passing coaches who found its hospitality to their liking. Not much has changed, the hospitality is still excellent and you will be very well cared for by   Heather and Tony Norden, the owners. It is a comfortable pub with a life style of its own. There is live entertainment on Tuesdays, Thursdays and Friday evenings and Klass Karaoke on Sundays. The Nordens have done much to make this pub special and are hoping to add accommodation before very long. You will probably be amused to read the old 'Auction Bills' which are framed on the walls. For example you can see that the pub was sold in 1804, during the reign of George III, for the princely sum of £400! It makes interesting reading. Tony is the chef and his love for high standards of presentation and taste ensures that a meal at The Mount Pleasant is something you will remember. There is a wide range of choice and a traditional Sunday lunch. Good value.

USEFUL INFORMATION

OPEN: Wed: 11-3pm & 5-11pm
  Thurs-Sat: 11-11pm
  Sun 12-3pm & 7-10.30pm
CHILDREN: In Restaurant only
CREDIT CARDS: None taken
LICENSED: Full Licence
ACCOMMODATION: Coming shortly

RESTAURANT: Good home-
  cooked fare
BAR FOOD: Wide choice. High
  standard
VEGETARIAN: Set menu.
  Lasagne etc
ACCESS FOR THE DISABLED:
  Yes from Car park
GARDEN: Not at present

THE GREAT WESTERN

Public House

42, Kidderminster Road,
Bewdley, Worcestershire.

Tel: (0299) 402320

This very friendly pub has served the locals faithfully for well over 150 years but not always as The Great Western; it was originally The Rifleman, so called because it was the unofficial headquarters of the local Volunteer Force. With the coming of the railway it was renamed The Great Western and from that day onwards it has given cheer to passengers and staff. It is situated next to the Severn Valley Railway Viaduct just below the station at Bewdley and a five minute walk from the bridge leading into the town.

Bewdley has a charm of its own. It was once a busy port on the River Severn and to remind us of this there is a working museum in the 18th century 'Shambles'. For the visitor the town offers a wonderful opportunity to browse through the antique and bric a brac shops, perhaps stopping for a cup of tea in one of the tea rooms. The Great Western was refurbished 5 years ago leaving the original intricately designed plasterwork still intact. The upstairs function room was transformed into a gallery room, housing a pool table but doubling up as a dining room for the monthly gourmet evenings. The one single lounge bar has comfortable seating and the bottom half serves as an eating area. Allan and Jane Harvey, the owners, have a well deserved reputation for the excellence of their food. The winter menu includes memorable stews, steak and kidney pies and liver and onions, whilst in the summer mouthwatering salads take pride of position. There are specials and good bar snacks.

USEFUL INFORMATION

OPEN: Mon-Thurs: 12-3pm & 6-11pm Fri/Sat: 12-11pm Sun: 12-3pm & 7-10.30pm
CHILDREN: Welcome if eating
CREDIT CARDS: None taken
LICENSED: Full Licence
ACCOMMODATION: Not applicable

RESTAURANT: Not applicable
BAR FOOD : Good, home-made reasonable
VEGETARIAN: One on the menu
ACCESS FOR THE DISABLED: Yes
GARDEN: Picnic tables on paved area

THE TERRACE RESTAURANT

9, Watling Street,
Brownhills, West
Midlands.

Restaurant

Tel: (0543) 378291/360456

It is almost impossible to believe that this elegant building which houses a fine restaurant, facilities for banqueting and conferences, started life as a transport cafe and a garage on the A5, the main trunk road, before the motorways altered everything. It could not be more conveniently situated just 4 miles from Lichfield, approximately 7 miles from Cannock and 7 miles east of the M6: with Walsall only 5 miles to the south east. The restaurant seats 150 comfortably and there is a large car park. Coaches are welcome but by appointment only.

Many companies use the conference room because it is so easy to get to, and once here every facility is available including excellent food, whether it be a full meal, a light meal or a snack. The Terrace certainly serves some of the best smoked salmon sandwiches you will taste anywhere. Party menus are available for groups of 10-25 people offering a good choice, at a set price. For the normal diner the range of dishes on the menu is extensive and delicious including Beef or Lamb Wellington, a hot Seafood Platter, Trout Cleopatra, Scampi Mexican or Lemon Sole Mornay. It is quite difficult to choose because it all looks so good. The set price Sunday lunch offers three choices of roast meats as well as Chicken and Turkey or Fish, plus some delectable sweets. Good value.

USEFUL INFORMATION

OPEN: Lunch 12-3pm Dinner 7-10pm
Sunday Lunch only (Book please)
CHILDREN: Welcome
CREDIT CARDS: All major cards
LICENSED: Beers, Spirits, Fine Wines
ACCOMMODATION: Not appliccable

RESTAURANT: A la carte.
Traditional cuisine
BAR FOOD : Extensive,
interesting, tasty
VEGETARIAN: Wide choice
ACCESS FOR THE DISABLED:
Easy access
GARDEN: Pretty garden

THE EAGLE AND SPUR

Public House

Castle Road,
Cookley, Kidderminster,
Warwickshire

Tel: (0562) 850184

Things were a bit different in 1834 when Joseph Morris opened his beerhouse in Cookley calling it The Spin Eagle. It was licensed to retail Ale and Cider under the authority of the Duke of Wellington Beer House Act of 1830. His license cost him two guineas a year and the opening hours were from 4am until 10pm seven days a week, closing only during Divine Service, Christmas Day and Good Friday.

The pub became the Eagle and Spur in due course and many changes have been made but it remains as it was originally intended by Joseph Morris, a Social Centre for the Community. The pub is situated in the Wyre Forest just three miles out of Kidderminster off the A449 to Wolverhampton. A turning signposted Cookley will take you right into the village and let you make the acquaintance of this friendly and hospitable hostelry. Tony and Sue Jay are the welcoming landlords. Apart from the bar and the lounge there is a small restaurant and a function room in which occasional live entertainment takes place on a Friday night. The food is extremely well cooked and presented, good pub fare at very reasonable prices. You can eat either in the restaurant or the bar whichever pleases you. On Sundays the traditional lunch offers you a choice of three roasts with several vegetables and crisp roast potatoes. This is a very good value establishment.

USEFUL INFORMATION

OPEN: Mon-Sat: 12-2.30pm & 6-11pm
  Sun: 12-3pm & 7-10.30pm
CHILDREN: Welcome
CREDIT CARDS: Visa/Access/Amex
LICENSED: Full licence
ACCOMMODATION: Not applicable

RESTAURANT: A la carte. Good choice
BAR FOOD: Wide selection
VEGETARIAN: Always 3 dishes
ACCESS FOR THE DISABLED: Yes
GARDEN: Beer Garden. Bowling Green. B.B.Q.

THE RED LION

Wall Hill Road,
Corley Moor,
Nr. Coventry.

Public House & Restaurant

Tel: (0676) 40135

Two hundred years ago the building which is now The Red Lion started off its life as the village morgue! You could not find anything less miserable today. The pub is a true traditional English country inn offering great hospitality and friendship especially to families.

The orginal pub was situated across the road and is now a farm and stables making the whole scene delightfully rural. The large garden with a well equipped play area is paradise for children. The addition of a menagerie of friendly domestic animals is something they all love. They can play in total safety there whilst their parents enjoy a well earned drink. In the summer barbecues are frequently held on the patio, to which people come from near and far because it is good fun and the food is excellent. Meriden is only 3 miles away, the N.E.C 6 miles and Birmingham 10 which allows The Red Lion to be close enough for business people to drive out at lunchtime if they wish. With a riding school just opposite the pub has been able to join with them and produce a 'Ride and Eat' lunch between 12-2.30pm. All the food is freshly prepared and it is good wholesome pub fare at sensible prices. The emphasis is on pies and home-made desserts which are delicious. Good value Sunday lunch is available too.

USEFUL INFORMATION

OPEN: Mon-Sat: 11-3pm 5-11pm
 Sun: 12-3pm 7-10.30pm
CHILDREN: In restaurant & garden
CREDIT CARDS: None taken
LICENSED: Full licence
ACCOMMODATION: Not applicable

RESTAURANT: Home-made,
 freshly cooked
BAR FOOD: Wide variety.
 Super pies & desserts
VEGETARIAN: 6 dishes daily
ACCESS FOR THE DISABLED: Yes
GARDEN: Yes. Play area & barbecue

THE PRINCE WILLIAM HENRY

Public House & Restaurant

252, Foleshill Rd,
Coventry,
Warwickshire

Tel: (0203) 687776

One mile from the city centre of Coventry on the main A444, which is Foleshill Road leading to the M6, 2 miles away is The Prince William Henry. This distinguished old coaching inn goes back over three hundred years and is probably the oldest hostelry in Coventry. It has seen many alterations not the least of them being the loss of the Ostlers cottages, which used to be attached to the building, until they were incorporated to give more space. It has not lost its charm or character and you can still warm yourself in front of a roaring open fire on a cold winter's day. Many of the regulars here have enjoyed The Prince William Henry's hospitality since before World War II, sure proof that the beer is good.

The situation of the pub is ideal for business people at lunchtimes and also for shoppers because Debenhams is close by. From the large garden, with its well maintained lawns you can glimpse the canal which runs behind. Mal Negra, the owner, has accomplished much here and his standards are very high indeed. It was in 1984 that he and his wife, Kulvinder, came to the pub and the reputation they have gained is well deserved. Here you can feast on Indian cuisine at its best, if that is your pleasure, or tuck into an excellent steak if you prefer it. Whatever your choice it will be beautifully presented and served with charm and efficiency. The Bar snacks are good, wholesome and more than sufficient if you just want something light. There is a large car park. It is all excellent value.

USEFUL INFORMATION

OPEN: Mon-Sat: 12-10pm.
Sun: 12-3pm & 7-10pm
CHILDREN: Welcome with diners
CREDIT CARDS: Major cards not
Amex
LICENSED: Full licence
ACCOMMODATION: Not applicable

RESTAURANT: Indian + Steaks etc
BAR FOOD: Reasonably priced
VEGETARIAN: Always 4 dishes
ACCESS FOR THE DISABLED:
Yes. Special toilets
GARDEN: Large, well maintained.
Car park

THE FOREST HOTEL

Hotel

Station Approach, Dorridge,
Solihull, West Midlands.

Tel: (0564) 772120
Fax: (0564) 770677

This warm and comfortable hotel is situated ten minutes from the M40, M42 and M6. The N.E.C and Birmingham International Airport are only 15 minutes drive from here.

The Muntz family have owned The Forest Hotel for several generations, passing to the present owner, Mrs Yvonne Walker (nee Muntz) in 1931 from her uncle W.E. Muntz, who still retains an active interest in the hotel. The family have created something very special. The Forest, is situated in the heart of Dorridge, a pleasant village, which is only 30 minutes from Stratford-upon-Avon and the Cotswolds, within easy reach of many historic and interesting places to visit, including Warwick Castle. The delightful restaurant serves dinner every evening and lunch on Sunday. Bar snacks, light or substantial, are served every lunch time except Sunday. English and French food is cooked in traditional style, from extensive menus, with the emphasis on fresh produce. All twelve bedrooms are ensuite, have direct dial telephones, colour TV, radio, tea, coffee making facilities, hair dryers and trouser press. The lounge and cocktail bars are pleasant and the function suite caters for 100 dining formally, or up to 150 buffet style.

USEFUL INFORMATION

OPEN: Food: 12-2.30pm & 7-10pm
CHILDREN: Welcome
CREDIT CARDS: All major cards
LICENSED: Full licence
ACCOMMODATION: 12 bedrooms
    all ensuite

RESTAURANT: Traditional English
    /French
BAR FOOD: Comprhensive menu
ACCESS FOR THE DISABLED: Yes
GARDEN: No

THE EAGLE AND SUN

Pub

Hanbury Wharf,
Hanbury Road,
Droitwich, Worcestershire

Tel: (0905) 770130

There is a long stretch of canal frontage at The Eagle and Sun at Hanbury Wharf, just one mile outside Droitwich. Canal pubs have a character of their own which is special and this is no exception. It was built in 1835 some twenty one years after the canal was opened and has served those working on the canal, passers by, and local trade ever since. On a good day you can sit out in front and enjoy one of the traditional beers including Theakston's 'Old Peculiar'. It is no good looking for Keg beer because it is not sold here.

Malcolm and Pat Giles, the owners of The Eagle and Sun have been publicans for almost a quarter of a century, and have a reputation for good innkeeping for miles around. It is no wonder that it attracts all sorts of people including some very well known names. If you can take a look at the Sunday Carvery set up just before they start serving, it will tell you all you need to know about the standard of food on offer.

You can eat at the pub both at lunchtimes and in the evenings, seven days a week, enjoying a menu that changes daily and is full of good home-made choices in which fresh produce has been used. As this book goes to press an extension is being built which will provide a super Conservatory and Garden Room with added accommodation. It is a delightful place now but this should add the finishing touches.

USEFUL INFORMATION

OPEN: 10.30-3pm & 5.30-11pm
CHILDREN: Welcome to eat
CREDIT CARDS: None taken
LICENSED: Full licence
ACCOMMODATION: Not Applicable

RESTAURANT: Not applicable
BAR FOOD: Daily changes.
  Fresh food
ACCESS FOR THE DISABLED:
  Level entrance
GARDEN: Yes + canal frontage

WHY NOT INN

Why Not Street,
2, Gates, Halesowen,
West Midlands

Public House

Tel: (0384) 61019

This small public house demands your attention with its sparkling exterior. It stands just 3 miles from the M5 at Junction 3 and off the A458 Stourbridge road. It is traditional in every way although it has recently been refurbished by the new owner, June Morton. This likeable lady has had the good taste and sense to make sure that it remains a locals pub in which visitors are warmly welcomed.

There are two attractive bars and a separate dining area for those who like to eat away from the drinkers. Sometimes the second bar is let out for private parties which is ideal and a great deal of fun. Coach parties frequently make The Why Not a port of call but they are always asked to ring June first especially if food is required. For those who enjoy good beer you will find that June keeps hers perfectly, particularly the Black Country Bitter brewed in Stourbridge. In the summer the outside paved area with rustic seating is a popular place in which to enjoy a drink and put the world to rights. Food is simple, nourishing and sustaining at very reasonable prices; you can still get a very good Sunday lunch here for less than a fiver. Grills, Lasagne, Seafood Platters, Ploughmans are all part of the daily fare plus Vegetarian dishes and the usual bar snacks.

USEFUL INFORMATION

OPEN: 12-3pm & 5.30-11pm.
   Normal Sun
CHILDREN: Welcome to eat
CREDIT CARDS: None taken
LICENSED: Full Licence
ACCOMMODATION: Not applicable

RESTAURANT: Good value,
   Grills etc
BAR FOOD: Wide selection. Home-
   cooked
VEGETARIAN: Always 3-4 dishes
ACCESS FOR THE DISABLED:
   Easy Access
GARDEN: Paved area with seating

THE LITTLE TUMBLING SAILOR

Public House

Mill Lane
Kidderminster,
Worcestershire.

Tel: (0562) 747527

This really is a pub with a difference! To find it you follow the road towards Bewdley off the Ring Road and then turn right towards Bridgnorth. Look out for the Lighthouse near the old Mill Street Hospital and you will see The Little Tumbling Sailor on the corner complete with a small·garden, a boat, a smaller rowing boat and a beach! It is worth finding.

It has been a pub since the early 1800's and until 6 years ago was known as The Old Tumbling Sailor. It is full of nautical memorabilia with pictures of ships and even hammocks. The bars are lively and the atmosphere friendly. Roy and Anthea Wilkes are the landlords and it is their personalities added to the general bonhomie of the pub that makes it so good. The pub is part of a group called 'The Little Pub Co.' owned by a man known as 'Mad' O'Rorke which probably accounts for a lot! Roy is fanatical about his beer and the condition of his Lumphammer is definitely the best in the Little Pub Co. Anthea is a superb cook and has gained a good reputation for the food she serves. She is imaginative and every dish is fresh and home made in the pub's kitchen using only the best of produce. If you have a sweet tooth you will be delighted with the 'Sweet Ship' which holds all the desserts and is an exact replica of a ship. In the summer months there are Barbecues and every Monday night there is live music. A super place to visit.

USEFUL INFORMATION

OPEN: Mon-Sat: 11-3pm & 6-11pm
Sun: 12-3pm & 7-10.30pm
CHILDREN: Not really
CREDIT CARDS: Access/Barclaycard
LICENSED: Full Licence
ACCOMMODATION: Not applicable

RESTAURANT: Home-made.
Fresh produce
BAR FOOD: Wide variety.
Imaginative
VEGETARIAN: 6 dishes
ACCESS FOR THE DISABLED:
Yes. Wide toilet
GARDEN: Yes with benches &
in the boat

THE WHITTINGTON INN

Kidderminster Rd,
Kinver,
Nr. Stourbridge,
Staffordshire

Public House, Restaurant & Bistro

Tel: (0384) 872110

Even if you have no great interest in history you will still delight in this wonderful Inn. It is as beautiful inside as it is out and has a quite remarkable atmosphere,which appeals to everyone who passes through its portals, whether they are customers or staff. It is a half-timbered Manor House built in 1310 by Sir William de Whittington, who owned all of Kinver. His famous grandson Dick Whittington, born in 1358, went on to be Lord Mayor of London four times. Some two hundred years later, Lady Jane Grey spent part of her childhood here.

The Whittington is situated in lovely countryside, close to the village of Kinver and Kinver Edge, a National Trust area. For those who enjoy shopping the Merry Hill Centre is 3 miles away and there is easy access to major motorways, Birmingham, the Black Country and Worcester. The 4 Lounge bars are charming and comfortable, the 100 cover restaurant is totally in keeping with the building, there are three function rooms, a Bistro restaurant, a large paved patio and a delightful garden. Inside there are beams everywhere and roaring log fires dispelling warmth in winter. It goes without saying that the food is of a standard that one would expect in such a superb place. The menu is traditional in the main, and offers a number of local specialities. Whether you want a Bar snack or to dine in style you will not be disappointed.

USEFUL INFORMATION

OPEN: Mon-Sat: 11-3pm & 5.30-11pm
Sun: 12-3pm & 7-10.30pm
CHILDREN: In all areas. Bouncy Castle
CREDIT CARDS: Access/Visa
LICENSED: Full Licence
ACCOMMODATION: Not applicable

RESTAURANT: Traditional dishes
BAR FOOD: Varied Menu. Local
specialities
VEGETARIAN: Approx 5 dishes
ACCESS FOR THE DISABLED:
Most areas
GARDEN: Walled Tudor garden.
Patio. BBQ

BADGERS WINE BAR

Wine Bar & Restaurant

75, Queens Road,
Nuneaton,
Warwickshire.

Tel: (0203) 371282

From the outside you might think that Badgers Wine Bar was pretty ordinary. It has no great architectural merit, but do not let that prevent you from going inside. Within its walls is a charming, lively and delightful wine bar downstairs and an equally attractive restaurant upstairs. Great thought and care has been put into the decor and the furnishings, to make that little bit of difference.

It is a relaxing, friendly establishment owned by Dennis Harding, who has a good understanding of the needs of his customers. His choice of wines ranges from the exotic to good, inexpensive house wines. If you look through the list you will see there are wines from all over the world and you will be encouraged to be adventurous in your choice, yet not pushed into spending far too much. Badgers is enjoyed by adults of all ages although the emphasis is on people in their twenties and upwards rather than youngsters.

Whether you eat in the restaurant or in the wine bar you will be regaled with some interesting and beautifully cooked dishes prepared by a skilled chef, who obviously loves his job. Every day there is a wide selection and on Sundays you will be offered a traditional lunch from a carvery which never has less than three joints as well as poultry and a selection of fresh, crisp vegetables. The food is good and the price is right.

USEFUL INFORMATION

OPEN: Wed-Sat eve 7-midnight
  Wine Bar: 11-2.30pm & 7-11pm
  Sun: 10.30pm
CHILDREN: In Restaurant
CREDIT CARDS: None taken
LICENSED: Fine wines. Good value
ACCOMMODATION: Not applicable

RESTAURANT: Wide selection.
  High standard
BAR FOOD: Not applicable
VEGETARIAN: A selection daily
ACCESS FOR THE DISABLED:
  Wine bar only
GARDEN: No

THE HOTEL MONTVILLE & GRANNY'S RESTAURANT

101, Mount Pleasant,
Redditch,
Worcestershire.

Hotel & Restaurant

Tel: (0527) 544411

A 'Home away from Home' would be an apt description of this pleasant hotel which has grown around a previously, privately owned, Victorian house. Redditch has grown, and in the old part, this hotel has achieved what is required for comfort today and for the needs of this growing town. Mary and Trevor Warner-Welch have been astute and realised that a homely atmosphere is what people want; something that cannot be built into a modern establishment. This they have managed to do with the help of their family and staff, who appear to be a part of the family.

The bedrooms are exceptional in their quality, each individually furnished and decorated by Mary. The cosy, friendly bar is the perfect place to unwind after a hard day at work or pleasure. Redditch is a perfect location for business people, just a short drive from Birmingham International Airport and the National Exhibition Centre, yet it is set amidst the beautiful rolling countryside of Worcestershire. Granny's Restaurant is a favourite with guests and very popular with locals, who are aware it is the only true English 'home cooking' kitchen in the area. All the food is home cooked and the fresh vegetables and salads are purchased daily. International cookery is also indulged in and the hot, home-made traditional puddings really are something to write home about! Vegetarians are also well catered for.

USEFUL INFORMATION

OPEN: Rest: 6pm-midnight
CHILDREN: Welcome
CREDIT CARDS: Mastercard/Access/ Visa/Diners
LICENSED: 24 hour if necessary
ACCOMMODATION: 16 bedrooms, en-suite

RESTAURANT: Fresh, English home cooking
BAR FOOD: Not applicable
VEGETARIAN: 3-6 dishes
ACCESS FOR THE DISABLED: Level entrance
GARDEN: No

THE RED LION

Public House/Restaurant

Bridgnorth Road,
Shatterford,
Kidderminster,
Worcestershire.

Tel: (02997) 221

Shatterford is a small village just outside Kidderminster going towards Bridgnorth on the A442. It used to be a very busy place in World War II when the American Air Force had an airfield at Stanmore. The bar of the Red Lion resounded to the lively voices of the airmen who used this friendly, welcoming pub as their local. Today it is a comfortable country pub with a roaring coal fire and a pleasant restaurant in which you dine beneath heavy oak beams. Gaming machines are taboo, and although there are plans to extend the Red Lion, the owners, Richard and Pam Tweedie, have promised that none of the rural atmosphere of the pub will be lost.

From here you can visit Dudmaston Hall, belonging to the National Trust, or take a trip on the Severn Valley Railway. Arley Victorian Railway Station is 1½ miles away, and has been featured in many films. You can stay in the pub if you wish in one of the two bedrooms, both of which have access to the jacuzzi and one is strictly non-smoking. Once a month there is live music and entertainment which is fun. The Tweedie's have their own flock of sheep closeby in Romsley and on the menu, in season, you will find the house speciality, Romsley Lamb Pie. This is only one of the many delicious dishes available, using local home produce. Very good value.

USEFUL INFORMATION

OPEN: 11.30-2.30pm & 6.30-11pm
Sun: 12-3pm & 7-10.30pm
CHILDREN: Welcome
CREDIT CARDS: Access/Visa
LICENSED: Full Licence
ACCOMMODATION: 2 double rooms

RESTAURANT: Traditional English
BAR FOOD: Comprehensive range.
Local produce
VEGETARIAN: Four varied daily
ACCESS FOR THE DISABLED:
Under construction
GARDEN: Yes & large car park

THE BLACK STAR
Public House

1, Mitton Street,
Stourport-on-Severn,
Worcestershire.

Tel: (0299) 822404

Mitton Street has produced some curious happenings in its time, none more so than the canalside pub, The Black Star. The present public bar is the original pub that was built in 1750, at much the same time as the canal. Just over a century later a building was erected next door as a non-conformist chapel, and used as a Sunday School to educate the Boat People's children. That building today has been incorporated into the pub and forms the lounge, the loos and the kitchen. In the garden on the other side of a walled yard there is a pretty building, sporting a weather vane; this was originally a brewery which worked to raise money for the support of the church and to ensure that the pub had good beer.

Upstairs there are two hideous gargoyles and outside on the guttering are faces looking down on the people beneath. What extraordinary conversations they must have heard when the non-conformists, all teetotal, met up with the sinful in the pub!

Ann Tunley and her daughter Libby Clewlow are the proprietors of this fascinating hostelry and their welcoming attitude sums up the essence of what this pub is all about today. It is a lively, friendly place with a wealth of activities going on, to which visitors are cordially invited. There is Jazz every Tuesday and a Folk night on the first Friday of every month. They produce their own Pantomime; Canal Theatre Groups visit and Sing-a Longs are very much the order of the day. The food is good pub grub at very reasonable prices. It is fun to be there.

USEFUL INFORMATION

OPEN: Sat: 11.30-11pm.
    Sun: 12-3 & 7-10.30pm
CHILDREN: In beer garden
CREDIT CARDS: None taken
LICENSED: Full Licence
ACCOMMODATION: Not applicable

RESTAURANT: Not applicable
BAR FOOD: Good pub grub,
    home-cooked
VEGETARIAN: 2 dishes
ACCESS FOR THE DISABLED: Yes
GARDEN: Canalside garden. BBQ

THE OAK INN
Public House

336, Green Lane,
Walsall,
West Midlands.

Tel: (0922) 645758

Town pubs do not always have a good atmosphere but that is definitely not so at The Oak Inn where Andy and Sally Button with their daughter Louise, run it as a family business. Perhaps it is this that makes it different from other pubs in the area. You are welcomed into a one room pub with an island bar. Its speciality is traditional cask ales something you will have discovered already if you are a reader of the CAMRA Good Beer Guide.

It has been a pub since the late 19th century but always had a slightly chequered career and it was not really until it was granted a full license in 1948 that it became a place beloved by the locals. This spirit has been advanced even further by the Button family. It is entirely unpretentious but the service is excellent and everyone is cheerful and enjoys looking after the customers. It is situated on the main A34 northbound from Walsall town centre and only a few minutes from the shopping area and railway station. You will find too that there is ample parking closeby; definitely a bonus in a town pub. Eating here is both sustaining and incredibly reasonable. At this present time there is not one dish over £3. Specials are available every day and everything is cooked to order. You can choose from a wide selection which ranges from chicken and chips to a bacon and egg sandwich. It is closed Sunday lunchtime.

USEFUL INFORMATION

OPEN: Mon-Fri: 12-2.30pm & 7-11pm
  Sat: 11.30-3pm & 7-11pm
  Closed Sun lunch. Eve 7-10.30pm
CHILDREN: No
CREDIT CARDS: None taken
LICENSED: Full Licence
ACCOMMODATION: Not applicable

RESTAURANT: Not applicable
BAR FOOD: Good pub grub.
  Inexpensive
VEGETARIAN: Omelettes &
  sandwiches
ACCESS FOR THE DISABLED:
  Level entrance
GARDEN: Available for customers

THE GATE HANGS WELL

Woodgate,
Hanbury, Bromsgrove,
Worcestershire.

Free House & Restaurant

Tel: (0527) 821459

In the past ten years Mark and Louise Giles have taken The Gate Hangs Well from a small and almost unknown pub to the large and successful business it is today with a reputation that is worldwide. It has always enjoyed the peace and beauty of the unspoilt Worcestershire countryside but it is now enhanced by the atmosphere and the charm that these two people have created.

The menu may not be extensive but has the best quality and the cheapest prices you are likely to find. Scottish Steak is the speciality of the house, renowned as the best in the world and the pub is also well known for the prime, fresh North Atlantic Cod. Every detail has received attention, from the training of the smiling and efficient staff, to the design and information on the menus. The section on the menu for children is called 'Codlings Corner'! On Monday and Wednesday nights they take bookings for their now famous Duck Supper which consists of half a seven pound duck roasted and served with twelve fresh vegetables and a delicious home-made orange and Grand Marnier sauce. On Sundays there are two sittings at 12 noon and 2pm for the carvery with a choice of prime beef, locally reared turkey and succulent leg of pork. The vegetable choice is immense and includes the pub's famous garlic potatoes. The wine list is simple and inexpensive. The Gate Hangs Well is an experience.

USEFUL INFORMATION

OPEN: 12-3pm & 6-11pm
CHILDREN: Welcome. Garden
CREDIT CARDS: None taken
LICENSED: Full Licence
ACCOMMODATION: Not applicable

RESTAURANT: Good value. High
 quality
BAR FOOD: Not applicable
VEGETARIAN: Always one dish
ACCESS FOR THE DISABLED: Yes
GARDEN: Yes, tables

The Imperial Vase, Worcester Porcelain, Dyson Perrins Museum

INCLUDES:

The Duke of York	*Berrow*	p. 121
The Old Bush	*Callow End*	p. 122
The Yorkshire Grey	*Earls Croome*	p. 123
The Bulls Head Hotel	*Inkberrow*	p. 124
The Huntsman Inn	*Kempsey*	p. 125
The Walter de Cantelupe	*Kempsey*	p. 126
The Red Hart Inn	*Kington*	p. 127
The Old Chestnut Tree	*Lower Moor*	p. 128
The Cottage in the Woods Hotel	*Malvern Wells*	p. 129
The Imperial Restaurant	*Pershore*	p. 130
The Crown Inn	*St Johns*	p. 131
Coppertops	*Worcester*	p. 132
The Real Sandwich Shop	*Worcester*	p. 133

*'And Noah he often said to his wife when
he sat down to dine,
I don't care where the water goes if
it doesn't get into the wine.'*
G. K. Chesterton

WORCESTERSHIRE AND THE MALVERN HILLS

'The bursting prospect spreads immense around ...'
James Thomson 1726-30

This is an area of richness and contrast in terms of it's agricultural wealth, historical associations and scenic beauty.the dark fertile soils of the **Vale of Evesham** produce the finest of vegetables and fruits while farmers throughout the region happily indulge in the old-fashioned concept of mixed farming with seeming success. Orchards, arable fields and pasture lie happily grouped together while on the ancient western hills, contented sheep graze on both enclosed and common land. Man's presence on this rich earth   dates back to Paleolithic times and its fertility was appreciated by Celt, Roman, Saxon and Norman as it is by the agricultural industrialists of today. Paradoxically, such pastoral splendour has also been the stage for savage blood-letting and the scene for king making and king-breaking. The power of the Barons was smashed at Evesham in 1265, **Tewkesbury** saw the Lancastrian claim defeated by the Yorkist Edward IV in 1471 and, nearly two centuries later, Cromwell's greatest victory over the Royalists was at **Worcester** in 1651. Such vicious yet decisive battles, seem strangely at odds amongst such a gentle landscape where rivers meander through a countryside of quiet moderation and simple continuity; violence appears ill-suited to rolling hills and broad blossom-strewn plains, lacking the bleak heathland or craggy peaks normally associated with such savageries.

The venerable Cathedral city of **Worcester** is capital to the region and reflects much of the contrasts to be found within the region as a whole with historical associations, architectural contrast and industrial, as opposed to agricultural wealth; yet even it's industry has a bucolic air to it, for the black smoke and noisome forges of the Industrial Revolution have little place in the manufacture of gloves, Royal Worcester porcelain or that secret blend of 'brown vinegar, walnut ketchup, anchovy essence, soy sauce, cayenne, and shallots' known world-wide as Worcestershire sauce.

I am extremely fond of the city for it has much of interest and has always been a welcoming and friendly face, but it has to be said

Hanbury Hall - Worcester

that the twentieth century has not treated it kindly. William Cobbett (1763-1835) described Worcester as 'One of the cleanest and handsomest towns I ever saw: indeed I do not recollect to have seen any one equal to it.' Sadly, his description no longer tallies; ring-roads, multi-story car-parks, power stations and other civic developments have changed forever what was once 'the noblest Georgian townscape in the Midlands'. Nevertheless, there remains much that is good and visitors will find their time amply repaid.

The small Roman market town known by the tongue-twisting name of Weogornaceaster was developed, fortified and provided with it's first major ecclesiastical building by a Saxon version of own Lady Thatcher, one Aethelflaed, Lady of the Mercians. The minster she founded was on the site of the present CATHEDRAL OF CHRIST AND THE BLESSED VIRGIN MARY and there is a gruesome legend concerning Danish pirates and the old minster; the raiding party stole the bell and the enraged citizens caught the leader, flayed him and nailed his skin to the oak door of the minster. On a more cheerful note, no less than three saints were associated with the Cathedral's early history - St Dunstan, St Oswald and St Wulfstan. All three are important figures in the history of the English Church and both Oswald and Wulfstan were buried within the choir and their tombs became notable shrines for mediaeval pilgrims. Fire and re-building in mediaeval times meant that their shrines were moved and the sites are now marked by two banners flanking the tomb of a rather less godly man who died more than a century after the last saint, Wulfstan, was laid to rest.

King John's Tomb (1216) is notable for two reasons; he was the first mediaeval king to be buried in England (his predecessors were all buried in France) and the black Purbeck marble figure is the oldest surviving royal effigy in the country. John visited the city a number of times and left instructions in his will (now in the Cathedral library) that he was to be buried there, flanked by the two saints and his body clothed in a monk's habit. A cynic, looking at his furtive and slightly twisted features and recalling his unpleasant record, might conclude that such instructions were some form of insurance policy against retribution in the life hereafter ... Another royal tomb of greater splendour and innocence is to be found on the south side of the sanctuary; that of Prince Arthur, the fifteen year old son of Henry VII, who died in Ludlow in 1502 and whose widow, Katherine of Aragon was re-married to Arthur's brother, Henry VIII.

The Cathedral contains much of interest, particularly if you have a sharp eye. The craftsmen of old were noted not only for their skills but often for their sense of humour, notably when it came to decoration; the 14th century choir stalls have a fine set of misericords (a rather grand name for a hinged support) and these represent a perfect riot of carver's fantasies - biblical characters, mythical beasts, scenes from both court and everyday life and even a wolf saying grace before devouring his victim! Memorials to the famous and the not-so-famous are scattered throughout but the real glory of the building, like so many of it's kind, is in the construction and harmony of the interior which was skillfully overhauled in the last century by the famous Victorian architect, Sir George Gilbert Scott. Scott was responsible for many such restorations and was something of a workaholic, indeed, he was so busy that he once telegraphed his London office from Manchester, with the perplexed request 'Why am I here?'

The Cathedral stands on a rise overlooking the River Severn and the WORCESTERSHIRE COUNTY CRICKET GROUND, where traditionally, touring Test teams play their first county matches. Ornamental gardens cluster around the WATERGATE at the bottom of the rise where a ferry once ran when the city was walled and a tablet on the gate records the impressive heights gained by the river during floods.

The Guildhall - Worcester

It is a splendidly English backdrop, ideally suited to our summer game but in 1651 the area now dedicated to peaceful recreation would have seen the Royalist forces stumbling in retreat before Cromwell's invincible Model Army. The clash of steel and thunder of guns rang out where leather meets willow today. Relics, displays and mementoes of the Battle of Worcester and other aspects of the Civil War are to be found in the COMMANDERY, a fine 15th century timber-framed building built on the site of an earlier hospital founded by St Wulfstan, and in the baroque 18th century GUILDHALL with it's sumptious assembly rooms. I have mentioned the friendliness of the inhabitants of Worcester but it obviously does not pay to cross them, since not only do they skin light-fingered Scandinavians but they also have an unpleasant habit of nailing effigies of their enemy's heads to public buildings by their ears. A careful study of the splendid facade of the Guildhall will reveal the likeness of Oliver Cromwell, affixed in the manner described, on the keystone of the central porch! Further evidence of such bloodthirstiness is to be found in the CITY MUSEUM AND ART GALLERY, which, apart from much of general local interest (including the ultimate fisherman's tale; an incredible eight-foot sturgeon caught in the Severn) contains the Regimental Museum of the Worcestershire Regiment, who rejoiced in the stomach-turning nickname of 'the Vein-Openers'! Their heroism and professionalism in battle earned them the approbation of Wellington, who called them 'the best regiment in this army', while the city's loyalty to the Crown was recognised by Charles II, who gave it the motto 'May the faithful city flourish'.

*Patriotism of a more peaceful variety is to be found in the music of that most English of composers, Sir Edward Elgar, who succeeded his father as organist at ST GEORGE'S ROMAN CATHOLIC CHURCH and who was born at nearby **Broadheath**, where his birthplace has been preserved as a museum. Music is an important part of Worcester life and every third year it plays host to the world's oldest musical celebration, the THREE CHOIRS FESTIVAL, which was started in 1717. The other cathedral cities involved are Hereford and Gloucester.*

SPETCHLEY PARK on the city's eastern edge is an early 19th century mansion with a deer park and splendid formal gardens that are open to the public. An ancestor of the present owners, one Robert Berkeley, founded the alms houses known as the BERKELEY HOSPITAL in Foregate Street, Worcester. Still in use today, they were built in 1692 and their design is Dutch in style. Architectural styles more familiar to the English eye can be seen in COLLEGE YARD, BRITANNIA and ST GEORGE'S SQUARES (Regency) and in the splendid half-timbered GREYFRIARS (Tudor with later additions) which has been fully restored under the aegis of the National Trust and which also has a most delightful walled garden. The five hundred year old TUDOR HOUSE FOLK MUSEUM is close-by and has fascinating displays of social history while in Severn Street, the DYSON PERRINS MUSEUM contains examples of Royal Worcester porcelain dating back to 1751 and includes the dinner service made for the Prince and Princess of Wales. The Royal Worcester Porcelain Company is the oldest factory to manufacture porcelain and was established in 1751.

I have made the point that the city repays close investigation and one of my discoveries was in the rather mundane surroundings of the FOREGATE RAILWAY STATION where there is a splendid example of private enterprise in the shape of THE REAL SANDWICH SHOP; a station cafe which serves excellent cakes, snacks and sandwiches with nary a stale BR bun in sight - and you don't have to be a traveller to enjoy their home-made produce.

Two very varied forms of entertainment are offered by the SWAN THEATRE and WORCESTER RACECOURSE, which was founded in 1718. A newspaper report of that time recounts that ' The company that appeared on the Course was very numerous and genteel. Peevishness and Debate were no-where to be found; but Cheerfulness, Harmony and Universal Satisfaction were everywhere visible .' Children will enjoy facilities at BENNETTS FARM PARK at Lower Wick, which apart from the animals and farm displays, also includes a children's adventure playground and coarse and game fishing. In the suburb of St John's, to the west of the city, I visited two extremely hospitable and professionally-run pubs that presented a neat contrast to each other. One was the modern COPPERTOPS in Oldbury Road, a large and cheerful establishment with function rooms and a restaurant full of people who had the air of those having a thoroughly good time. The other was the neat little CROWN INN in Bransford Road; a quieter and more traditional pub but every bit as welcoming and friendly.

Setting out to the east from Worcester, one crosses the M5 and enters fruit growing country; an area stretching from Worcester across to Stratford and home, amongst many other varieties, to that most ancient of apples, the Worcester Pearmain. The Romans were the first to introduce this delicious and versatile fruit to our islands and the Pearmain is the first named variety of which there is any note being first recorded as early as 1204.

The first village I visited was Crowle, an attractive village with a tree-lined main street and pleasantly varied architecture. Although the CHURCH OF ST JOHN THE BAPTIST was rebuilt in the 19th century it has a fine 14thcentury timber porch with a carving of the Annunciation under the gable and a remarkable marble lectern which is thought to be over 700 years old. Possibly from the Abbey at Evesham, it lay in the churchyard until 1845 until rescued by the vicar of that time, and is carved with the figure of a kneeling man clinging to two vine tendrils. Nearby, but seemingly far more remote, is the 15thcentury moated house of HUDDINGTON COURT which once belonged to the Winter or Wyntour family. The handsome old house has intimate connections with the Gunpowder Plot of 1605, for the Winters were party to the intrigue with their cousin Robert Catesby, and when the plot failed, they and other conspirators paused here on their flight from retribution. Appropriately, the house has both priest-holes and a headless ghost, said to be that of Robert

Winter. The fine little church which stands outside of the moat, contains the arms of the Winters and some excellent 15th century glass together with linenfold panelling.

*The Gunpowder plot was a minority Catholic reaction to persecution under the rule of James I; the majority of Catholics practiced their religion in private and their priests travelled incognito and were hidden in houses both great and small. The RED HART INN at **Kington** well may have had such associations for it is thought that the original sign was that of the 'Red (i.e. Bleeding or Sacred) Heart '. Situated just to the south of the A422 Worcester-Stratford road, this 400 year old half-timbered pub now has a reputation for cheerful company, excellent food and drink and is a great favourite with the sporting fraternity - cricketers and fishermen in particular and touring Test teams are not unknown ! **Dormston**, a hamlet lying to the north of the main road is worth visiting to see the CHURCH OF ST NICHOLAS, with it's black and white timber-framed tower and MOAT FARM with it's timbered dovecot.*

*This part of Worcestershire is an ideal situation from which to explore the charms of the county and the neighbouring areas and **Inkberrow**, a couple of miles to the east of Kington is a fine base for any such expeditions. A handsome church overlooks the village which slopes away and which is composed of houses both modern and old Mature trees surround the area and the black-and-white facade of THE BULL INN looks out across the village green. Farmland surrounds the whole and there is an air of rural calm - a very picture of bucolic bliss. Sounds familiar? Well, the BBC based the mythical 'Ambridge Village' of the 'Archers' on Inkberrow and when I stayed at the hospitable BULLS HEAD HOTEL in the High Street, I could swear that the originals of both Dan Archer and Eddie Grundy were in the bar that night! the Bulls Head is a family run business with a brick facade but the cosy interior reveals clear evidence of a far older establishment with exposed beams, inglenook fireplaces and flagstone floors.*

*My first stop heading south was at **Church Lench** ('lench' means a hill) in orchard country where the much re-built parish church contains the remains of a faded 16th century blue velvet cope, beautifully embroidered with figures of the saints. Decorative skills are also on show at the ANNARD WOOLLEN MILL, a working mill which stocks both ready-made garments and exclusive designs for knitting at home.*

Further to the south and east there are two quite different National Trust properties well worth visiting. The first is the magnificent TITHE BARN at **Middle Littleton**. Around 140 feet long and some 40 feet wide, it was built in 1376 and used as the great barn for **Evesham Abbey**. This no doubt accounts for its faint ecclesiastical air provided by the slender buttresses and gable crosses. It is still in use as a farm building and has a happy air of continuity for just that reason - as does the second property which is best visited during licensing hours! This is the FLEECE INN at **Bretforton**, a converted mediaeval farmhouse with a fine collection of pewter and furniture. There is a delightful small square facing the CHURCH OF ST LEONARD, which is 12th century in origin and contains a list of incumbents dating back to 1191, as well as some splendid carvings.

The River Avon almost entirely encircles **Evesham**, a town which owes it's beginnings to a vision of the Madonna seen by a local swine-herd called Eoves. Egwin, Bishop of Worcester, established a monastery on the site in 714 and became it's first Abbot. THE ABBEY rapidly became an important place of pilgrimage and a town grew around the site. The original shrine of Eoves' vision increased in importance with the canonisation of Egwin and then, 560 years after the Abbey's foundation came the battle which would lead to a third shrine within it's precincts. The barons, led by Simon de Montfort, fell out with Henry III over the interpretation of the Magna Carta and a short but bloody war resulted. The barons held Henry captive after defeating him in battle but had failed to hold on to his son, who later became Edward I. The Battle of Evesham, which took place on the 4th August 1265, resulted in a crushing defeat for the barons and was an astonishing feat of arms by the young prince who had left Worcester on the morning of August the 2nd, marched to Kenilworth and captured it, then turned to the south to approach Evesham on the morning of the 4th - sixty miles in forty-eight hours, not forgetting the hand-to-hand combat on the way! De Montfort's body was dismembered but the trunk was buried before the High Altar of the Abbey where it soon became the shrine of a man the common people considered a folk-hero, and who is remembered today as the 'Father of Parliaments'. The Abbey grew ever-more wealthy and two churches were built outside the monastic grounds to cater for the townsfolk and the pilgrims respectively, and these churches, dedicated to ST LAWRENCE and to ALL SAINTS, still remain. The Abbey was pulled down during the Dissolution and the principal remains include the magnificent Perpendicular bell-tower, built by the last *rightful abbot, Clement Lichfield, who is also remembered in both churches.*

Evesham Abbey

The ALMONRY MUSEUM *chronicles much of Evesham's history and, although the town is a busy marketing and light industrial centre, it's fascinating history is reflected in the ancient buildings and streets. It is also very much a town of, rather than by, the river since the Severn has acted as a means of both defence and transport in times past and of recreation today.*

The Vale of Evesham was described by the American writer Henry James as 'The dark rich hedgy flats of Worcestershire'. Since he wrote those words in 1875, the majority of the hedges have long gone in the pursuit of intensive cultivation of fruit and vegetables. All manner of varieties are grown in the fertile tilth including such exotics as asparagus and peppers, but it is the fruit that gives the area it's greatest glory - albeit for only a short time. Generally around late March and early May, depending on the climate, the area becomes almost magical with blossom from cherries, apples, pears and plums. There are well marked SPRING BLOSSOM TRAILS that can be followed on car, bike or foot and it is one of the most wonderful sights that the English countryside has to offer. It is nothing less than a total transformation and there are many who come back year after year to view the splendour. It is an interesting fact that although local farmers had appreciated the fertility of the Vale's soil for centuries, it was left to a foreigner to reveal its true potential. Francesco Bernardi was a Genoese envoy in the 17th century who settled in the Vale after a dispute with his country. He spent the enormous sum of £30,000 to begin, in effect, the local industry of market-gardening.

The area between Evesham and Pershore has a number of most attractive villages which are worthy of investigation. Cropthorne with it's CHURCH OF ST MICHAEL, which contains the finest Saxon Christian relic in the country; an intricately carved cross dating from 250 years before the Conquest. CROPTHORNE MILL is an exceptionally fine picturesque water-mill which is a great favourite with artists and photographers. Nearby Fladbury also has a mill which was in use from Domesday until the 1930's and a number of handsome 18th century buildings. It is a village with a long history since excavations have revealed traces of Bronze Age settlement, as well as Roman and Saxon. At Lower Moor there is a most hospitable half-timbered inn, THE OLD CHESTNUT TREE, where even the resident ghost is of a genial disposition !

Pershore is the second town of the Vale and was once the 'third town' of the county after Worcester and Droitwich. A handsome town with a predominance of seemingly Georgian architecture (many are facades built onto older buildings) it lies to the north of Bredon Hill amongst water-meadows beside the Avon's meanderings. It too, has an Abbey although considerably more survives than that of neighbouring Evesham. PERSHORE ABBEY is still a magnificent building although much reduced in size; it has a splendid pinnacled tower supported on high Norman arches and a wonderful vaulted roof to the choir with much fine carving. The original religious settlement dates back as far as 689 but depredations from Danish pirates and disbelieving Saxons meant that little of import was established until the Benedictines founded a monastery dedicated to King Alfred's grand-daughter, St Eadburh. Over the centuries the Abbey grew, surviving set-backs like the fire in 1288 which led to the re-building of the present tower, until the Dissolution of the Monasteries when the faithful citizens of Pershore bought the monastic part of the building for their own use at a cost of £400. Pershore's prosperity, like Evesham, is strongly linked to the surrounding fertile land and to the River Avon which for many years enabled agricultural produce to be sent downstream to Bristol, including the famous Pershore Plums.

THE LOWER AND UPPER AVON NAVIGATION TRUSTS have done tremendous work in restoring the numerous locks and weirs dating back to the 17th-century that enable the river to be fully navigable. The advent of the railways meant that many of these riverine structures fell into disrepair and the work done by the Trusts has been extensive and of benefit to all. I recommend a boat trip to appreciate not only the beauty of this unique part of England but also to see and appreciate the work that has, and is being done.

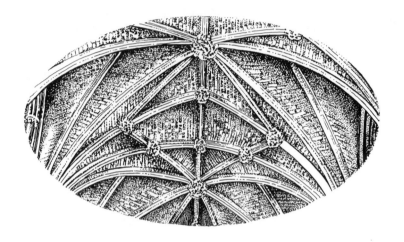

The Lierne Vault of Pershore Abbey

Pershore is a most attractive town with many handsome buildings including the Regency-style ROYAL THREE TUNS (with it's handsome ironwork balcony), the Georgian PERROTT HOUSE and the ancient half- timbered ALMONRY.

Sight-seeing has a tendency to make one hungry and I was fortunate to discover the IMPERIAL RESTAURANT in the High Street; a most pleasant and welcoming Chinese restaurant with cuisine and service of a very high standard.

To the south-west lies another small town of considerable appeal whose fortunes have also been linked to a river: **Upton upon Severn.** *The Severn is stronger and more direct than the meandering Avon and for many years Upton possessed the only bridge across the river between Gloucester and Worcester and was such an important* meeting place for river craft that what became known as the 'Bridge Parliament' was held there. Obviously, the bridge was of major tactical importance during the Civil War and the Royalists, based at Worcester, blew out two of the spans to prevent an outflanking movement - but in vain. Due to the negligence of a sentry, a small party of Roundheads crept across the plank that had been left across the gap and barricaded themselves in the church, resisting all efforts to displace them until relieved by their own cavalry which had crossed at an unguarded ford. Upton fell to the Parliamentarians and the church was partially destroyed. There is a romantic sequel to the brief but savage skirmish; that evening Cromwell himself arrived to congratulate his men and saw, at an upstairs window, a beautiful girl in obvious distress. He asked her name and when told that it was a Miss Morris, he pardoned her brother whom he had just condemned to be shot. It is nice to know that Old Ironsides had the human touch..

Upton-upon-Severn is a charming little town where such a story seems eminently believable. The mediaeval church tower survives, crowned with a copper-covered cupola and is now used as an heritage centre, whilst in the churchyard can be found that well-known epitaph:-

> 'Beneath this stone, in hope of Zion,
> Doth lie the landlord of the Lion,
> His son keeps on the business still,
> Resigned unto the heavenly will.'

Apt lines for a town that has a greater number of pubs per head of resident population than most - probably as a result of the old river traffic. Incidentally, the (WHITE) LION is still thriving and all the pubs do a roaring trade during the many Summer events that take place here, such as THE STEAM RALLY, THE WATER FESTIVAL, and THE JAZZ and FOLK FESTIVALS.

Earl's Croome received it's title from the mediaeval earls of Warwick and is a peaceful little place close to the north-east of Upton. It has a fine Elizabethan manor house where Samuel Butler (1835-1902) the author of Hudibras once worked as secretary to the Squire, and a good-looking church which, with the exception of the tower, is largely Norman. There is also a cheerful and welcoming pub with a large restaurant in the shape of THE YORKSHIRE GREY. Good value, good fun and a quite overwhelming collection of tankards!

The next village to the west also has a fine church and manor house and once had a castle, too. HANLEY CASTLE was the site of a fortification built by King John to command the important high road from Worcester to Upton-upon-Severn and was the residence of the Keeper of Malvern Forest until Tudor times, when it was pulled down as part of Henry VII's policy of reducing the power of the barons. Much of the stone has gone into the construction of buildings such as the alms houses and the old grammar school; all that remains of the fortifications is a few mounds and depressions to the south of the church.

Worcestershire's greatest natural glories is to be found to the west of the Severn. The Malverns are perhaps the originators of that well-known phrase 'as old as the hills' for this ridge of pre-Cambrian rock is more than 500 million years old. The name means 'the bare hills' and they rise gently from fertile soils and woodlands to stand guardians against the prevailing winds. Although of no great height (the highest point is only 1394 feet) their appearance is impressive in contrast to the lowlands from which they spring, and the infinite permutations of light and shade sweeping over their bracken-strewn slopes and barren summits have inspired musicians, poets and artists over the centuries. The wilder and less inhabited southern end has long been my favourite and I stayed with old friends living just over the border in neighbouring Herefordshire in order to explore the area more fully. The small village of **Eastnor**, a mile to the east of **Ledbury**, has a distinctly Wodehousian air to it and one feels that at any minute the tweedy shambling figure of the Earl of Emsworth, accompanied by his favourite pig, the Empress of Blandings, could appear sauntering along the twisting lanes at the foot of the hills. Perhaps this feeling is explained by the fact that much of the village is still part of a large estate based on the splended 19th century Norman-style EASTNOR CASTLE, a wonderful confection designed by Robert Smirke for John, first Earl Somers, with additional works by Pugin, Fox and the indefatigable Scott (who also had a hand in the restoration of the Church and the Rectory). The castle, enclosed by arboretum, lake and deer-park has a magnificent ornate interior with collections of armour, furniture and works of art. The well-kept village is composed of farms, cottages (including a delightful half-timbered post-office complete with rose-bowl) a school, and a handsome Norman church with a fine gilded weathervance in the shape of a cockerel. The Earl's descendants still live there and on neighbouring MIDSUMMER HILL there is an obelisk erected in *memory of a relative killed in the Peninsular War. The Hill bears traces of an ancient hill fort, a companion to the better-known Iron Age BRITISH CAMP, on the HEREFORDSHIRE BEACON.*

Walking the beautiful hills is a sure way to work up both thirst and appetite and there is an excellent old hostelry which caters to both at Berrow, just off the A438, some 6 miles to the east of Ledbury. THE DUKE OF YORK has a long history of catering to travellers for it dates back to the 14th century when it was used by pilgrims making their way from Tewkesbury to Hereford. The old stone cross in the churchyard of the mediaeval ST FAITH'S is reputed to have once stood outside the inn. Birtsmorton is less than a mile from the hamlet of Berrow and the squire to Henry VI, Sir John Nanfan, once lived at the ancient moated BIRTSMORTON COURT. Cardinal Wolseley was also resident when he was a young man and acting as chaplain to Sir Richard Nanfan, sometime Deputy Constable of Calais - The 14th century CHURCH OF ST PETER AND ST PAUL, adjacent to the Court, contains a number of memorials to the family, including the tomb of Admiral William Caldwell who was the second husband of the four-times married Catherine Nanfan, last of the family. The Admiral's tomb is a splendidly nautical affair with a ship and all manner of naval impedimenta and one cannot help but wonder how Birtsmorton's most famous son would have fared had he been buried there. William Huskisson was a 19th century politician and cabinet minister whose manner of death is remembered rather than his statesman-like qualities; he was the first railway fatality, having been crushed to death at the opening of the Liverpool and Manchester Railway in 1830.

At nearby Castlemorton there is the MALVERN HILLS ANIMAL AND BIRD GARDEN.

Moving away from the woodland, furze and common-land of this part of Worcestershire I made my way north into the very heart of the Malverns. The name is not only applied to the hills but to the straggle of six distinct settlements often referred to collectively as Malvern. These are Little Malvern, Malvern Wells, Malvern Link, Great Malvern, North Malvern and West Malvern this is an area of extraordinary beauty, interest and entertainment and if you are going to stay hereabouts and really enjoy yourself then I can do no better than to recommend THE COTTAGE IN THE WOODS HOTEL at Malvern Wells. Described as having the 'best view in

WORCESTERSHIRE

England', an opinion I would not disagree with, this superlatively comfortable small hotel sits high in wooded countryside overlooking the Severn Valley with the Cotswolds in the distance.

Little Malvern is the smallest and southernmost of the Malverns and nestles cosily in the lee of the steep slopes. THE CHURCH OF ST GILES is all that remains of a larger priory church and was treated roughly by the Parliamentarians during the Civil War who removed the misericords and damaged some of the beautiful 15th century glass. They also left a sword behind in the graveyard which is now kept in a glass case. It is a somewhat un-Christian thought but one can only hope that losing a weapon was courts-martial offence in those days ! Next to the church is LITTLE MALVERN COURT, parts of which date back to the 12th century and which was the refectory of Prior's Hall of the original monastic foundation. Long a family home, it contains a priest-hole, a magnificent 14th century roof and a number of treasures including a travelling trunk and silk quilt belonging to Catherine of Aragon.

The shifting play of light and shadow on the ancient hills, sometimes dramatic, more often subtle and complex is nowhere better artistically represented than in the wonderful music of Sir Edward Elgar. It seems only right that this man of Worcestershire whose genius was acknowledged worldwide but who remained a countryman at heart, should be buried, together with his wife and daughter, in the quiet peace of the Malverns at ST WULFSTAN'S ROMAN CATHOLIC CHURCH.

Another great musician is buried not far away in the Wilton Road Cemetery; the 'Swedish Nightingale' , Jenny Lind. The greatest soprano of her day, she was adored and mobbed wherever she went; in New York, the police department had to turn fire-hoses on the crowd who had turned out to see her disembark. Although born in Stockholm, she too ended her days in the shelter of these beautiful hills.

The strict contemplative life of a monastic order would seem ideally suited to this region and MALVERN PRIORY CHURCH is the sole, but impressive, remnant of a large priory which dates back to 1088. Unfortunately, the monastic order was not always strict or contemplative for, in 1282, the prior was accused of adultery with twenty-two women! Although the conventual buildings (the living quarters) were nearly all pulled down in the Dissolution, the church was retained by the payment of £20 (in two instalments) - a wonderful bargain for a building which is externally a fine example of Perpendicular architecture with a light and airy interior which includes a six-bay Norman nave of the early 1100's. The 15th century stained glass is wonderfully complimented by some beautiful tiles of the same period, together with a fine set of misericords. Once again, the humour of the old craftsmen has been given full sway, for example, there are three mice hanging a cat and a drunkard being beaten by his wife to name just two. THE MALVERN MUSEUM is housed in the other surviving part of the priory, The Abbey Gateway.

Great Malvern surrounds the church and is essentially late 18th and early 19th century in character and is a product of the period's preoccupation with spa waters. There are distinct parallels with life today; our pre-occupation with health, diet, fitness and beauty has led to the establishment of fashionable 'health farms' while the Georgians and Victorians had their spas and hyaros.

Perhaps the only difference being the emphasis our ancestors placed on ailments affecting digestion - hardly surprising when one considers the amount that they ate! Four meals a day, breakfast, lunch, dinner and supper were the norm, even for the lower middle classes and a menu from a local hotel, now defunct, offers the following delights :-

Caviare
Soups : Mulligatawney or Julienne
Fish : Brill or Stewed Eels
Entrees : Salmi of Wild Duck or Chicken Cream
Roast : Sirloin of Beef or Haunch of Mutton
Sweets : Orange Fritters, Benedictine Soufflee or Ices
Savouries : Angels on Horseback or Cheese Straws

All this was accompanied by copious quantities of the appropriate wines and liqueurs and eaten in tight restricting clothing; well-laced whalebone corsets being de rigeur for the women and the vainer men. Consequently, anyone offering relief from such embarrassing disorders as 'Constipation, Flatulence, Diarrhoea and Indigestion or similar ailments arising from Impure Blood or Disordered Stomach' was undoubtedly on to a winner.

The first entrepreneur to exploit the area's waters was the founder of the Royal Worcester Porcelain Works, one Dr John Wall. He had, however, one slight problem in extolling the curative properties of the liquid; it tasted pleasantly fresh and sparkling - quite the reverse of the generally foul-flavoured mineral-rich fluids experienced in other fashionable resorts. Dr Wall was evidently made of stern stuff and had a marketing ability that would have made him a target for all major executive recruitment agencies were he still alive today.

'Malvern Water, said Dr Wall,
Is famed for containing nothing at all.'

This was the essence of the campaign and it worked! His premise was quite simply that, since the water was so pure, the cure was effected faster 'as it could pass more rapidly through the vessels of the body'.

The town quickly became fashionable and hotels, pump rooms and lodging houses were built. The Victorians added a further refinement by introducing a form of 'water-cure' that was horrific by anyone's standards. This consisted of being wrapped tightly in cold wet sheets for hours on end, having hundreds of gallons of icy water dropped on you from a great height, cold baths, long walks, a strict diet and naturally nothing but water to drink. Recreation was strictly controlled with even reading being banned as 'too demanding' . It was a wonder that anyone survived; nevertheless, the resort attracted the likes of the Royal Family, Gladstone, Florence Nightingale, Macaulay, Carlyle, Wordsworth and Charles Darwin to name but a few.

It was not long before the more artistic visitors started organising entertainments and concerts, and from these beginnings evolved the MALVERN FESTIVAL. This was closely linked in it's early days with the playwright George Bernard Shaw, and is now an internationally-known annual event involving music and drama. The world's first film festival was held here and has been revived in recent years with great success. These events are based upon the MALVERN FESTIVAL THEATRE and the WINTER GARDENS, which also hosts numerous other concerts, productions and exhibitions.

The waters have not been forgotten and are bottled and exported all over the world by Cadbury Schweppes, while the awful Victorian *water treatments have been replaced by the delights of a 'water activity centre'. THE SPLASH, an indoor complex complete with water-slide, wave-making machine and 'beach'.*

Malvern is not merely a resort and retirement area; it has a wide range of enterprises which include both the unusual and the eccentric. Education plays a big part in the life of the town with a quite phenomenal number and variety of schools including the famous MALVERN COLLEGE. MORGAN CARS build hand-crafted sports cars and follow on a long tradition that dates back to the fact that the country's first internal-combustion powered vehicle, the Santler, was built here. Other products manufactured in and around the town include high-quality porcelain, kites, musical instruments and electronics.

Above all (literally) are the hills and to walk their eight mile length and savour the amazing views is to see England at its very best. The MALVERN HILLS CONSERVATORS were set up by Parliament in 1884 to protect the common land from commercial exploitation and they have done their job wonderfully well. There are more than twenty-six miles of footpaths, together with a number of discreet car-parks so that the hills can be enjoyed by all.

The Malvern Hills

Madresfield meaning the 'Field of the Mowers' is home to the MADRESFIELD AGRICULTURAL SHOW, a delightfully local show featuring all manner of events including equestrian events, vintage agricultural machinery displays and innumerable animal classes. It is held in the grounds of MADRESFIELD COURT, a handsome Victorian mansion built on mediaeval and Elizabethan foundations and which is considered to be the inspiration for Evelyn Waugh's revisited 'Brideshead'.

A good family pub to visit after exploring the Malverns or visiting an agricultural show, is to be found a couple of miles north-east of Great Malvern; THE OLD BUSH at *Callow End* is a cheerful old black and white building which provides a play-ground for children and has barbeques and pig-roasts on Saturday night throughout the summer.

Powick is just to the north and saw much conflict in the Civil War. This is where the River Teme merges with the Severn and the area surrounding the narrow stone bridge was of particular tactical importance. Nine years to the day before Charles II fled from defeat after the Battle of Worcester, a crack Royalist cavalry squadron wiped out a similar-sized Parliamentary force. It is hard to imagine Prince Rupert's troopers galloping with sword and lance across the modern housing estate of today.

Echoes of that earlier battle at Evesham are to be found at *Kempsey*, a mile to the east of Callow End. The village has grown over the years but the old centre stands grouped around the CHURCH OF ST MARY, close to the Severn. Here, Simon de Montfort heard Mass for the last time before his defeat and brutal death. With him was his prisoner, Henry III, and they were given hospitality that night by Bishop Cantelupe, later canonised as St Thomas of Hereford. The church, which contains some rare 13th and 14th century glass and the fine tomb of Sir Edmund Wylde is also noted for the strange fact that, for many years, a horse-chestnut grew out of the tomb. Legend has it that it grew from a conker confiscated from a mischievous choir-boy during a service!

Bishop Cantelupe's name is given to the hospitable and attractive WALTER DE CANTELUPE INN which makes a speciality of serving excellent local produce including at least a dozen local cheeses. The inn also has a most attractive and secluded walled garden, perfect for eating and drinking during the summer.

*A mile away from the village, just off the A38 Worcester to Tewkesbury road is another splendid pub, THE HUNTSMAN INN. Close to the commons of Kempsey and **Stonehall**, this is a massively-built country pub of the 'traditional' type with a most cheerful and friendly atmosphere.*

*Skirting the city of Worcester, I made my way towards the north-east and the Teme Valley, back amongst rich farmland running down to the looping river. I stopped off to visit the ELGAR BIRTHPLACE MUSEUM at **Lower Broadheath**. A modest little cottage which has been beautifully restored, and, together with the fascination of seeing so many relics relating to the great man, has a most friendly and welcoming atmosphere.*

*To the north, at the end of a lane in meadows bordering the Severn, lies the village of **Grimley**. Apart from some gravel pits and a number of farms, this would seem a quiet and prosaic country community. However, in the churchyard lies Sir Samuel Baker (1821-93), an African explorer of renown, discoverer of Lake Nyanza and the Murchison Falls, big-game hunter and colonial administrator, while at neighbouring **Thorngrove** lived an even more exotic character, in the shape of Lucien Bonaparte. He was the younger brother of Napoleon and offended the Emperor by marrying the ex-wife of a planter. Napoleon offered Lucien the Kingdoms of Spain and Naples if he would renounce the woman but Lucien refused and, in trying to escape to America, was captured by the British. He eventually settled with his wife in this remote corner of Worcestershire, where they happily whiled away the remaining war years by writing turgid epic poetry together.*

*At **Wichenford** the National Trust has restored a marvellous 17th century half-timbered Dovecote and the nearby WICHENFORD COURT is said to play host to two female ghosts, both members of the Washbourne family. One stalks around holding a bloody dagger aloft (she was reputed to have murdered a French prince) and the other plays a harp whilst sitting in a silver boat drawn by white swans. Makes a change from grey ladies and headless horsemen !*

__Martley__ is a large village on the B4204 that is worth visiting for it's CHURCH OF ST PETER. Lichen grows on the red sandstone walls and in the churchyard grows a huge cross of clipped yew, but it is the interior that is of greatest interest. We tend to forget how ornate the insides of our churches were before the Reformation swept away so much decorative work. Martley is worth visiting to see the amazing mediaeval wall paintings including 'St Martin and the Beggar' and the 'Adoration of the Wise Men'. There are numerous patterns and animals both strange and familiar and there is also a fine tie-beam roof.

In the north-western corner of the region it is worth making a detour to visit the derelict grandeurs of GREAT WITLEY COURT and the baroque CHURCH OF ST MICHAEL. The court, originally a Jacobean mansion with Georgian additions was given an Italianate facade in the last century when the Earl of Dudley was said to have spent a quarter of a million pounds on its renovation, an enormous sum of money in today's terms. The result was a palace-like building where royalty frequently stayed, but in 1937 it was largely destroyed by fire and plans to auction the remainder were thwarted by the 1938 Munich Crisis. Today, the great house is a truly noble ruin amongst the remains of landscaped gardens, complete with two massive fountains. The church is perhaps even more extraordinary; described as Britain's finest baroque church, it is best thought of as an ornate Venetian or Bavarian chapel languishing in the very depths of rural England. It is a quite extraordinary confection of gold and white inside inside a comparatively plain exterior. Brilliant colours warm the interior from the glass and paintings and there is an almost overwhelming monument to the chapel's creator, Lord Foley.

The landscape of the county reveals many such gems whether man-made or natural. The glorious blossom, the ancient buildings and the views from the hills - even in the most mundane little corner there is always something to interest and delight.

THE DUKE OF YORK

Berrow,
Malvern,
Worcestershire.

Public House & Restaurant

Tel: (0684) 81-449

This is a pub with a tremendous history that goes back as far as the 14th century. It was used by pilgrims travelling from Tewkesbury to Hereford and by local Yorkists during the War of the Roses. The pub was also the meeting place for the wild boar hunt on Malvern Chase and features in the book of that name. It is said that the 'Pilgrims Cross' which now stands in the porch of Berrow Church used to be at the front of the pub on what was then the village green

Berrow is a quiet, tranquil place, close to the Malvern Hills making it a centre for people who enjoy walking. Pam Harber is the lively, informally professional, owner of the pub and she is ably assisted by a first class staff. The Duke of York is frequented by many regular customers who have discovered how good the food is both at lunchtime and in the evenings, seven days a week. Newcomers revel in the atmosphere of this ancient inn with its beams, nooks and crannies and warmth. It is the sort of place that once discovered is never forgotten.

The extensive menu is full of intriguing dishes including traditional favourites which frequently appear on the chef's 'Specials of the Day'. From a choice of 8 starters you can choose Wings of Fire, marinated chicken wings flash roasted or an excellent Seafood Salad. The main dishes offer anything from pasta and fish to the chef's steaks and house specialities. Crisp salads, Ploughmans, a Childrens Menu, and delectable sweets from the trolley are all available.

USEFUL INFORMATION

OPEN: 11-3pm & 6.30-11pm
CHILDREN: Yes. Menu & play area
CREDIT CARDS: Access/Visa/
    Mastercard
LICENSED: Full Licence
ACCOMMODATION: Not applicable

RESTAURANT: Wide choice
BAR FOOD: Good, wholesome food
VEGETARIAN: Always 6 dishes
ACCESS FOR THE DISABLED: Yes
GARDEN: Patio at front. Childrens
    garden

THE OLD BUSH

Public House

Upton Road,
Callow End,
Worcester.

Tel: (0905) 830792

The Old Bush is a typical country pub in the traditional manner. Black and white on the outside with a large car park and an enormous garden, the inside is friendly, warm and comfortable with one large bar which has an open fire that greets you with its cheery glow in winter. The dining room is secluded and a delightful place in which to eat the well prepared meals.

Matthew and Jane Williams are the proprietors whose enthusiasm for their job is infectious and makes The Old Bush a happy place to visit. During the summer months they stay open all day long and the garden is much in use. In it there is a children's play area complete with one of those fantastic bouncy castles which delight young ones for hours. Barbeques and 'Pig Roasts' are the order of the day every Saturday throughout the summer,weather permitting, whilst indoors there is live music or a Quiz night every week.

The food is simple, wholesome and mostly home-cooked. The Steak and Kidney Pie is very popular served with chips or Jacket potatoes. You can choose from quite a range of dishes from plaice, and scampi to curry, chilli, steaks and gammon or vegetarian dishes. Chips are served with everything but they are crisp, golden and delicious. Cream teas are offered in the afternoons in the summer months. Good value, generous portions.

USEFUL INFORMATION

OPEN: 12-3pm & 5.45-11pm
All day Sat. & every day in summer
CHILDREN: Yes & in play area
CREDIT CARDS: None taken
LICENSED: Full Licence
ACCOMMODATION: Not applicable

DINING ROOM: Good
traditional fare
BAR FOOD: Wide range,
traditional
VEGETARIAN: Always 3 dishes
ACCESS FOR THE DISABLED:
Yes, no facilities
GARDEN: Large. Childrens
area. Bouncy castle

THE YORKSHIRE GREY
Public House & Restaurant

Worcester Road,
Earls Croome,
Worcestershire.

Tel: (0684) 592155

Just two miles away from the popular riverside town of Upton on Severn and on the main Worcester to Tewkesbury road, is the little hamlet of Earls Croome in which is The Yorkshire Grey, originally built in the 18th century as a cottage. It has grown elegantly and charmingly over the years. Today it has comfortable bars and a very attractive restaurant which can seat 100 comfortably and yet still remains intimate.

Many people have discovered the delights of the Yorkshire Grey and come from Malvern which is 5 miles away or drive the 7 miles from Tewkesbury or 12 miles from Worcester, to sample the wide selection of keg and traditional beers and lager, or the interesting wine list and cider. Food, of course, is very important and The Yorkshire Grey has a super chef who has been there for years, as indeed have many of the staff. This continuity has done much to endear the pub to its faithful followers. There is no doubt that guests like to see familiar faces. Everyone is given a sincere welcome especially by Eric Little and Dena Davis, the joint proprietors. In addition to enjoying the food and drink, you can also have great fun on the dart board or enjoy a quiet game of Crib or Dominoes. In summer the front lawn and back patio are favourite places in which to drink, under the gaily coloured umbrellas. This nice pub deserves its good reputation and is one to be savoured.

USEFUL INFORMATION

OPEN: 11an-11pm
CHILDREN: Welcome. Highchairs
CREDIT CARDS: None taken
LICENSED: Full Licence
ACCOMMODATION: Not applicable
GARDEN: Garden & patio. Tables, umbrellas etc

RESTAURANT: Good food at sensible prices
BAR FOOD: Wide choice. Good value
VEGETARIAN: Always several dishes
ACCESS FOR THE DISABLED: By arrangement

THE BULLS HEAD
Public House & Hotel

High Street
Inkberrow,
Worcestershire

Tel: (0386) 792233/793090

Situated in the very heart of Worcestershire countryside, Inkberrow is very well known by the many 'Archers' listeners as being the basis for the village of Ambridge. In its main street is an old pub, The Bulls Head which offers everything a traditional inn should. Real log fires glow in the Inglenook fireplaces, original 14th-century flagstone floors gleam with the patina of age and there are a wealth of exposed beams. The cosy, well furnished bars open their arms in welcome, and the well appointed table areas tempt you to sample some of the items on the extensive Bar Food Menu.

This is a family run business with Ray and Sonia Millward at the helm, assisted by their three delightful daughters and a friendly staff. If you stay here you will find the bedrooms all have en-suite facilities, colour TV and tea/coffee making equipment. You will come down in the morning after an excellent night's sleep to a huge English breakfast which is included in the tariff.

The Bull is only 15 minutes from Stratford on Avon and Worcester Cathedral, within minutes of Ragley Hall and Caughton Court plus many other places of interest. The menu at The Bull is simple but beautifully cooked, steaks come to table exactly as you have instructed and the 'Enormous North Sea Cod' is the best you will taste anywhere. There is a childrens menu. The Sunday Carvery is superb with succulent meats and a choice of over 10 vegetables. Why stay at home and eat?

USEFUL INFORMATION

OPEN: 11-3pm & 5-11pm
  Sat: All day
CHILDREN: Highchairs & menu
CREDIT CARDS: Access/Visa/
  Master/Euro
LICENSED: Full Licence
ACCOMMODATION: En-suite rooms

RESTAURANT: Not applicable
BAR FOOD: Superb, fresh food
VEGETARIAN: 1-2 dishes daily
ACCESS FOR THE DISABLED: Yes
GARDEN: Fenced garden. Tree
  house etc

THE HUNTSMAN INN

Inn

Green Street,
Kempsey,
Worcestershire

Tel: (0905) 820336

Just one mile outside the delightful village of Kempsey off the main A38 Worcester to Tewkesbury road is the charming, intimate and oak beamed Huntsman Inn. It is a place that is essentially part of the local community used by farmers and villagers. Occasionally you will see a sprinkling of city dwellers who have been lucky enough to discover it. Once having done so they return regularly either just to drink at the bar revelling in the warmth of the log fires in winter or perhaps to bring their children in summer so that they may play on the slides and swings in the garden. Sometimes it will be to lunch or dine in the pretty restaurant.

The Harris family run the business with just the right balance of professionalism and informality that makes it such a pleasure to come here. The Malvern Hills are quite close by and beckon to those who enjoy walking. For others a walk on Kempsey and Stone Hall Commons might be the answer after lunch.

You will find the food is good pub fare offering fresh, home-cooked dishes as well as all the time honoured favourites. Bar snacks are described by the Harris's as 'cheap and cheerful' but they would better be described as wholesome, substantial and reasonably priced. It is a pub that is just waiting to welcome you and one that you will enjoy.

USEFUL INFORMATION

OPEN: 12-3pm & 6-11pm
CHILDREN: Yes. Swings & slides
CREDIT CARDS: None taken
LICENSED: Full Licence
ACCOMMODATION: Not applicable

RESTAURANT: Good wholesome pub food
BAR FOOD: Wide range. Inexpensive
VEGETARIAN: Always 3 dishes
ACCESS FOR THE DISABLED: Level entrance
GARDEN: Lawn and play area

WALTER DE CANTELUPE INN

Inn

Main Road, Kempsey,
Worcester.

Tel: (0905) 820572

Just by the village Post Office and set back from the busy A38, one of the most used holiday and tourists routes in the country, the Walter de Cantelupe brings not only a colourful name but a wonderful array of various hues in the hanging baskets and window boxes that adorn the outside of the building.

The history of the village is fascinating going back to 1237-1266 when Walter de Cantelupe was Bishop of Worcester and chose to live in Kempsey. It was he who helped Simon de Montfort, Earl of Leicester to cross the River Severn at Kempsey. He discovered that the ford was unguarded and under cover of darkness he led de Montfort and his 5,000 troops across the river. The following morning, August 3rd 1265, the Bishop said Mass in the church for the troops and blessed them before they left for Evesham expecting to be joined by reinforcements. This was not to be, Royalist troops led by Prince Edward defeated them. Simon de Montfort was killed and his men massacred. Bishop Cantelupe fled but was captured, excommunicated and deprived of office.

The interior of the pub is delightfully furnished with antiques some of which come from India. The bar is one large area and from it French windows lead to a paved hidden garden which is wonderful on a balmy summer's night. The inn is a joy to visit and the food lives up to the high standards set by Martin Lloyd-Morris, the proprietor. Everything is fresh, home-made and good to eat.

USEFUL INFORMATION

OPEN: Easter-Mid Oct: 10am-11pm
  Oct-April: 10am-3pm & 5.30-11pm
CHILDREN: Welcome
CREDIT CARDS: Access/Visa
LICENSED: Local Real Ales.
  Good wines
ACCOMMODATION: Not applicable
RESTAURANT: Traditional
  British. Local produce

BAR FOOD: Super food, wide
  range
VEGETARIAN: At least 1 dish
  daily
ACCESS FOR THE DISABLED:
  Easy access
GARDEN: Hidden garden. Seats in
  front of inn

THE RED HART INN
Public House & Restaurant

Kington,
Flyford Flavell,
Worcestershire.

Tel: (0386) 792221

The Red Hart Inn, in the village of Kington, is wonderfully situated for anyone wanting to enjoy the countryside roundabout and is in easy reach of the Cotswolds, the Vale of Evesham and the Malvern Hills. You will find it on the A422, half way between Worcester and Stratford-upon-Avon.

The pub is over four hundred years old and much of the original black and white building remains, together with a tasteful extension built in 1992, which is in total harmony with its ancient counterpart. Over the years it has become known as 'The Sportsmans Pub' because of its great cricketing connections. Regular 'Sportsmans' lunches are held here and you are very likely to find a well known sporting personality or two in the bar who have just popped in to visit 'Drinkers', the landlord, David Drinkwater, who played for the World International Wanderers. It is a fascinating place and you will get as much pleasure in looking at all the bits and pieces of cricketing memorabilia and a substantial number of fishing rods, as you will in the excellence of the food and drink. The A La Carte restaurant seats 50 and there is a comfortable lounge area with a bar where 40-45 people can be seated. The new banqueting suite is used for all sorts of purposes including the Sunday Carvery Lunch, wedding receptions etc. From Easter to September breakfast and a super afternoon tea are available. It is one of the happiest pubs to be found.

USEFUL INFORMATION

OPEN: Mon-Sat: 11-2.30pm & 6-11pm
    Sun: 12-3pm & 7-10.30pm
    longer Easter-Sept
CHILDREN: Welcome
CREDIT CARDS: Access/Visa
LICENSED: Full Licence
ACCOMMODATION: Not applicable

RESTAURANT: Traditional menu
    & vegetarian
BAR FOOD: Trusted favourites &
    specials
VEGETARIAN: 6-10 dishes daily
ACCESS FOR THE DISABLED:
    Yes, disabled toilet
GARDEN: Large with wooden
    seats and tables

THE OLD CHESTNUT TREE
Inn

Manor Road,
Lower Moor, Nr. Pershore,
Worcestershire.

Tel: (0386) 860380

This small village in a pleasant rural setting has an excellent inn, The Old Chestnut Tree. Behind the pub is the gently flowing river, along whose banks is a delightful walk. For fishermen it is ideal.

This Grade II Listed Building is full of the character and atmosphere of centuries. Built in 1547 it was originally a Granary for the Manor House which used to be next door. Imagine what a wonderful place it is with a black and white exterior, with ancient leaded windows; inside it is still black and white with heavy beams. In the lounge there is a big open fireplace which has a gravestone in the hearth, on which is engraved 'Ann the daughter of Sarah Hantley, Died 1766, aged 15 years.' Charles, the ghost, lives in the pub. There are two stories about him. The first is that he was the Manor House priest, hiding from the Roundheads in a priest hole in a chimney. The night was cold and they lit the fire, burning the poor man to death. The second story is that he stays in the pub to guard his daughter, Sarah, whilst she lies in her grave in the hearth. He is a friendly man and there is no doubt that his presence can be felt. There are two letting rooms, a comfortable lounge, bar, and dining room. The menu is good traditional food at extremely reasonable prices. Barbecues and bands are a feature of the summer. David and Jayne Vale are the landlords of this exceptionally nice place.

USEFUL INFORMATION

OPEN: Mon-Fri: 11-2.30pm & 6-11pm
   Sat: 11-11pm
   Sun: 12-3pm & 7-10.30pm
CHILDREN: Welcome. Garden with
   slide
CREDIT CARDS: None taken at present
LICENSED: Full on Licence
ACCOMMODATION: 1 double, 1 family

RESTAURANT: Good food.
   Available for weddings
BAR FOOD: Full range of meals &
   snacks
VEGETARIAN: 6 dishes always
ACCESS FOR THE DISABLED:
   Level entrance
GARDEN: Yes with tables & chairs

THE COTTAGE IN THE WOODS HOTEL

Holywell Road,
Malvern Wells,
Worcestershire.

Hotel & Restaurant

Tel: (0684) 573487

The Cottage in the Woods is outstanding in many ways and not the least because of its stunning location. Perched high on the Malvern Hills like an Eagle's Eyrie, its magnificent vista unfolds across 30 miles of the Severn Vale to Bredon Hill, and beyond to the Cotswold Hills, which form the horizon.

The main hotel building is a Georgian Dower House, once part of the Blackmore Park Estate, home of Thomas Hornyold. Beech Cottage which has four delightful bedrooms was built in 1700 as a woodmans cottage, but was also a Cider House in which walkers on the hills found refreshment. It is a place of enchantment, with 7 acres of grounds giving direct access to the nine mile range of the Malvern Hills, which is criss-crossed with over 100 miles of paths and tracks. The hotel has a 3 star AA/RAC rating and is, deservedly, 4 Crowns Commended. John and Sue Pattin, the owner/managers have not always been hoteliers but no one can doubt that here they run a faultless establishment.

Open to non-residents, there is a cosy and well stocked bar and an elegant restaurant in which you may lunch or dine. The Luncheon Option menu allows you to have as much or as little as you like, choosing from the Light Bite Menu or indulging in a full luncheon of superb standard known as The Mega Bite. Dinner is a gastronomic dream, essentially English at heart, but influenced by styles and flavours of the world. The Cottage in the Wood is an experience no one should miss.

USEFUL INFORMATION

OPEN: 7am-11pm all year
CHILDREN: Welcome. Baby listening service
CREDIT CARDS: Access/Visa/Amex
LICENSED: Restaurant & Residential 200+ wines
ACCOMMODATION: 20 en-suite rooms

RESTAURANT: Essentially English
BAR FOOD: High quality, good choice
VEGETARIAN: 2+ on every menu
ACCESS FOR THE DISABLED: Level entrance
GARDEN: Lovely garden, tables on lawn

THE IMPERIAL RESTAURANT

Restaurant

62, High Street,
Pershore,
Worcestershire.

Tel: (0386) 556746

For anyone who enjoys Chinese cooking at its best, the gracious, Imperial Restaurant, in the High Street of Pershore, is worth seeking out. The elegant frontage is the first thing that attracts one. Once inside, the sparkling, crisp cleanliness of the table linen, the pretty floral arrangements and the smiling, welcoming staff, confirms that you are about to enjoy a feast of Peking, Szechuan or Cantonese Cuisine. Next door to the Imperial is a delightful small flower shop called 'Bloomin' Lovely' and one cannot help but think that name applies equally to the restaurant.

One of the difficulties for anyone inexperienced in Chinese cooking, is choosing the right combination from the extensive menu. If you are unsure, well trained staff will guide you through the menu and make sure that your meal will be a delicious combination of dishes. There are 'Seafood Dishes' including Spicy Sea Scallops or Fried Squid in Black Bean Sauce

'Sizzling Dishes' of Oyster, Lamb, Chicken or Fillet Beef are much in demand. 'Vegetable Dishes' are designed especially for Vegetarians but are equally popular with those who are not. The names of some of these dishes sound exotic; for example, Shaolin Temple Vegetables and Peking Mixed Vegetables. Aromatic Crispy Duck, Lobster, Crab and Sea Bass, all have their place on the menu. There is also a Take Away menu.

USEFUL INFORMATION

OPEN: Tues-Sat: 12-2.30pm & 6-11.30pm
Mon: 6-11.30pm. Closed Sundays
CHILDREN: Welcome
CREDIT CARDS: Amex/Visa/Access/
Euro/Master
LICENSED: Full Licence
ACCOMMODATION: Not applicable

RESTAURANT: Peking, Szechuan,
Cantonese
BAR FOOD: Not applicable
VEGETARIAN: Many choices
ACCESS FOR THE DISABLED: Yes
GARDEN: Not applicable

THE CROWN INN
Public House

66, Bransford Road,
St Johns,
Worcester

Tel: (0905) 421091

This well appointed black and white inn is set back along the A38 to Hereford Road. It faces the beauty of the Malvern Hills and is surrounded by local amenities. Because it is only three miles from the M5 and one mile from Elgar's birth place it is a popular and well used pub.

Once upon a time it was a Cider house but in 1987 it underwent a complete refurbishment which has made it a very attractive and comfortable place to be. Gone is the private access to the cellar which was a trap door under the bar and was reported to have been responsible for many an accident, particularly at the close of day when quite a few ales would have been consumed! The cellar is no more but it is not missed by those who enjoy their food and drink in the comfort of the new lounge, and take an interest in the pictures, adorning the walls, of the old St John's area at the turn of the century. Children are welcome here and there are special dishes for Vegetarians.

Lunch time meals are good value and generous in portion offering a wide range of dishes on the menu and several interesting specials. The home-made Leek and Potato Pie and the Sweet 'N' Sour Pork are especially popular. You can book a table and order your meal in advance if you are in a hurry. The sandwiches and Ploughmans are great for a simple meal. On Sundays a traditional lunch is available at a reasonable price.

USEFUL INFORMATION

OPEN: 11-2.30pm & 6.30-11pm
  Sun: 12-3pm & 7-10.30pm
CHILDREN: Allowed to eat with
  parents
CREDIT CARDS: None taken
LICENSED: Full Licence
ACCOMMODATION: Not applicable

RESTAURANT: Not applicable
BAR FOOD: Home-made fare
VEGETARIAN: Several
  home-made dishes
ACCESS FOR THE DISABLED:
  Level & toilets
GARDEN: No garden

COPPERTOPS

Public House & Restaurant

Oldbury Road
St Johns
Worcester.

Tel: (0905) 421230

This modern building situated on the western side of Worcester in St Johns, is a busy, bustling place enjoyed by regulars and visitors. Local people know it as the home of cabaret on Saturday nights in addition to its good reputation for food. It is also a place where people meet to enjoy companionship whilst having a drink.

It is an interesting building with several attractive features, including gardens with seating for eating and drinking 'al fresco'. Laughan (Bubble) Brook runs adjacent to the gardens.

The 2 large function rooms have many facilities, including a chair lift for the physically disabled. From Monday to Friday the function rooms are available for entertainment, with an Organist for dancing or sing-a-longs. Saturdays are Cabaret Nights. The 120 seater A la Carte Restaurant caters for parties large and small. Prices are realistic and the atmosphere is great. One of the function rooms also offers a skittles venue.

Brian and Ann Abbott with their son Andrew own and run Coppertops with the assistance of a cheerful and efficient staff who all hold Food Hygiene Certificates. There are three full time chefs who produce well cooked and well presented meals to suit everyone, children and vegetarians included. The restaurant offers both Table d' Hote and A La Carte whilst the bars have their own wide ranging menus of tempting foods.

USEFUL INFORMATION

OPEN: 11-3pm & 7-11pm
   Last orders 9.30pm
CHILDREN: Welcome
CREDIT CARDS: None
LICENSED: Full Licence
ACCOMMODATION: Not applicable

RESTAURANT: Freshly cooked
   food
BAR FOOD: Comprehensive list.
   Freshly cooked
VEGETARIAN: Always 6 dishes
ACCESS FOR THE D ISABLED:
   Yes. Chair lift
GARDEN: Yes. Seats for 50

THE REAL SANDWICH SHOP

Cafe

Platform 1,
Foregate Street Station,
Worcester.

Tel: (0905) 20651

This is an unusual venue. Not many of us would think about going to a 'Station Cafe' but visit this one and you will find it is different and a very pleasant place to be. Obviously it is well known to commuters and welcomed by them, but you do not have to be a traveller to eat here. It is not in the least pretentious but what it does offer is good quality, freshly prepared snacks throughout the day starting at 7am and closing at 6pm. Sundays is the exception, the shutters are up, whilst the efficient and friendly staff, take a well earned rest from the normal strenuous day.

People who have discovered this friendly spot tend to become regulars. Sometimes one only wants something light and here the well prepared snacks are more than satisfying and the home-made cakes will delight anyone with a sweet tooth. They will tell you that it is a good place to pop into if you are visiting the city. Worcester is a wonderful place to be in for several reasons. Historians will not need to be told that the first clash of arms in the Civil War took place here. Music lovers venerate it as the birthplace of Sir Edward Elgar, and you would have to be without heart or soul if you did not enjoy the majestic beauty of the Cathedral. For shoppers, Platform 1 is right in the centre and could not be a better place to rest your weary feet even if you do have to climb steps to reach it.

USEFUL INFORMATION

OPEN: Mon-Sat: 7.30am-6pm
CHILDREN: Welcome
CREDIT CARDS: None taken
LICENSED: Not applicable
ACCOMMODATION: Not applicable

RESTAURANT: Snacks, sandwiches. Super cakes
BAR FOOD: Not applicable
VEGETARIAN: Snacks available
ACCESS FOR THE DISABLED: No
GARDEN: No

Goodrich Castle, Herefordshire

INCLUDES:

The Green Dragon	*Bishops Frome*	p. 176
The Cottage of Content	*Carey*	p. 177
The New Inn	*Eardisley*	p. 178
The Crosskeys Inn	*Goodrich*	p. 179
The Harewood End Inn	*Harewood End*	p. 180
Gilbies	*Hereford*	p. 181
The Bridge Inn	*Kentchurch*	p. 182
The Queens Head	*Kington*	p. 183
The White Pheasant	*Kington*	p. 184
The George and Dragon	*Knighton*	p. 185
Barons Cross Inn	*Leominster*	p. 186
The Black Horse Coach House	*Leominster*	p. 187
The White Lion	*Leominster*	p. 188
The Swan Inn	*Letton*	p. 189
The Red Lion	*Madley*	p. 190
The Bridge Inn	*Michaelchurch*	p. 191
The Yew Tree Inn	*Priors Frome*	p. 192
Cloisters Wine Bar	*Ross-on-Wye*	p. 193
Fresh Grounds	*Ross-on-Wye*	p. 194
Pheasant's Restaurant	*Ross-on-Wye*	p. 195
The Rosswyn Hotel	*Ross-on-Wye*	p. 196
The Lough Pool Inn	*Sellack*	p. 197
The Lamb Inn	*Stoke Prior*	p. 198
Cadmore Lodge Hotel	*Tenbury Wells*	p. 199
Royal Oak Hotel	*Tenbury Wells*	p. 200
Ye Olde Salutation Inn	*Weobley*	p. 201

'Go thy way, eat thy bread with joy,
and drink thy wine with a merry heart . . .'
Ecclesiastes

HEREFORDSHIRE AND THE WELSH BORDERS

Pulchra Terra Dei Donum
(This fair land is the Gift of God)
County Motto.

Although Herefordshire is joined with Worcestershire for administrative purposes, the characters of the two counties have little in common. A perfect illustration of this is gained from the viewpoint atop the **Herefordshire Beacon** in the Malvern Hills. To the east lie the rich fertile lowlands of Worcestershire through which the Severn and Avon wander, whilst to the west, the undulating wooded scenery of Herefordshire extends to the lowering ridge of the **Black Mountains,** some forty miles away.

A further clue to the disparity between the two countys is given by the nature of the viewpoint, for this is the site of that ancient Iron Age fortress known as the **British Camp.** Although the sleepy rural calm of the region to the east was brutally disturbed by three of the most decisive battles in English history, it's western neighbour was engaged in continuous territorial struggle for many centuries and rarely turned to more peaceful pursuits once the din of battle had died away. Here, people were always on their guard with billhook, sword or spear close to hand and a wary eye cocked to the western horizon. Herefordshire was the last English territory to be seized from the Celtic Welsh by the Anglo-Saxons - and neither race has ever been noted for their expertise in turning the other cheek. Norman intervention hardly helped matters and for generations blood was shed in ambush, foray, raid and battle. Following the example of their predecessors, the Romans, in their dealings with the Scots, the Saxons expended an enormous amount of time and energy in the construction of **Offa's Dyke**, named after the King of the Mercians and which ran north to south, from 'sea to sea'. Although the great ditch was, in reality, more of an official boundary than a defensive work, fortifications were built and these works were accelerated by the Normans who constructed a chain of castles along the border, known as the **Welsh Marches.** The barons who commanded these castles were known as the Marcher Lords and their conduct was not always above reproach. William the Conqueror was evidently a believer in the

136

dictum 'Divide and Rule', for the noblemen he appointed to the Marches were the most scheming and potentially disruptive in the Kingdom. Far from the intrigues of Court, they were left to their own devices - harrying the Welsh, bullying the Saxons, plotting against each other and generally feathering their own nests (or castles - it is interesting to note that, over the centuries, the number of fortifications built in the county has only been succeeded by those of Northumberland). This was border country where the King's Law was of little import and territory was all.

With such a turbulent history, the casual visitor might be forgiven for imagining the county a gloomy introspective place, much given to brooding over past injustices and full of ghost-ridden ruins. Nothing could be further from the truth for the region as a whole, including the Welsh border county, has a cheerful bucolic atmosphere; a land of great beauty where the stranger is welcome, not suspect. Perhaps this owes much to the six 'W's': Wool, Water, Wheat, Wood, Women and Wine (or cider). Herefordshire has long been a rich agricultural county and is famed for its cattle, whose robust constitution have resulted in their export all over the world. The Normans established a wool and cloth industry and sheep still graze the hills and slopes while the many apple orchards contribute to that well-known beverage, cider. Beer-drinkers are catered for by the cultivation of hops and the rich red earth produces fine cereal crops. It is still an intensely rural landscape with few great houses - though many are of great age and antiquity - and is, in some senses, an almost forgotten region of England with but a few miles of motorway intruding into its south-eastern corner.

This motorway, the M50, is a western spur of the M5 and runs some five miles into Herefordshire before ending at **Ross-on-Wye**, a delightful market town overlooking the **River Wye**. Agriculture, light industry and tourism form the basis of the local economy and Ross (from the Welsh ros, meaning a spit of land) is ideally situated for exploring the glorious country of the Wye Valley. Its friendly and welcoming atmosphere owes much to the example set by the town's best loved inhabitant, John Kyrle (1637-1724). Trained as a lawyer, he inherited a small fortune and never practiced, preferring to spend his time and money on good works and acts of great public generosity. He died, a bachelor, at the age of 89, having given all his money away but never incurred a debt. He is remembered as the 'Man of Ross', and among his many philanthropies were the provision of a town *water-supply, a causeway enabling the bridge to be used when flooding occurred, and a walled public garden, still known as Kyrle's Prospect. He built a summer-house in the grounds of his home, now known as KYRLE HOUSE, and paid the poor and unemployed to find horse's teeth from animals killed in a nearby cavalry skirmish during the Civil War; these were then set into mortar to create a mosaic in the shape of a swan. Kyrle is buried in the CHURCH OF ST MARY'S, and his monument is modest and restrained. Inevitably, he did much for the church including the casting of the tenor bell (to which he also contributed his favourite silver tankard) and the re-building of the elegant spire which he had raised by nearly fifty feet. He provided help for the needy, aid for the sick, and education for the illiterate and remained a modest and much-loved man. Also in the church are a number of interesting monuments to the Rudhall family to whom the Kyrles were related and who also acted with generosity towards the town; building, in 1575, the RUDHALL ALMSHOUSES. Another, but unrelated benefactor, was Frances, Duchess of Somerset, who provided the handsome sandstone 17th-century MARKET HALL, raised on sixteen pillars and where market-stalls gather to this day. In the north-eastern corner of the churchyard is a stone cross in memory of the 315 victims of an outbreak of the plaque in the year of John Kyrle's birth.*

The little town on its steep rocky outcrop has been a favourite with visitors since the early Victorian era when, as now, the attractions of the surrounding countryside and the excellent salmon-fishing brought people back year after year, prompting a testy local parson, Thomas Fosbrooke, to comment in the 1830's that the tourists 'during summer and autumn poke about the Wye like snipes and woodcocks, and after rummaging through everything, re-emigrate to London'. Around that time, a conscious effort was made to romanticise the town by 'mediaevalising', constructing walls and a round tower. Thankfully, the soft red local sandstone has eroded fast and what could have looked uncomfortably twee now looks uncommonly like the real thing. Hotels, pubs and restaurants are plentiful, and I was impressed by the enthusiasm and high standards to be found. In Edde Cross street stands the deservedly award-winning PHEASANTS RESTAURANT, just around the corner from the unique BUTTON MUSEUM. The high culinary standards of the restaurant are matched by the warmth of welcome, decor, and service; limited accommodation is also available, Another friendly establishment which also describes itself as 'restaurant with accommodation' is to be found at FRESH GROUNDS AT RAGLAN HOUSE. Raglan House is in Broad Street, in the heart of the town, and is an early Georgian building that has recently been extensively renovated. There are seven bedrooms, all en-suite, and the restaurant serves excellent food using local produce. In the nearby High Street is the ROSSWYN HOTEL, which dates back to the 15th-century and is complete with priest-hole, Jacobean staircase and a wonderful Elizabethan fireplace. Non-residents can enjoy the food and hospitality of the restaurant and wine-bar. Also in the High street is CLOISTERS WINE BAR, distinguished from the outside by its impressive stained glass windows and rightly popular with visitors and locals alike for its cheerful atmosphere, good food and drinks. All of these establishments are pleasantly small in scale and have a distinct 'family' feel without any loss of professionalism.

Raglan Castle

This matter of scale is very much a keynote to the town; THE LOST STREET MUSEUM is a charming, and very well-thought out museum in the form of an arcade of Edwardian shops containing all manner of period items including amusement machines, musical boxes, toys, costumes and gramophones. An unusual local industry is candle-making and ROSS-ON-WYE CANDLEMAKERS open their workshop to the public in Old Gloucester Road. Horticulture, as well as agriculture, is important locally. WOLF TOOLS make all manner *of garden implements from dibbers to mowers, while the HILL COURT GARDENS AND GARDEN CENTRE to the east of the town and HOW CAPLE COURT GARDENS to the north are a gardener's delight.*

South of Ross, there are a multitude of attractions to be found as the Wye loops its way round to enter the precipitous limestone gorge known as Symonds Yat, one of the most beautiful and spectacular views in England. The 400-foot high Yat Rock (yat being Old English for a gate or gorge) is a favourite spot to admire the scenic splendour of the Wye curling its way sinuously through the wooded countryside. Peregrine falcons nest in the precipitous limestone cliffs and at the bottom of the path from the Rock down to the river there is an unusual man-powered rope ferry.

Symonds Yat

*At **Symonds Yat West**, THE JUBILEE PARK offers a wide range of family entertainment, including a maze, craft shops and a butterfly farm. THE HEREFORDSHIRE RURAL HERITAGE MUSEUM, set in an attractive rural location, houses one of the country's largest collections of historic farm machinery and agricultural implements.*

About 3 miles downstream, in the wooded Doward Hills above the river, is KING ARTHUR'S CAVE where excavations have revealed that its occupancy by man dates back nearly 60,000 years! Five miles south of Ross and upstream from Symonds Yat are the romantic and massively impressive ruins of GOODRICH CASTLE. **Goodrich** is an entertaining, though somewhat scattered little village and the 12th-century castle is sited on a high rocky spur overlooking a crossing of the river. Square in shape with a tower at each corner and surrounded by a moat hewn out of the red rock, Goodrich was besieged by the Parliamentarians, under the command of Colonel Birch, in 1646. Legend has it that Birch's niece, Alice, was inside the castle with her Royalist lover, and that they were both drowned in the Wye whilst trying to escape. Her shrieks of distress can still be heard on stormy nights when the river is in spate.

The castle was slighted at the end of the Civil War, having suffered severe damage during the siege, and some idea of it's immense construction can be gained by a contemporary account of the oaken roof timbers which were described as 'without knotte or knarle and being sixty-six feet long and two feet square'. These would have come from the nearby **Forest of Dean,** in **Gloucestershire.**

Goodrich Castle

The CROSS KEYS INN in the village is a welcome stop after walking to the castle and back, and should you wish to stay longer the inn offers accommodation.

*Heading north-east from Ross on the **A449** and lying close to the eastern border of the county is the attractive village of **Much Marcle**, blessed with a fine church of 13th-century origins, ST BARTHOLEMEW'S and two historic houses. By the church porch is a splendid hollow yew with planked seats inside reputed to sit seven. The church has an ornate reredos carved by Queen Victoria's talented niece Lady Feodora Gleichen, and contains a number of beautifully-sculpted memorials dating over three centuries. Blanche Mortimer, who died in 1347, being the earliest, an Audley tomb of 1400 where puppies are carved pulling at the wife's dress, and the Kyrle Chapel with Sir John Kyrle, who died in 1650, and his wife, Sybil Scudamore, lying in elegant state. There is also a rare wooden effigy of Walter Helyon, once steward to a 13th-century lord of the manor. He is also remembered by the name given to the lovely house he once lived in, a gentle corruption of his surname from Helyon to HELLENS. Rebuilt in the Jabobean period, the house was originally started by Yseult, Lady Audley, in 1292 and has been occupied by her descendants ever since. Pictures, tapestries, furnishings and armour used by the family are on display. Nearby lies HOMME HOUSE, now converted into flats, but once the family home of the Kyrles. In the 17th century, the Kyrles also bought the site of the CASTLE, sited on the earthworks to the north of the church, but the stone had gone two centuries earlier, much of it being used in the construction of the church tower. Much Marcle is also renowned for a quite different attraction, WESTON'S CIDER FACTORY, where the locally-brewed cider and perry can be sampled and purchased.*

*Just over 4 miles further along the **A449** is the delightful ancient market town of **Ledbury**. Set by the ancient cross-roads to Tewkesbury, Hereford, Gloucester and Malvern, it has been inhabited since around 1500BC. In common with Much Marcle it also has connections with an Audley, the saintly Katherine of Edward II's reign, whose name is associated with the almshouses of ST KATHERINE'S HOSPITAL - although they were founded long before Katherine and her hand-maiden arrived in the town to live a simple religious life in a hut beside THE CHURCH OF ST MICHAEL AND ALL ANGELS. Herefordshire's premier parish church was built on an earlier Saxon foundation, has a Norman chancel and west doorway and a magnificent mediaeval north chapel. The tall and elegant detached spire was built by Nathaniel Wilkinson who was commisioned by John Kyrle to replace the spire at Ross-on-Wye, and a further connection between the towns can be found in the* *belfry; the bells were presented by the Rudhalls in the 17th century. Their restoration in this century was made possible by the poet John Masefield, a native of Ledbury, who donated the profits from many of his books towards the work. Further poetic connections are provided by the memorial to Elizabeth Barrett Browning's parents. Other interesting memorials include a 13th-century monk complete with Mass vestments, a number of family groups and one to a lady of the Pauncefoot family, flanked by a mass of heraldic shields.*

The Clock Tower - Ledbury

The wide main street, flanked by many half-timbered houses including the Elizabethan FEATHERS INN, was the scene of a desperate charge by Prince Rupert's cavalry during the Civil War, when a Parliamentarian force was routed. Bullets are still embedded in the church door and in the walls of the dining room of the TALBOT, in New Street. CHURCH LANE, cobbled and narrow, offers a delightful period view of St Michaels and opens out into a small close with some handsome houses surrounding the church. The attractive MARKET HALL was built in 1633 and stands on 16 pillars of Spanish chestnut while BUTCHER ROW HOUSE and the OLD GRAMMAR SCHOOL contain a Heritage Centre and collections of local interest. Ledbury stands at the southern end of the Malverns and the beauty of the surrounding countryside has, as we have seen, inspired many notable works of art. One of the central works of Early English literature is the poem, 'Piers the Plowman', which has its setting in the area and its author, William Langland (c.1332-1400) was probably born in Ledbury:-

'Ac on a May morwenyng on Maluerne hulles, Me byfel to slepe for weyrenesse of wandryng.' To the east lies the astonishing EASTNOR CASTLE (see Chapter 3), while at Bosbury, to the north, the mediaeval traditions of wine-making are continued at THE BOSBURY VINEYARDS AND GARDENS, which grows and sells top-quality English wines, offers wine-tastings in a converted oast house and has a most attractive rose-garden with aquatic features. The big CHURCH OF HOLY TRINITY is particularly notable for the fact that the massive tower is completely detached from the main body of the building. This unusual feature is found more in Herefordshire than in any other county and is thought to have been a defensive measure; a refuge for the villagers when danger threatened.

Eastnor Castle

The south-eastern quarter of Herefordshire is the main hop-growing region, and hopyards, with their trellis-work of poles, wires and strings can be seen throughout the area. At **Bishops Frome,** on the Ledbury to Bromyard road, THE HOP POCKET HOP FARM is open to visitors interested in a form of cultivation that is regrettably in decline. Drying kilns, hop-picking machines and the hopyards are all open to inspection and there is a very good craft shop with a large display of local work. Finally, in order to sample the end-product, the *splendid GREEN DRAGON INN keeps an excellent cellar of traditional ales on its 400-year old premises.*

Further information on the history, traditions and practices of hop-growing can be found at the BROMYARD HERITAGE CENTRE along with other displays relating to matters of local interest. **Bromyard** *sits in a natural bowl amongst rolling downland and was one of the most important towns in Herefordshire long before the Norman clerks started to compile the Domesday Book. It had a Saxon church in 840 AD and the present CHURCH OF ST PETER was probably built on the same site in about 1160. The town's wealth came principally from its market and local agriculture - later came an added bonus in the form of its geographical position half-way between Worcester and Hereford which led to its development as a coaching centre. Notable amongst the inns catering to this trade was THE FALCON, whose post-boys wore a smart uniform of white hats, breeches and yellow jackets. Somehow, I cannot believe that they stayed smart for very long.. BROMYARD DOWNS, with their splendid views is a popular picnicking area, and the National Trust have created some lovely woodland walks at* **Brockhampton,** *a couple of miles east towards Worcester. LOWER BROCKHAMPTON consists of a late 14th-century moated manor house with an unusual detached half-timbered gatehouse across the moat and the ruins of a 12th-century chapel. It is a most idyllic scene, particularly in summer when dragon-flies can be seen flitting over the moat where golden carp lazily turn. The moat was multi-purpose, providing protection against attack, keeping out animals and supplying fish for meatless days.*

The B4214 running north from Bromyard runs through beautiful hill country and down to **Kyre Park,** *where the large house, now a council establishment, is of interest because of the diary the owner, Sir Edward Pytts, kept during the period that he rebuilt the house from 1586-1611. Obviously a gentleman of a practical nature, he took part in many of the activities and faithfully recorded the exact costs and amounts of the various materials involved. The names of the workmen and their descriptions have a splendidly Shakespearian ring:' Roo, Lem, boy Jack, the drunken Reve and Thomas his unthrifty son'. Anne Pytts founded the PYTTS HOSPITAL in 1715, almshouses for the 'provision of eight aged widows', and close-by lies the CHURCH OF ST MARY, which has some good Georgian woodwork and a fine painting of the Madonna.*

The **River Teme** *wriggles through the three counties of Herefordshire, Worcestershire, and Shropshire in the area around* **Tenbury Wells.** *A borough since 1248, Tenbury has remained an attractive small market town surrounded by hopyards and apple orchards. Hopes of fame and fortune came its way in the 19th century, with the discovery of saline springs - but the town lacked an entrepreneur of the quality of Dr Wall at Malvern and the spa never became fashionable - in fact, before it was closed during the First World War, the owners were rather desperately advertising it 'as suitable for the middle and lower classes, with every convenience at the lowest popular price.' Potential customers may also have been put off by the somewhat ambiguous remarks made by the wonderfully-named Dr Augustus Bozzi Granville, who was quoted as saying 'Immediately upon swallowing half-a-tumbler of the Tenbury water, a disturbance, or rather commotion, is set up in the abdomen, which, upon repetition of the same quantity of the fluid, after a proper interval, will be found, in most cases, to end in a way desirable under such circumstances.' Little wonder the waters never gained great popularity! The incongruous PUMP ROOMS survive, known locally as the 'Chinese Temple', because of the style of architecture.*

Failed spa apart, 'The Town in the Orchard'is a cheerful, bustling place set in the attractive Teme Valley and has an interesting sideline in trade at Christmas time; holly and mistletoe are auctioned off in the town for distribution all over the country. THE CHURCH OF ST MARY was rebuilt in 1770 after flooding had undermined part of the foundations but retains its 12th-century tower and mediaeval chancel, and contains a handsome tomb of 1581 with fine alabaster effigies to Thomas and Mary Acton. In Market Street, there is THE ROYAL OAK HOTEL, whose half-timbered black and white facade is both complex and attractive. The handsome heavily-beamed interior is cosy and welcoming, with food and hospitality of a very high standard.

Two miles to the west is another splendid family-run hotel - but of a quite different type. THE CADMORE LODGE HOTEL is a new development, standing within its own wooded estate which has been laid out to provide golf, fishing and other sporting facilities. Appetites sharpened by such activities are more than adequately catered for by the hotel's excellent restaurant.

Leominster *(pronounced 'Lemster', or 'Lempster') lies nine mile to the south-west and is Herefordshire's second largest town, set* *amongst a gentle landscape of fields, hills and meadows where river, stream and brook wander. The town's fortunes were based on the fine quality of the wool from the local breed of sheep, the Ryeland, an animal that thrives on the poorer grazing to be found on the neighbouring hills and the less fertile outcrops of sandy soil from which the name is derived. The demand for this wool was so great that at one time the fleece was known as 'Lempster Ore'.*

The area is also known locally as John Abel country, after the master-craftsman who was responsible for many of the fine timber-framed buildings; a rural architectural genius who was awarded the title of 'King's Carpenter' for his works during the Civil War and who died in 1674, at the ripe old age of 97. Leominster contains what is probably his finest work; GRANGE COURT, a magnificently carved and beautifully proportioned building that was originally the Town Hall and is now, fittingly, the Council offices. Built in 1633 with money contributed by the local gentry, it had a somewhat chequered career, being auctioned in 1855 under the description 'To all lovers of such curious antiquated Buildings, an opportunity of gratifying their tastes now presents itself which may never occur again, and which should not be lost sight of'. A local landowner bought the building for £95 and had it moved from Broad Street to its present site at The Grange. Now on a masonry base, it originally stood on massive wooden timbers, similar to the Market House at Ledbury. Leominster Council bought it in 1939, when there was a chance of it being sold and dismantled for export to the USA.

There are a good mix of architectural styles in the town, principally Jacobean and Georgian, and HIGH STREET, CHURCH STREET and ETNAM STREET all contain good examples, and in the last-named sight-seeing thirst and hunger can be appeased in the cheerful 14th-century surrounds of THE WHITE LION INN. Very much a family pub, there is a large garden, children's play area, and a large patio for summer barbecues. The LEOMINSTER FOLK MUSEUM is also in Etnam Street.

Leofric, Earl of Mercia, and husband of that well-known naked equestrienne, Godiva, is supposed to have given his name to the town with the establishment of a religious order in the 9th century (Leofric's Minster). This is thought unlikely since the order was a nunnery (although he may have hoped that his wife would enter and stop embarrassing him) and anyway, the family cannot have been

147

over-popular in the area since Leofric's son promptly ran off with the Abbess! A second legend concerns a lion who cornered a Christian missionary but spared the man's life in return for a share of his bread, whereupon the missionary took this to be a remarkably good omen and founded a church on the spot (Leo's minster). The most likely story is rather more prosaic and has no connection with either embarrassed Saxon aristocrats or vegetarian lions; Leominster simply means 'the Church on the Lene'- Lene being the old name for the Arrow Valley. Nevertheless, carved into the head of one of the huge pillars of the west entrance to LEOMINSTER PRIORY CHURCH are the figures of a monk and a lion..

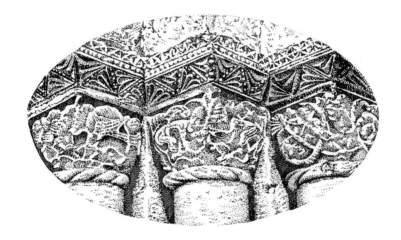

Romanesque Capitals - Leominster Priory

The Priory succeeded earlier religious foundations, including Leofric's nunnery, that dated back to a Celtic settlement of about 660AD. Rebuilt as a monastery in the 11th century, it suffered much damage during the Dissolution and also as a result of a severe fire in 1699, but for all these disasters it remains a most handsome and dignified building. The unique tower reflects it's history incorporating work of the Early Norman, Transitional, Early English, Decorated and Perpendicular periods. The south aisle contains extensive examples of a form of early 14th-century decoration to be found all over Herefordshire - the ball-flower, a three-petalled carving enclosing a ball. There is also a fine Chalice of the same period, and, in the north aisle, the town's Ducking Stool. This was the last such stool to be used in England and the victim was one Jenny Pipes, immersed in the Arrow in 1809 (there would have been a later ducking in 1817, but the river was too low!).

A thriving market town with a sprinkling of light industry and a large number of antique shops, Leominster stands surrounded by hopyards and apple orchards, and the products of the former find special favour with the landlord of the BLACK HORSE COACH HOUSE, on the southern edge of town. This is because the attractive old pub has recently begun to brew its own ales. One would have thought the town would be a natural brewing centre because of the availability of hops and water, but this is the town's first brewery since 1926. Good luck to them.

A mile to the west on the A44, is another cheerful and welcoming establishment, THE BARONS CROSS INN. A large and handsome half-timbered building of mediaeval origin, the warmth of hospitality ensures that, even if you were a baron and were cross, you wouldn't remain so for long!

The Romans had an encampment at **Stoke Prior**, *a couple of miles or so to the south-west of Leominster, and archeological excavations continue to investigate the extent of the site. Due west of the village is HUMBER MARSH, a mecca for naturalists with its diverse range of habitats and wildlife and which has been developed as an environmental education centre. Courses and lectures are run at the marsh, which is administered by the BRITISH SCHOOL OF CONSERVATION, based in Broad Street, Leominster.*

Naturalists, archeologists and the rest will find a warm welcome in THE LAMB INN, at Stoke Prior. Built in the 1700's, the inn offers comfortable accommodation as well as good food and ale, and is a most cheery and friendly establishment.

Dinmore *is Welsh for 'Great Hill' and its great mass, situated to the south of Leominster, has presented the countys' engineers with numerous problems over the decades. A tunnel was driven through the rock for the railway and the road has to wriggle its way up the steep gradient. Trees cover the hill-top plateau and the entire area is a delight, being a combination of an arboretum with species from all over the world, as well as large tracts of native woodland. Called the*

Humber Marsh Wetland Reserve - Herefordshire

QUEEN'S WOOD, *it was purchased by the Herefordshire branch of the Council for the Protection of Rural England to commemorate the Silver Jubilee of King George V, and the Royal Family have continued to plant trees in this wonderful spot. The hill also shelters the historic building of DINMORE MANOR, built on the site of a Commandery of the Knights Hospitallers, and their small 14th-century chapel is there to this day. A Commandery acted as a centre for training, as a hospital, as a sanctuary and as a shelter for the poor and needy. Because of the immunity granted to the Hospitallers by Pope Paschal II, in 1113, the Parish of Dinmore paid no rates until the middle of the 19th-century! The simple little chapel dedicated to St John of Jerusalem has an oaken tablet listing the early Commanders of Dinmore and the priests who served there. At the bottom of the tablet are the words:-*

The Knights are dust,
Their swords are rust,
Their souls are with the Saints we trust.

The manor house, parts of which date back to the 16th-century, is a splendid affair, lying in beautiful grounds beside fish ponds which would have supplied the Knights with carp on meatless days. The manor was bought in 1927 by Mr Richard Hollins Murray, the inventor of the 'cat's-eye' lens, who spent both money and care on the house, adding a magnificent music room and cloisters.

Dinmore Manor

Cider orchards along the road heading south to **Hereford,** hint at one of the city's major industries. BULMER'S have been making cider in Hereford for well over a century, and their premises in Plough Lane are open for tours and sampling. The contrast with modern automated production techniques with those of yesteryear are enormous, and a visit to THE CIDER MUSEUM AND KING OFFA DISTILLERY, in Ryelands Street, is a real eye-opener. There are numerous displays and reconstructions, including a farm Cider House and an apple orchard, massive presses and mills and cellars where Champagne Cider was stored. The Distillery is where Cider Brandy is made in a 40-gallon copper pot, bought over from the Calvados region of France. The spirit was popular in the 16th and 17th centuries but has now been revived under licence from HM Customs and Excise - who were responsible for enforcing the whopping taxes that led to the original demise of the liquor!

Any town or city engaged in the convivial pursuits of brewing or distilling has a rather jolly atmosphere, and Hereford is no exception, although its early history would suggest otherwise. Never free of strife until the end of the Civil War in 1651, the city suffered numerous attacks and sieges over the preceding centuries, yet during *that time managed to become one of the most thriving mediaeval cities in England; a centre for both trade and scholarship.*

Its tactical importance can be judged by its name, which means' an army river-crossing'. The Saxons built the earliest defences against the Welsh, who managed to destroy them in 1055, and William Fitz-Osborne, first of the Marcher Lords, built the CASTLE in 1067. The power of these Lords of the Marches grew rapidly and they were rightly perceived as a threat to the Crown, for their rule was absolute and they commanded large and well-disciplined armies whilst their allegiance was often doubtful. Their weakness was in the fact that they quarrelled as often with each other as they did with Celt or Crown; feudal law existed in the Marches long after the rest of England had peaceably settled down. One result of this was that the unfortunate citizens of Hereford, and indeed, of the entire region, were subject to attack, not only by the Welsh, but by forces of the Crown attempting to break up unwelcome alliances, or simply by rival barons seizing an opportunity to take a neighbour's property. Hereford and its castle were attacked many times, and changed hands with (almost) monotonous regularity. The last time the castle was rebuilt was in 1402, during Owen Glendower's Welsh revolt. It suffered its final siege during the Civil War and was demolished in 1660, with a large part of the city walls being removed for redevelopment in the 18th century. CASTLE GREEN, east of the Cathedral, bears no trace of the long-suffering fortress which stood guard above the Wye - but does have a monument to a famous freeman of the city, Admiral Lord Nelson. Unfortunately, money ran out so the sixty-foot column has an urn rather than a bust at the top. For many years, 'Roaring Meg', an immense siege mortar that fired 200-pound cannon balls, was to be found on the Green. Responsible for inflicting much damage to Royalist strongholds during the Civil War, including Goodrich Castle, the huge weapon has been moved to the peaceful, if slightly incongruous, surrounds of Churchill Gardens. Other items relating to the turbulent past, as well as to more peaceful interests, such as bee-keeping, can be seen in THE HEREFORD CITY MUSEUM AND ART GALLERY, in Broad Street. The modern military presence in the city is restricted to the HEREFORDSHIRE REGIMENTAL MUSEUM at the TA Centre in Harold Street, and to the discreet gentlemen of the SAS, at Bradbury Lines. Hereford is rich in museums; apart from those already mentioned there are the BULMER RAILWAY CENTRE, for steam enthusiasts, THE CHURCHILL GARDENS MUSEUM, displaying fine furniture, costumes and paintings of the late 18th and 19th centuries,THE ST JOHN MEDIEAVAL MUSEUM, containing armour and other relics relating to the Order of St John, and THE OLD HOUSE, built in 1621 and beautifully furnished in period. The area around the Old House is a pedestrian precinct and in nearby St Peter's Close weary feet can be rested, thirsts quenched and hunger satisfied at GILBIES BISTRO AND BAR. A splendidly secluded spot with a distinctly Continental flavour, it has a continually changing menu which the proprietor modestly describes as 'good, but not great' and some real bargains in the wine-list.

The medieaval visitors to the city - scholars, men-at-arms, and traders - would have had their numbers swelled by large numbers of pilgrims, visiting THE CATHEDRAL OF ST MARY THE VIRGIN AND ST ETHELBERT THE KING. The Cathedral was begun in the 11th century on Saxon foundations dating back to the 7th century - in fact, the appointment of the first Bishop of Hereford dates back to that time. A large proportion of the Norman masonary work survives, particularly inside, but siege and structural collapse in the 17th and 18th centuries led to extensive re-building and renovation.For all this, it is still a wonderfully handsome building, quite small compared to most cathedrals, and full of many unique treasures. Chief amongst these is the Mappa Mundi, a map of the world drawn around 1290 and of great importance because it shows us how the scholars of that

Hereford Cathedral Triptych

time saw their world in both spiritual, as well as geographical, terms. Although it shows the known world centred on Jerusalem, the topography of Europe and the Middle East is surprisingly accurate. The medieaval draughtsmanship is superb with all manner of beasts, both fabulous and familiar. The cathedral also has a notable collection of manuscripts and early printed material in the Chained Library,including the 8th century Anglo-Saxon gospels still used when Hereford's bishops are sworn in.

The pilgrims were attracted by two shrines. The first was that of St Ethelbert, Christian King of East Anglia, who was treacherously murdered in 794AD while visiting the palace of the Mercian King, Offa, at Hereford. His death was not the usual form of saint's martyrdom - in fact, it was more a case of 'cherchez la femme', since it would appear that he was killed on the instructions of the Queen Cynefrith, having rejected her passionate advances. His shrine was destroyed by the Welsh in the raid of 1055, but when the cathedral was rebuilt, the tomb was replaced and continued to be popular until the Dissolution. The second saint to be interred was Thomas de Cantalupe, Bishop of Hereford 1275-82, and who died from the plague on his way to Rome. His chaplain, being required to bring the Bishop home for burial, boiled the body and brought back the bones which were then deposited in the Lady chapel. Miracles were almost immediately attributed, with sick animals a speciality - Edward I

The Tomb of St. Thomas Cantelupe

interceded on behalf of a pet falcon although history does not relate the outcome. Cantelupe's tomb bears carvings of figures of Knights Templars, an order founded to guard the pilgrim's routes to the Holy Land, for he was their Provincial Grand Master.

The choral traditions of the Cathedral are long and the origins of the magnificent Three Choirs Festival can be traced back to an 18th-century chancellor, Thomas Bisse. To listen to magnificent music in such surrounds is surely close to 'the rudiments of Paradise'.

The two other principal churches in the city are ST PETER'S, which has an excellent Early English interior and from the tower of which the Norman Marcher Lord, Walter de Lacy, fell to his death in 1085 (doubtless to the cheers of the Saxon workmen) and ALL SAINTS, which also has a notable collection of chained books, some truly outstanding carving and decorative work, including frescoes, and a crooked spire. This was caused by building the tower over an old ditch, so that when the spire was added in the 14th century, the result was partial collapse and an alarming tilt. Later restorers were responsible for the crooked effect since they rebuilt the top section of the tower to make it as vertical as possible. In 1717, David Garrick, the actor, was christened in the font - which raises the interesting point that the city and surrounding area have no theatrical traditions but have nevertheless produced some great figures of the English stage, such as the Kembles, Sarah Siddons, Kitty Clive, Garrick and Nell Gwynne.'Poor Nell' has a plaque to honour her birthplace near the gateway to the medieaval BISHOPS PALACE, and is also remembered at the St John Medieaval Museum. This is because the building was originally an almshouse, known as the Coningsby Hospital, founded in 1614 'for worn-out soldiers, sailors and servants' and it is said that when Nell told Charles II all about this splendid institution in her old home town, he promptly founded the Chelsea Pensioners.

The Wye, the cleanest major river of England, loops its wandering way around the town and then is joined, to the east by the more turbulent **River Lugg,** second river of the county. Both rivers were utilised for transport, and above the stone bridge leading to **Mordiford** there are traces of ancient docks along the Lugg's banks. Both rivers were, and are, subject to sudden flooding and the ancient Celtic name for the Wye has been only slightly altered - Gwy, meaning White Stream. Attempts were made to control the river in the same manner as the Severn, but were never really successful.

The bridge at Mordiford had an interesting tradition attached to it; in Norman times, the local lords of the manor paid their rent to the Crown in the shape of a pair of golden spurs, payable each time the King rode over the narrow stone bridge. There is an equally good, but less true, story attached to the beautiful HAUGH WOODS which surround the area, now largely administered by the National Trust who have laid out nature trails and picnic areas. Legend has it that, in the Dark Ages, the area was inhabited by one of those splendid fire-breathing dragons that crop up in all the best stories. This one subsisted entirely on male villagers (maidens were obviously not on his diet-sheet) and had such an appetite that the local population was on the verge of extinction. Eventually, a condemned criminal named Garson volunteered to deal with the beast in exchange for a full pardon. Being a good Herefordshire dragon, the animal was extremely fond of a drop of scrumpy, so Garson hid himself in a cider barrel and killed the brute with a well-aimed arrow, fired through the bung-hole. Sadly, brave Garson perished in the conflagration caused by the dragon's dying breath. Until its restoration at the beginning of the 19th century, the church tower wore a dragon's effigy with the following inscription:-

This is the true Effigies of that Strange
Prodigious monster which our Woods did range,
In East Wood it was by Garson's hand slaine
A truth which old Mythologists maintaine.

The 18th-century SUFTON COURT was designed by James Wyatt and the grounds laid out by Humphrey Repton. Repton was known for the skill with which he prepared paintings and drawings of the 'before-and-after' type. These were usually bound in leather for presentation to the client and known as 'Red Books', and the lovely little Palladian mansion has Repton's book along with a fine collection of china.

THE YEW TREE INN provides welcome hospitality at nearby **Priors Frome,** *and has excellent food with some distinctly unusual items including Wild Boar in Whisky Sauce - Dragon Cutlets are no longer on the menu! South of Hereford, the loops of the Wye become ever-greater as it wriggles its way towards Ross-on-Wye. One can only admire the endurance and tenacity of the salmon as they make their way upstream to their spawning-grounds. The river has long been renowned for the quality of its fishing, and the acknowledged* master of the Wye was Robert Pashley, who, between 1908 and 1947, caught 9122 salmon weighing an astonishing total of 63 tons! However the record for a single fish, is held by Miss Doreen Davey. In 1923, after a battle of one hour and fifty-five minutes, much of the contest by the sole light of a bonfire, she landed a Wye salmon weighing 59½ pounds! This immense fish, with a length of 52½ inches and a girth of 29 inches, remains the record for a rod-caught fish, not only for the Wye, but for the whole of England. Strangely, the United Kingdom record was also taken by a young woman - Miss Georgina Ballantine,who caught a monster 64-pound fish on the River Tay in Scotland.

Leaping Salmon

The Wye is still a mecca for fishermen and women and fishing rights nowadays exchange hands for immense sums of money, although it is still possible to fish by the day for reasonable prices. Salmon-fishing with rod and line became really popular in the Victorian era and the number of smart fishing-lodges in the area bear testimony to that fact, and the demand continues to this day. When in season, salmon is often on the menus of the many excellent local pubs and restaurants, as it is in THE COTTAGE OF CONTENT, an aptly-named and quite delightful old inn at **Carey**, near **Hoarwithy**. Atmosphere, service and comfortable accommodation make this a perfect spot for a fishing holiday, but it is equally popular with the many walkers and tourists who visit the area - not to mention the locals. The CHURCH OF ST CATHERINE at Hoarwithy is reached by a steep flight of steps and is worth visiting for it is Mediterranean in appearance and even possesses a campanile. Its exotic appearance is due to an eccentric and wealthy vicar who spent most of his fortune on it - even to the extent of importing Italian craftsmen, giving the church its present Byzantine look, and decorating the interior with gold mosaics and lapis lazuli.

Mediterranean influence also extends to the food found in the 16th-century, and totally English, surrounds of THE LOUGH POOL INN at **Sellack**. The landlord, once a chef on the QE2, has brought back some unusual and delicious recipes from his travels, including a Greek goat casserole. Very good it is too, but the extensive menu also caters for more traditional tastes - prime Herefordshire beef a speciality - and has large and pleasant gardens next to the pool from which the pub gets its name.

A mile or so to the west, on the A49, is THE HAREWOOD END INN, in the village of the same name. A favourite touring spot, in the midst of fruit-growing country, the fine old pub has a detached restaurant in a well-converted old barn and its own 4-acre camp site. The inn sign is a splendid visual pun; a hare, back to the artist, facing some trees.

This south-western region of Herefordshire and the Welsh Borders was known as **Archenfield** and stretched from the western bank of the Wye to the long ridge of the Black Mountains, twenty miles away. It remained a Welsh enclave in England for around six centuries until well after the Conquest. Many of the laws and customs remained peculiarly Welsh until as recently as the present century. An attractive, yet sparsely populated region, with few large villages but a wealth of churches, which point to the fact that this area has had possibly the longest history of continuous Christianity in England.

Welsh Newton is still the scene of a yearly pilgrimage since the graveyard contains the last of Herefordshire's many saints. John Kemble, who was canonised as recently as 1970, was a Jesuit priest who administered to the many Catholics in the area, including the wife and daughter of the man who arrested him for complicity in the Popish Plot. An innocent and greatly loved man, he was executed in the most barbaric manner at Hereford, in August 1679. He was eighty years old.

In the 1644 siege of PEMBRIDGE CASTLE, John Kemble had behaved with great gallantry, bringing succour to the wounded and saying mass in the chapel. Much of the castle survives and is thought to date back to the early 13th century. It passed through a number of hands before 1644, when it was held by Sir Walter Pye, a Royalist, who held out against Colonel Kyrle's Parliamentarian forces. Damaged during the attacks, it has now been considerably restored. The history of the castle during the Civil War and for a time after, has a number of strange coincidences; the final successful assault on the castle was led by a Scudamore, probably the father of the man who arrested John Kemble some thirty years later. The castle was bought after the war by one George Kemble, and in 1715, it changed hands again - to a Scudamore.

*At **Kilpeck**, just off the A465 from Hereford, is the most famous of Archenfield churches,THE CHURCH OF SAINTS MARY AND DAVID. Saxon work remains in the north-east wall of the nave, but the church is principally Norman and the local red sandstone from which it was built has survived the weathers of time remarkably well (exactly where this extraordinary stone was quarried is still a mystery). The real glory of the little church is it's carvings; work of the skilled masons who are sometimes referred to as the Herefordshire School, and who flourished during the 12th-century. The carvings are a strange mixture of Christian and pagan, the obscene and the secular. Dragons, warriors, patterns of leaves, the Lamb of God, a mermaid and a sheila-na-gig, a strange female figure supposed to represent either fertility or to act as a warning against lechery, are all represented. Even on the exterior, the work remains crisp and clear, almost if it was done yesterday; rather than more than 700 years ago. Behind the church can be found the remains, little more than a stump, of KILPECK CASTLE, built around the same time that the carvers were indulging their strange fantasies with hammer and chisel. King John visited here a number of times, and it is recorded that a pretty widow, Joan de Kilpeck, offered him a bribe of fifty marks and a palfrey (a small horse) if he would allow her to marry who she pleased.*

It was to the men of Archenfield that England looked in time of strife. From this area came the mediaeval equivalent of the machine-gun; the long-bow, made from yew, and in the hands of a master capable of piercing through the mailed thigh of a horseman and nailing him to the saddle at fifty paces or more. More importantly, the next arrow would be on its way within seconds, whereas the rival cross-bowman would still be tensioning his weapon. Once the major disputes between English and Welsh were settled, it was the bowmen of Archenfield who led the English armies in attack and held the rear in retreat.

The Church Porch - Kilpeck Church

Men-at-arms of higher rank, but of common experience, are remembered amongst the high, sheep-grazing hills of **Garway**. These were the Knights Templar, soldiers of Christian belief and noble birth who wore a red sign of the cross on the simple white surcoats that covered their armour. Formed to protect pilgrims on the long and dangerous journeys to and from Jerusalem, they showed great bravery during the Crusades and later founded numerous religious houses throughout Europe. Garway was one of their estates and THE CHURCH OF ST MICHAEL is one of only six Templar foundations left in England. The massive detached stone tower is not only the belfry, but also acts as a refuge, or, if necessary, a prison. The slightly odd shape of the body of the church is accounted for by the fact that the Knights liked their churches to have round naves, in imitation of the Temple at Jerusalem. Although this feature has long gone, traces of it can be detected outside - however, the chancel has a distinctly oriental look about it. Their Preceptory, or headquarters, has disappeared, and the only other reminder of their presence is a large dove-cote, which would have supplied food for the Templars and their *guests. It seems strange to think of those grim monastic soldiers, used to the blazing sun and the desert battles with the Saracens, ending their days on these damp hillsides. The place is moving in its simplicity and well worth the meandering drive south.*

On the subject of meandering, Chesterton may well have had Herefordshire in mind when he wrote those splendid lines:-'Before the Roman came to Rye or out to Severn strode, The rolling English drunkard made the rolling English road.' The highways and byways do wander and roll, yet the delight of the county is in its many surprises and delights - there is always something interesting around the corner.... Giraldus Cambrensis (1147-1223), a famous priest and scholar of Norman-welsh descent, wrote about the Welsh in words that still ring true:-'

In musical concerts they do not sing in unison like the inhabitants of other countries, but in many different parts; so that in a company of singers, which one very frequently meets with in Wales, you will hear as many different parts and voices as there are performers.'

Harmony in church, chapel or pub is still part of that tradition, and I was delighted to hear the landlady and her daughter singing most beautifully in the handsome little BRIDGE INN at **Kentchurch.** *Lying beside the waters of the Monnow and at the southern approach to the* **Golden Valley,** *this 400-year old pub provides excellent straight-forward food and is everything a good country pub should be.*

If the lands to the east of the Wye seems full of Kyrles and Rudhalls, then the western region of Archenfield is that of the Scudamores. They built two great houses, HOLME LACY (now a hospital) and KENTCHURCH COURT, a medieaval house with a great tower. Altered by Nash in 1800, the house contains some wonderful carvings by Grinling Gibbons, together with furniture, porcelain and other works of art. One of the most interesting paintings of local relevance dates back to around 1400, and depicts Jack-of-Kent, a local boy made good. He was a stable-lad who impressed the then Sir John Scudamore with his ready wit and intelligence; so much so, that Sir John sent him to Oxford University and then retained him as his personal chaplain. Jack o'Kent became an almost mythical figure in Welsh folklore, in league with the Devil but always managing to get the best of Old Nick. One of the stories concerns the little bridge by the Bridge Inn and tells of how Jack and the Devil built it on the understanding that the first passenger to cross over was to belong to the Devil. On completion, Jack promptly threw a bone over and an unfortunate dog chased after - so all the Devil got for his pains was a mangy cur.

Naturally, Jack had sold his soul to the Devil on the understanding that when Jack died, his soul would be forfeit,'whether he was buried within the church or without'. Consequently, he was buried within the church wall - neither in nor out. His actual burial place is contested, but some claim that it was just over the Welsh border, in the walls of the chapel of GROSMONT CASTLE. If so, this would provide another link with the Scudamores for the castle was besieged by Owen Glendower, whose daughter, Alice, later married the said Sir Jonn Glendower was a romantic and charismatic figure who, during the uncertain reign of Henry IV, exploited the state of feudal anarchy existing in the Marches to brilliant effect. However, the few years of virtual freedom that he achieved for Wales while the English were preoccupied with dynastic strife and trouble in France, were to cost his country dear and he is said to have ended his days in the tower at Kentchurch Court, alone and embittered.

Driving north-west along the B4347 into the Golden Valley one passes through the now peaceful border community of **Pontrilas**, the scene of far more recent 'raids' by the Welsh - although only on Sundays. This was because, until very recently, their licensing laws kept their own pubs shut on the Sabbath- Perhaps the Saxons and Normans would have had more success pacifying their Celtic neighbours if they had built pubs rather than castles?

EWYAS HAROLD CASTLE (pronounced Yewas) on the west side of the Valley is unusual in that it was a Norman castle built before the Conquest. It is often forgotten that ties were close between the two races and that the Conquest was a result of William's legitimate claim to the throne. The 'Harold' of Ewyas Harold was not the unfortunate counter-claimant who happened to look up at the wrong moment in 1066, but Harold de Clifford, second Earl of Hereford-'Ewyas' is the Welsh for 'sheep-district' and presumably the origin of the word 'ewe'. The castle was first built around 1050 with further rebuilding in 1067-71, and is of the familiar motte-and-bailey type -the motte being the earth of rock mound upon which the central *fortification stood, and the bailey being the wall that either surrounded this central tower or was set to one side of it. In 1645, the castle was noted as being 'ruynous and gonne' and only the earthworks survive today. This was often the case with large buildings such as abbeys and castles; once damaged and allowed to fall into disrepair, they became a natural site for scavengers; medieaval yuppies, keen to improve the looks of their bothy with a bit of fancy stonework. Farmhouses, churches, pubs and cottages all became the last repository for many such stones, and can often be identified as such today.*

The Golden Valley gets its name from a justifiable piece of linguistic confusion on the part of the Normans; they muddled the Welsh 'dwyr', meaning water, with their own 'd'or', meaning gold - hence Golden Valley and the River Dore. Also ABBEY DORE, a mile or so from the castle and a great Cistercian monastery until the Dissolution. The remains were carefully restored under the direction of the first Viscount Scudamore, and he and his craftsmen did a most excellent job. The present building possesses a simple grandeur and contains good glass, some interesting glazed tiles, and a knightly effigy of the grandson of the founder of the Abbey, Robert de Clifford. John Abel, the King's Carpenter, contributed the wooden screen which has the royal arms of Charles I flanked by those of the Scudamores and Archbishop Laud.

Several centuries later - but sadly no longer - there was a railway in the valley which was described as 'the loveliest and most inefficiently-run line in England', and there is a splendid account of it, written in 1892:-'...

that most eccentric of lines...where we have seen the linesman, when not engaged in hay-making, deeply engrossed in his occupation of weeding between the rails, as we waited for the train which, if we are to believe the tongue of rumour, sometimes fails to put in an appearance, the company's only locomotive having been seized for distraint of rent.'

Those lines may well ring a bell with one or two modern commuters...

Michaelchurch Escley *sits tight under the lee of the Black Mountains, truly a dark and brooding mass, frequently blue or purple* *in tint. From these slopes the Celtic warriors of long ago would rush in ambush, only to vanish into the woods and hills when ambush threatened.*

*The trout-laden waters of the **Escley Brook** run parrallel to those of the Mannow, into which it eventually merges, and the area is border country at its best - remote and beautiful. Here the drovers, on their way to Hereford market, would stop to water their beasts and refresh themselves at the lovely BRIDGE INN at Michaelchurch Escley. A pastoral atmosphere still clings to the 14th-century building, sitting in tranquillity beside the brook, and it is a wonderful place to enjoy a drink or meal.*

*The road running north alongside the Mannow passes through **Craswall**, with **Hay Bluff**, the source of the river, rising high over the hamlet. The Order of the Grandmontines, an offshoot of the Cistercian order and named after their founding-house in Limoges, had their abbey here. The remote situation must have suited an order which emphasized strict discipline and reliance on alms and agricultural labour.*

*The road continues northward, climbing to around 1500 feet, before dropping down through steep wooded slopes and into Wales at **Hay-on-Wye**. Hay changed hands several times in its turbulent early years, being burnt down five times, which may account for the fact that there are the remains of two castles in the small town. The motte by the church is all that remains of the first, while the second, which dominates the town centre, dates back to the 13th century. Glendower took it in 1402 and the remains were later converted into a private dwelling which suffered considerable further damage as a result of a fire in 1977. Nevertheless, the castle is still in use (although for far more peaceful purposes than its creators would have envisaged), as is almost every other redundant building in town, for Hay is known world-wide for its bookshops. Second-hand books in their million line the shelves of the castle, the cinema, a garage, and shops that once catered for the more mundane demands of the local populace- Rare first editions and fine leather bindings lie in close proximity to heaps of dog-eared paperbacks and bundles of yellowing magazines. Sleepy little Hay has woken up to the fact that it is now a tourist attraction in its own right - thanks to the wonderfully eccentric, but undoubtedly shrewd local entrepreneur, Richard Booth, who started the whole idea.*

An elegant Victorian clock-tower presides over the market area with its two small halls once dedicated to the sale of cheese and butter and for all the proliferation of gift and antique shops, literary festivals, galleries, and eating houses, Hay still retains the friendly charm of a border market town.

Turning back towards Hereford, it is worth taking a detour to view the remains of CLIFFORD CASTLE, whose ivy-clad ruins tower over a shallow bend in the Wye. It was built by Walter de Clifford in the early 1200's and first saw action not long after when it was captured, not by Celt or fellow Norman Marcher Lord, but by Henry III. This unfortunate episode was as a result of Henry's request that Walter's debts should be paid off. Walter's reply was to make the King's messenger 'eat the King's Writ, waxe and all', so the incensed Henry promptly sacked the castle. The 'fair Rosamund', an earlier de Clifford who was mistress of Henry II, was probably born here. The King kept her hidden from the jealous Queen Eleanor, but eventually the Queen found Rosamund and forced her to drink poison. The Mortimers succeeded the Cliffords, so the old fortress was held by two of the greatest Marcher families.

'Of all noxious animals, too, the most noxious is a tourist. And of all tourists the most vulgar, ill-bred, offensive and loathsome is the British tourist.'

Those words have a sadly contemporary ring to them, but they came not from some long-suffering late 20th-century bar owner on the Costa Brava, but from a 19th-century cleric, Francis Kilvert, who ended his days as the vicar of THE CHURCH OF ST ANDREW at **Bredwardine.** *Kilvert is remembered for his diary, which he kept with no thought of publication, while he performed his duties as a parish priest. He wrote movingly of the remote country and the people on both sides of the border, which he loved, and of the hills which he seemed to endlessly walk - writing this about the Black Mountains:'It is a fine thing to be out on the hills alone. A man can hardly be a beast or a fool alone on a great mountain.'*

He died of appendicitis a few weeks after he was married, and is buried in 1879 in the churchyard beside a great yew. Sadly, his wife who survived him by thirty-one years could not be buried beside him - lack of room means that she is laid to rest in the new cemetery several hundred yards away.

*Kilvert's old vicarage looks across the river to BROBURY HOUSE GARDEN AND GALLERY, with its seven acres of semi-formal gardens, while a couple of miles to the north-west, in the village of **Eardisley**, lying in the hills that separate the Wye and Arrow Valleys, is the very hospitable NEW INN, the second pub on the site since the 17th century. This latest building was put up as a result of a fire in the early 1900's and, fittingly, the inn sign shows a phoenix arising from the ashes. The village is a large one by Herefordshire standards with a long main street crossing two streams, and was once the terminus for a horse-drawn tram-way which carried iron-bar, lead, lime and guano from Hay. Surprisingly, the tram-way remained in use long after the age of steam materialised. Perhaps the horses were more reliable and less likely to be seized for non-payment of debts than their smoke-belching rivals in the Golden Valley! The motte of the castle is all that remains of fortifications once belonging to the Baskerville family, the name made famous by Conan Doyle in his 'Hound of the Baskervilles', and the church has a wonderful font, another product of the Herefordshire School of Carvers, which illustrates Christ's descent into Hell and defeat of Satan.*

South of **Merbach Hill** is **Dorstone,** typical of a settlement village of the Norman period. It has the mound of the protecting castle, a minute market place and a Norman Church. The Marcher Lords created many such settlements, hoping to establish thriving communities in the heart of disputed territory, encouraging such places with land grants and rights to markets. Not unlike the far later pioneers in the far west of the USA - a country to which many in the region later emigrated. THE CHURCH OF ST FAITH was founded by William de Brito in 1171. He is principally remembered as one of the four knights involved in the murder of Archbishop Thomas Becket in Canterbury Cathedral. He was banished to Palestine for fifteen years, and, as an act of contrition returned to England to this isolated community and built the church.

On the thousand-foot hill are the far earlier remains of a different people. ARTHUR'S STONE is a megalithic burial chamber dating from around 3000 BC, and consists of a huge slab of sandstone nearly twenty feet long supported by a number of vertical stones. Close to this ancient site is the spot where Charles I met the Scottish Army in 1645.

Arthurs Stone, Dorstone - Herefordshire

*Back to the Wye, and a mile downstream from Bredwardine is the hamlet of **Moccas** and MOCCAS COURT. The unusual name comes from the Welsh 'Moch-rhos', meaning swine-pastures, and the pigs of long ago must have enjoyed the acorns to be founded in the ancient woods around the area. Moccas consists of a few houses, the Norman village church, and the Court, a classic small country house designed by Robert and James Adam. Built in 1775 for the Cornewell family, the grounds were laid out by Capability Brown and it must be one of the most perfect river-side settings anywhere.*

*THE CHURCH OF THE NATIVITY in **Madley** is a large, almost barn-like affair, with a font to match. Originally Norman, and re-modelled in the 13th century, its size serves it well during the summer when the village's annual music festival takes place. THE RED LION is the village pub, which must be one of the county's oldest since it dates back to the 1100's. Family-run, it is in the best tradition of English country hostelries. GREAT BRAMPTON HOUSE contains a wonderful and varied collection of fine antique furniture and paintings but differs from most stately homes in that everything is for sale!*

*From Madley, it is worth doubling back on the other side of the valley and heading north to **Weobley** (pronounced 'Webley'). The*

167

tough Hereford strain of cattle, dark red with white faces, bellies and hocks, were first bred here, on the GARNSTONE ESTATE. The village was evidently one of the more successful Norman settlements. Only the castle's earthworks remain today, but Weobley's prosperity is indicated by the wealth of half-timbered housing and the large parish church, containing a fine memorial to Colonel John Birch, the most successful local Parliamentary commander during the Civil War, and who once owned Garnstone. Weobley is the place where the expression 'pot-walloper' was first coined; the term referred to Shropshire tenants of the Marquess of Bath who had the right to vote in local elections - providing they had set up their cooking fires in the main street the previous night. Needless to say, during the corrupt political era of the 18th century, His Lordship took full advantage of this strange custom to ensure the successful return of his chosen candidates. Pot-walloping is no more but another tradition, that of fine food and good accommodation, existed in YE OLDE SALUTATION INN long before the political chicanery described, and is happily continued to this day. A fine half-timbered building, in keeping with so much of its neighbours, the Inn is set at the top of Broad Street and commands a fine view of the village.

The half-timbered black-and-white theme is continued at **Eardisland**, *to the north of the A44. A picture postcard village by the banks of the Arrow, the enchanting Mill Stream Cottage was once the*

The River Arrow at Eardisland

village school and was built in the 1700's at a cost of fifty pounds. Close-by was the site of an ancient British settlement, now the site of BURTON COURT, a Georgian house of 14th-century origins which houses a fascinating collection of European and Oriental costumes and curios, together with natural history displays, ship models and a working model fairground.

About seven miles further to the west is **Kington**, *a small market town virtually on the border, and a favourite with walkers exploring Offa's Dyke. The GRAMMAR SCHOOL is particularly interesting as one of the few buildings built out of stone by John Abel. Below the castle mound is THE CHURCH OF ST MARY which contains the tomb of Thomas Vaughan and his wife, Ellen Gethin. Thomas was beheaded for being on the wrong (Yorkist) side at the Battle of Banbury in 1469. Known as Black Vaughan for both the colour of his hair and his evil deeds, he returned to haunt the town and caused so much trouble that his spirit was eventually exorcised by the combined efforts of twelve parsons and forced into a snuff-box which was thrown into the pool at HERGEST COURT, their family home which is now a farm-house. Unfortunately, the pool was drained a hundred years later and his spirit released, whereupon it promptly took the form of a great black dog, which is said to roam the Marches to this day. It is likely that the combination of this story and the local name of Baskerville were sufficient to inspire the famous Sherlock Holmes' adventure. Conan Doyle stayed nearby, at what is now HERGEST CROFT GARDENS, with its wonderful arboretum and old-fashioned kitchen garden. Other gardens containing acid-loving plants such as rhododendrons and azaleas, or roses and hydrangeas, ensure that there is colour throughout the season.*

Black Vaughan's wife was hardly much better than her ill-tempered husband and rejoiced in the name of Ellen the Terrible, earning her soubriquet by killing her brother's murderer after disguising herself as a man. This enabled her to enter an archery competition where she 'accidentally' put an arrow straight through the murderer's heart.

Climbing the hills, visiting gardens and searching for ghosts is a fine recipe for hunger and thirst, and two excellent and quite different establishments in the town can happily solve the problem. THE WHITE PHEASANT RESTAURANT, in the High Street, is one of those proper little steak-and-chop houses, serving good straightforward food at very reasonable prices, that were once so (deservedly) popular all over the country. In Bridge Street, echoes of the cheerful past are to be found in THE QUEEN'S HEAD, a pub built in the 1600's, which has still not got over the shock of being renovated in 1740 and proudly boasts that it is the only pub within a nine-mile radius that has a double set of ladies and gents toilets! Further eccentric claims in the town maintain that Kington has the highest golf-course in Britain - on the top of **Bradnor Hill**.

Offa's Dyke continues it's impressive way northwards through the hills passing three miles to the west of Presteigne. Owen Glendower defeated the English under Mortimer in 1402 where the Presteigne to Pilleth road crosses the path of the great Dyke. The town is divided by the River Lugg, with half the town being in Wales and the other in England. It has some handsome buildings and the church has an unique carillon, dating back to the 18th-century and reputedly the last of its kind to be working in the country.

Another five miles to the north lies another divided town; although this time the two halves are in Powys and Shropshire. **Knighton** has the Welsh name of Tref-y-Clawdd (The Town on the Dyke) and is a pleasant little town with a very steep main street. Two castles once stood here, but little remains now and sheep graze peacefully on the steep hills, once the scene of innumerable fierce clashes. An even earlier conflict, although belonging to myth rather than fact, is remembered by the name of THE GEORGE AND DRAGON, in Broad Street. A cosy and atmospheric place with a separate restaurant, it has an attractive lounge with 200-year old panelling acquired from the old church.

Back across the border into Herefordshire we come to **Brampton Bryan**, where a 17th-century lady of the manor, Lady Brilliana Harley, conducted a valiant defence of the castle while her husband was away, serving with the Parliamentary forces. A clever and resourceful woman, of great intelligence and learning, she led her small household into defying a 16-week siege by Royalist forces. When the siege was over, the castle and church were severely damaged, the village burnt to the ground, the stream poisoned and the cattle stolen. While preparing for the enemys return, Lady Brilliana died, worn out from malnutrition and exhaustion. The second siege reduced the castle to rubble and by it's side now stands a Georgian manor house. Six hundred years earlier, another gallant battle was fought between the Romans and the British King, Caractacus, on Coxall Knoll to the north. Tradition has it that he ended his days in honourable captivity in Rome and that his daughter, Claudia, returned to spread the Christian faith.

Fishing and walking must be two of the most popular recreational activities in the area, and I met afficianados of both pastimes in the excellent SWAN INN at **Letton**, a mile or so to the South-West of Brampton Bryan. The little village has an attractive grouping of half-timbered houses, with the 17th-century Inn standing opposite a small nursery. Family-run pubs nearly always have a most welcoming atmosphere and the Swan is no exception, with good food and company in abundance.

It really does seem extraordinary that such an area, outstanding in its natural beauty, combining peace and solitude with the scenery of the hills, woods and rivers, should have been the scene of so much strife - yet reminders lie all around. WIGMORE CASTLE has a connection with Brampton Bryan in that it was briefly owned by the Harleys before being dismantled by Parliamentarian troops, but it was first built by William Fitz-Osborn, Earl of Hereford, and then owned by the Mortimer family. The castle is impressively and strongly sited on a ridge in a most commanding position. It was to this great fortress that Prince Edward fled, before rallying his forces against Simon de Montfort (he had been imprisoned at Hereford and escaped by the simple ruse of challenging his captors to race their horses. When the animals were exhausted, the cunning Prince produced a fresh beast that had been kept hidden by a sympathiser and disappeared in the proverbial cloud of dust).

Of this great family who held the castle, perhaps the most astute and savage of the Marcher Lords, little remains but a tablet in the nearby gatehouse, where once stood an Augustinian abbey: 'In this abbey lie the remains of the noble family of Mortimer who founded it in 1179 and ruled the Marches of Wales for 400 years.' Henry VIII took little notice, even though his mother was a Mortimer, and the tombs vanished with the Abbey. Their name is, however, commemorated a little further down the road where the A4110 intersects the B4362. This innocent-looking junction in the valley of the River Lugg, was the scene, in 1461, of 'an obstinate, bloody and decisive battle.' Four thousand men died at what is now known as **Mortimer's Cross;** the first defeat to be inflicted on the Lancastrians by Edward, Duke of York - himself half a Mortimer, and later to become Edward IV. Before the fight began, an extraordinary sight was to be seen in the sky - three suns appeared. We now know that this phenomenon is caused by the refraction of light through particles in the atmosphere, and is called a parhelion, but to the superstitious medieaval warriors it appeared as an omen, a sign from God. The Yorkists took the three suns to represent the triumvirate of Edward, Duke of York, Richard, Duke of Gloucester, and George, Duke of Clarence, and the 'sun in splendour' became a favourite heraldic badge with the House of York.

Turn to the east at Mortimer's Cross, and you will come to three large houses lying within a few miles of each other, the first of which acted as a rendezvous for the Yorkist forces. The Croft family have lived at CROFT CASTLE since the time of Domesday, with the exception of a break of 177 years - due to some unfortunate debts incurred by an 18th-century Croft - and still live there, although the house and estate is now administered by the National Trust. The present castle owes its origins to fortifications of the 14th and 15th-centuries and was probably one of the last Marcher strongholds built. During the Civil War, the castle and the family fared badly; Sir William Croft, a Royalist, was killed in a skirmish at Stokesay, and the building was first plundered by Irish Royalists levies who claimed they had not been paid, then partly demolished, or 'slighted', again by Royalists to prevent its use by Parliamentarian forces. In its present guise, the castle is a massive but handsome house with turrets at each corner, and stands in beautiful parkland with an avenue of Spanish chestnut-trees - said by some to have been grown from chestnuts carried in a galleon of the Spanish Armada. For all its troubled history, it is a wonderfully peaceful and attractive home. A strong feeling of continuity and service hangs in the air; as exemplified by the memorials in the little church to two more recent members of the family. Both the tenth and eleventh baronets, father and son, were killed while serving with the Herefordshire Regiment in the First and Second World Wars, nearly eight hundred years after their ancestor, Jasper de Croft, was knighted during the Crusades.

In the north-west corner of the estate, on the crest of a high limestone escarpment, is an earlier fortification; the remains of the Iron Age CROFT AMBREY.

The other two houses stand almost side-by-side to the east of the Leominster to Ludlow road. The smallest is EYE MANOR, a neat

Restoration house, built for a slave-trader and plantation-owner from Barbados, with the exotic name of Sir Ferdinando Gorges. Known as the 'King of the Black Market', he spent a good deal of his ill-gotten gains on the interior decoration, particularly the ornate and well-crafted plasterwork.

BERRINGTON HALL has links with Moccas Court and Brampton Bryan, for the estate once belonged to the Cornewells who sold it to the Harleys in 1775. Thomas Harley, a prosperous banker, employed Henry Holland, later responsible for the original Brighton Pavilion, to design the house, and Holland's father-in-law, Capability Brown, to lay out the grounds. They succeeded splendidly and Berrington is surely one of the most attractive and elegant Georgian houses in the country. Thomas Harley's daughter, Anne, married the son and heir of Admiral Lord Rodney. It is doubtful whether the aloof and austere Admiral would have had much time for the delicate neo-classical interior of the Hall, but he would undoubtedly have approved of Thomas Luny's paintings of his principal sea-battles.

Berrington Hall is now run by the National Trust but from 1901, it belonged to Lord Cawley, and there is a moving memorial in the Norman church at Eye to his three sons, all killed in the First World War.

Hereford Cattle

It is tragic that they, like their neighbours the Crofts and so many other thousands of Herefordshire's sons and daughters, could not have been laid to rest in the soil of their birth, the land that Henry James described as 'The copse-chequered slopes of rolling Hereford, white with the blossom of apples.'

Goodrich Castle, Herefordshire

THE GREEN DRAGON
Inn

Bishops Frome,
Hereford & Worcester

Tel: (0885) 490607

If you are a traditionalist when it comes to pubs you will find The Green Dragon Inn, at Bishops Frome just on the borders of Hereford and Worcestershire, the ideal place for you to visit. The Inn is located in the heart of Hop farming country, with relentless discussions and exaggerations on the topic, which have to be heard to be believed.

The Inn retains a cosmopolitan atmosphere which blends well with the past traditions of the area. As you enter the door you feel a sense of history. The old flagstones are worn to a sheen with age. You look up and there are the old oak beams which were put in when the Green Dragon was built, over 400 years ago. In winter the large fireplaces hold the welcoming warmth of log fires, which add to the atmosphere. There is an air of peace and tranquillity, almost as if you are stepping back in time, away from the hurly burly of modern day living.

Real Ale enthusiasts can sample the unusual ales, with Timothy Taylors prominent, due to its excellent record of quality, and consistent winner of ale championships. The food complements the ale, with large doorstep sandwiches, excellent Pasta dishes and home cooked pies. The menu is extensive, catering for all tastes.

USEFUL INFORMATION

OPEN: 12-3pm & 5-11pm All year round
CHILDREN: Welcome
CREDIT CARDS: Access/Visa
LICENSED: Full. Large range Real Ale
ACCOMMODATION: Not applicable

RESTAURANT: Not applicable
BAR FOOD: Good food home cooked
VEGETARIAN: Always several dishes
ACCESS FOR THE DISABLED: Yes
GARDEN: Large beer garden

THE COTTAGE OF CONTENT

Public House

Carey,
Nr. Horwithy,
Herefordshire.

Tel: (0432) 840242

With a name like The Cottage of Content who could resist trying to find it? You would not be disappointed. It is in the heart of the country between Ross on Wye and Hereford, very near the M50 and conveniently situated for anyone wanting a meal, a drink or accommodation, before or after exploring some of the many interesting tourist attractions in the vicinity.

It is reached down a winding lane, which opens out slightly to reveal the beauty of this lovely old pub. Surrounded by beautiful gardens and an attractive patio, it is wonderful to drink outside on a summer's day. Inside it is full of 'olde worlde' character with oak beams and an open fire, which throws out a welcoming warmth in the cold winter months. In the years that The Cottage of Content has been a pub it has given thousands of people refreshment and great pleasure. It is doubtful if anyone ever left here discontented. The traditions of the past are continued today, with a landlord and his staff working so well together, that the pub exudes friendliness. Regulars will tell you of the great team spirit within the pub and no doubt crow about the success of their cup winning darts team. The menu, which is changed every month, includes super home-made pies, trout, salmon and many excellent home-cooked dishes. On Sundays there is a traditional Sunday lunch with succulent roast meats, crispy roast potatoes and a selection of fresh vegetables.

USEFUL INFORMATION

OPEN: Mon-Sat: 12-2.30pm & 7-11.30pm
CHILDREN: Permitted
CREDIT CARDS: Visa / Access
LICENSED: Full licence
ACCOMMODATION: 4 en-suite rooms

RESTAURANT: Not applicable
BAR FOOD: Home-made good
pub food
VEGETARIAN: 2-3 dishes daily
ACCESS FOR THE DISABLED: Yes
GARDEN: Lovely garden, patio, tables

THE NEW INN

Public House

Church Road,
Eardisley, Herefordshire.

Tel: (0544) 327285

There has been a pub on this site ever since the 17th century, but sadly, the original black and white timbered building was burnt down in 1901. It was replaced in classic Victorian/ Edwardian style, designed to suit travellers on the local railway. It has plenty of character and atmosphere which no fire could ever destroy. The village is just 15 miles from Hereford and 7 miles away from the Welsh Border and Offa's Dyke.

Local people come here regularly for the fun and the beer as well as the good pub food. Throughout the winter months the sporting instincts of the regulars turn to Darts, Pool, Crib and other pub games, most of them played against opposing teams from other hostelries. Live music sessions on Sunday lunchtimes with local musicians, and a live music night once a month are good entertainment. Mr and Mrs Baxter are the owners of this family run pub in which their aim is to give value for money, and ensure that people have a good outing.

There is no restaurant but good meals are served in the bar. In addition to a range of basket meals; steaks, gammon, fish and sausages are served with chips or rice. There is a small Vegetarian Menu and a range of bar snacks, including Jacket Potatoes, with a variety of tasty fillings. Children are welcome and there is a large play area with swings, slides and other equipment.

USEFUL INFORMATION

OPEN: 11.30-2.30pm & 6-11.30pm
  Sat: All day
CHILDREN: Yes. Play area
CREDIT CARDS: Not applicable
LICENSED: Full Licence
ACCOMMODATION: Not applicable

RESTAURANT: Not applicable
BAR FOOD: Good. Value for money
VEGETARIAN: 3-4 basic dishes
ACCESS FOR THE DISABLED: Yes
GARDEN: Large play area with
  swings etc

THE CROSS KEYS INN

Public House

Goodrich,
Nr. Ross-on-Wye,
Hereford

Tel: (0600) 890650/890203

Sometimes because of the outstanding beauty of Ross-on-Wye some of the surrounding areas get forgotten. No one should be allowed to forget Goodrich on the A40 between Ross and Monmouth. It is a place encompassed in glorious countryside and with many attractions such as Goodrich castle, Symonds Yat and the splendid walks along the River Wye and in the valley.

In the village is a good pub, The Cross Keys, where Mike and Lynn Sherwood own and run it in the manner of a traditional country pub complete with a resident ghost - so local gossip has it. The pub has 5 comfortable double bedrooms and 2 single rooms where you can stay and come and go as you please. Breakfast is a plentiful feast and for the rest of the day you can have food if you require it. The pub has two friendly bars where local people and visitors mingle happily together. One of the characters of the pub is the Scottish Chef, John who is not only talented in the kitchen but has a sense of humour that entertains everyone. The menu is a simple one with the food beautifully cooked and presented. Fresh vegetables are always used. There are Salad Platters and a selection of freshly prepared sandwiches toasted or plain. The Childrens Corner menu is outstanding value. In the inclusive price is ice-cream, coke and a lolly-pop with every clean plate! It would be hard not to enjoy the hospitality of The Cross Keys.

USEFUL INFORMATION

OPEN: 11-3pm& 7-11pm. All day.
CHILDREN: Children's Menu.
CREDIT CARDS: None taken.
LICENSED: Full Licence.
ACCOMODATION: 5 Double, 2 Single

RESTAURANT: Not applicable.
BAR FOOD: Good simple Pub fare.
VEGETARIAN: Yes, several dishes.
ACCESS FOR THE DISABLED: No.
GARDEN: Large Garden. Play area.

THE HAREWOOD END INN

Inn

Harewood End,
Herefordshire.

Tel: (098937) 637

There is a little inn that nestles into the countryside some four miles from Ross on Wye, and 9 miles from Hereford, in the pretty and tranquil village of Harewood End. The pub bears the name of the village and is quite enchanting. Built about 400 years ago it exudes warmth and happiness in its combined lounge and bar. Old oak beams and a roaring open fire simply add to the atmosphere and the general well being of The Harewood Inn.

Surrounded by some of England's most beautiful countryside and with the River Wye and a major fruit growing area within ¾ mile, this inn is just the place to visit, either for lunch or for an evening meal. If you know the place already, you will be aware that on 4 acres of land belonging to the pub, there is a registered Camp Site with space for 40 caravans. It must be wonderful to wake up here on a lovely summer's morning knowing that you have a blissful day ahead of you exploring the surrounding area. If you enjoy market towns then Hereford will suit you very well. This lovely, historic city has a Cathedral which is breathtaking.

David and Jill Headon are the cheerful and welcoming hosts. It falls to Jill's lot to produce the excellent food. Her insistence on fresh produce, including fish and game, has given her a reputation for miles around which is second to none. She obviously enjoys the task. As well as the restaurant menu there are 'Daily Specials' and a whole range of first class bar snacks. A traditional 'Sunday Lunch' is a firm favourite.

USEFUL INFORMATION

OPEN: Weekday: 11-2.30pm & 6-11pm
  Sundays: 12-3pm & 7-10.30pm
CHILDREN: Yes if well behaved
CREDIT CARDS: None taken
LICENSED: Full Licence
ACCOMMODATION: Not applicable

RESTAURANT: Fresh food inc.
  fish & game
BAR FOOD: Extensive & daily
  specials
VEGETARIAN: 6 dishes. Very
  good choice
ACCESS FOR THE DISABLED: Yes
GARDEN: Beer garden & mature
  garden

GILBIES
Bistro

4, St Peter's Close,
Commercial Street,
Hereford.

Tel: (0432) 277863

In the middle of the busy city of Hereford there is an oasis. Gilbies Bar and Bistro is something different and special. Somewhere you can go early in the morning for breakfast - as early as 7am if it is pre-arranged - have coffee, maybe a snack or a full meal throughout the whole day.

Modelled in many ways on the kind of Bistro you might find in any of the larger French or Spanish cities, Gilbies will make you feel a little more European, so flexible are the opening hours. Music also plays an important part in the everyday life of Gilbies. The music played is very much influenced by the customers. Regular jazz evenings are held on the first Wednesday of every month. The food, Kevan Gilbert, the proprietor describes as 'good but not great, at reasonable prices, eaten in a completely relaxed atmosphere'. Their menu changes hour by hour and always covers all styles of cuisine: from steaks to kebabs - from fish to sea-food or simple snacks like bacon sandwiches through to New Zealand Mussels. The wine includes a selection of more than 30 varieties from around the world; the choice is both interesting and reasonably priced. As is their choice of both traditional and unusual lagers and beers. The mixture of cuisine and culture under one roof is a piece of magic and a real asset to Hereford. Kevan Gilbert is to be congratulated.

USEFUL INFORMATION

OPEN: 10am-11pm every day
CHILDREN: Good children welcome
CREDIT CARDS: Visa/Access
LICENSED: Full Licence
ACCOMMODATION: Not applicable

RESTAURANT: One menu
   available all day
BAR FOOD: Competitive prices.
   Wide range
VEGETARIAN: At least 3 daily
ACCESS FOR DISABLED: Limited
GARDEN: Pleasant, secluded
   patio area

THE BRIDGE INN
Public House & Restaurant

Kentchurch,
Herefordshire.

Tel: (0981) 240408

This is a wonderful 400 year old building complete with a resident ghost. It lies on the banks of the Monnow River with a delightful riverside restaurant and a large beer garden. The views from here are superb, reaching out as far as the Black Mountains from the shelter of the Golden Valley. Kentchurch is not difficult to find, it lies mid-way between Hereford and Abergavenny.

It is not often that you will find yourself in a bar on a Sunday evening where the entertainment will be provided by the landlady and her daughter. Gill Bunce and her husband Phil own The Bridge and with Becky, Gill sings. Their voices are in total harmony and add to the general enjoyment of this happy establishment. Gill has sung semi professionally as Jill Bailey for many years. When she is not singing she is cooking and her freshly cooked food is rapidly gaining a following, deservedly so. The dishes are imaginative and very tasty.

There is nothing pretentious about the menu in the restaurant or the bar. For example you could start with a Mushroom Salad with Garlic Sauce and follow that with a perfectly cooked steak or if you are a Vegetarian a Vegetable Wellington. The bar food has home-made soups, daily specials and several other good choices including Jacket Potatoes and well filled Crusty Rolls.

USEFUL INFORMATION

OPEN: 11-2.30pm & 6-11pm
CHILDREN: Yes. No special facilities
CREDIT CARDS: None taken
LICENSED: Full Licence. Freehouse
ACCOMMODATION: Not applicable
GARDEN: Very large, riverside beer garden. Play area. Camping & Caravans

RESTAURANT: Freshly cooked, varied menu
BAR FOOD: Mainly home-made. Reasonable
VEGETARIAN: Always 4 dishes
ACCESS FOR THE DISABLED: Easy access to pub

THE QUEENS HEAD
Public House & Accommodation

Bridge Street,
Kington,
Herefordshire.

Tel: (0544) 230680

Just 1½ miles from the Welsh border and a third of the way along Offa's Dyke on the A44 is Kington, a very old and attractive market town which abounds with interesting buildings, amongst which is The Queens Head in Bridge Street. It is a great experience to visit this fascinating pub which is full of history and has a father and son as licensees. One part of the pub was built in 1690 and the new part in 1740 and it has never been anything else other than a hostelry. It is remarkable not because all the oak beams are original but one bar is almost literally as it was when it was built.

Thankfully the Henchliffes have no intention of altering anything. In the other bar certain modern things have crept in like a Jukebox and a Fruit Machine, but even these 20th century intruders have not changed the feeling of age and history that pervades The Queens Head. If you have never seen a double set of Ladies and Gents toilets then this too is an experience!

Father Henchliffe does all the cooking himself and he will tell you that he learnt his expertise from his mother. The recipes are all good, old traditional English ones. He uses local fresh produce whenever possible. The quality of the cooking is a credit to the meat and the local butcher. If you stay here for bed and breakfast you can be sure that breakfast will be a feast and the eggs, free range. The pub has a ghost living in the cellar, a female who is not averse to sampling the beer!

USEFUL INFORMATION

OPEN: Weekdays 11-11pm
Sun: 12-3pm & 7.30-10.30pm
CHILDREN: Permitted
CREDIT CARDS: None taken
LICENSED: Full Licence
ACCOMMODATION: 4 letting rooms

RESTAURANT: Home-cooked.
Local produce
BAR FOOD: Bar menu & A la Carte
VEGETARIAN: Always available
ACCESS FOR THE DISABLED:
Fairly easy
GARDEN: Garden, patio, car
park

THE WHITE PHEASANT
Restaurant

9 High Street,
Kington, Hereford.

Tel: (0544) 231291

If you want to enjoy what is possibly the best steak to be found in the county, then you should make for The White Pheasant where the chef, Mike Passey is the proprietor. That is not unusual, but what is different is that Mike was a butcher and he uses this expertise to cut and prepare your steak as it is ordered. Both he, and his wife Gladys, have been in the restaurant business some time and have a reputation for good food throughout Hereford and Worcester.

The White Pheasant is a listed building in the High Street with two separate dining rooms at present, a third will be available before Christmas. Each room is charming, the second one especially so, with oak panelling which stretches from floor to ceiling. The furniture is comfortable and the tableware gleams. The Passeys are friendly people and you can be sure that Gladys will welcome you either for a drink at the bar before your meal or to conduct you to your table. Each dining room is small enough to feel intimate and it is certainly relaxing.

In addition to steaks there are many other dishes on the menu and on Sundays throughout the year, there is a roast lunch which is extremely generous in the portions and naturally the quality of the meat is superb. From April to October they are open for lunches, when you can have the steak menu or snacks from Tuesday to Saturday. They are open every evening except Mondays from October to April, unless pre-booked. The wine is good and the prices are right.

USEFUL INFORMATION

OPEN: 12-2pm Tues-Sun6.30-10.30pm
CHILDREN: Welcome
CREDIT CARDS: none taken
LICENSED: Restaurant/Bar Licence
ACCOMMODATION: Not applicable

RESTAURANT: Steaks a
  speciality. Fresh food
BAR FOOD: Not applicable
VEGETARIAN: Several dishes
ACCESS FOR THE DISABLED: Yes
GARDEN: No

THE GEORGE AND DRAGON

Public House & Restaurant

4, Broad Street,
Knighton, Powys

Tel: (0547) 528532

Almost on the Shropshire border with Powys is the small and ancient market town of Knighton. Right on the path of Offa's Dyke walking trail and in the town centre, just below the clock tower, is The George and Dragon, which has given hospitality to travellers for over 350 years. It is one of those comfortable pubs where everyone feels at home almost immediately. A lot of this is to do with the pub itself but most of it comes from the way in which Jim and Rena Sidley, the owners run it. Their philosophy is that everyone who comes through the door is potentially a friend, and a welcome guest and this is the way that customers are treated. It is Jim who runs the bar and he is helped by Rena's mother Vera. Rena does all the cooking. The pub has a separate restaurant with thirty covers, a public bar, lounge and a games room. It is a regular meeting place for the local Bike club, and many firms hold business meetings in the restaurant which can be booked in advance, except at weekends. People book too for private parties knowing that Rena's cooking will be excellent and the atmosphere good.

Bar meals are extremely good value. There is a good choice of dishes including a Spicy Persian Lamb and a Mushroom Stroganoff. In the restaurant, succulent steaks are very popular and so too is the Chicken cooked in Cream, and the Welsh Lamb. If it is just a quick snack you require you will not be disappointed with what is on offer.

USEFUL INFORMATION

OPEN: Weekdays 12-3pm & 6.30pm-11pm
Sundays normal hours. Closed
Tues lunch. No meals Tues eve
CHILDREN: With diners or in garden
CREDIT CARDS: None taken
LICENSED: Full Licence
ACCOMMODATION: Not applicable

RESTAURANT: Steaks,
chicken, lamb, duck etc
BAR FOOD: Wide range. Fresh
produce
VEGETARIAN: 6-8 dishes daily
ACCESS FOR THE DISABLED:
Easy access
GARDEN: Small with
town/country views

THE BARONS CROSS INN
Public House

Barons Cross Road,
Leominster,
Herefordshire

Tel: (0568) 615114

Barons Cross Inn lies in a delightful, rural setting, one mile west of the old town of Leominster. It is an ideal spot to break your journey if you are travelling between the Midlands or South and Mid-Wales; the car park makes it simple to pull off the main A44. It is also a pub that is just right for people wanting to escape from the town at lunchtime or at weekends.

Many places of interest lie conveniently near Barons Cross Inn. The elegant Berrington Hall is 5 miles to the north west. Going south on the A49 you will find Dinmore Manor and Gardens - there is a Yew tree there that is 1200 years old! 3 miles east is the British School of Conservation, an exciting place in which you will learn to have a keener understanding of our natural world and the need to protect it. Or you can escape to Eardisland, 5 miles to the west, the centre for the Land of Black and White Villages. Add this to lunching in a pub where the hospitality is great and you will have a super time.

Steve and Carol Pusey own and run the Barons Cross. They are both members of the Guild of Master Caterers and have been running pubs for over eighteen years. They have three children and understand children's needs. The Beer is well kept, and the food offers a wide range of home-made dishes 7 days a week, lunch and dinner. You will not find a better Steak and Kidney Pie or Cottage Pie anywhere in the county. The prices are reasonable and the portions generous.

USEFUL INFORMATION

OPEN: Mon-Fri: 11-2.30pm & 6-11pm
 Sat: 11-3pm & 6-11pm
 Sun: 12-3pm & 7-10.30pm
CHILDREN: Yes for food. Childrens menu
CREDIT CARDS: None taken
LICENSED: Full Licence
ACCOMMODATION: Not applicable

RESTAURANT: Not applicable
BAR FOOD: Wide range, home cooked
VEGETARIAN: At least 3 dishes daily
ACCESS FOR THE DISABLED: With assistance
GARDEN: Yes. Eating & drinking & play equipment

THE BLACK HORSE COACH HOUSE

74, South Street,
Leominster,
Herefordshire.

Public House

Tel: (0568) 611946

The early months of 1992 saw the establishment of beer brewed on site at The Black Horse, the first time beer had been brewed in Leominster since 1926. Had the pub not been popular already, this excellent Real Ale would have made it so, very quickly. One would not suppose from the modest frontage what an exciting hostelry this is.

Inside, this Listed Building is spacious and very comfortable, with an attractive restaurant. A pleasant beer garden and a sizeable car park are the finishing touches to this good pub. The Black Horse is the first pub in Leominster, many say the prime pub, for those travelling North from Hereford leaving Leominster by-pass at the Cadbury factory. Ideally situated for anyone wanting to explore the town's historical buildings or to enjoy the shopping facilities.

Peter Hoare and his father, Douglas are the Licensees. Peter once a dispensing optician, now dispenses spirits from the optics! He specialises in serving excellently kept Real Ales and the pub is noted in the Good Beer Guide. Peter's wife, Jessica looks after the restaurant and cooks many of the delicious home-made dishes herself. There is an excellent choice of food and all at very reasonable prices.

USEFUL INFORMATION

OPEN: 11-2.30pm & 6-11pm
  Sat: 11-11pm
  Sun: Normal hours
CHILDREN: Welcome
CREDIT CARDS: None taken
LICENSED: Full Licence
ACCOMMODATION: Not applicable

RESTAURANT: Home-cooked.
  Good value
BAR FOOD: Wide range. Modest
  prices
VEGETARIAN: Several dishes
ACCESS FOR THE DISABLED:
  Good access
GARDEN: Beer garden. Play area

THE WHITE LION
Inn

Etnam Street,
Leominster,
Herefordshire

Tel: (0568) 612422

Leominster is one of Hereford's prettiest small market towns, which holds out its welcoming arms to the many visitors who come to seek out all its fascinating small antique shops, and those selling all manner of bric a brac. Its busiest day is Market Day on Fridays, when people come in from the surrounding areas. It is then you feel the benefit of the Free Parking system in the town.

Close to the town centre, the railway station and the interesting Leominster Grange, is a black and white 14th-century inn, The White Lion, surrounded by a large Beer Garden, a Play area for children, and with a vast Patio on which Barbecues are held regularly in summer. It really is a super place and very lively. Furnished in keeping with its age you will find much to intrigue you including the gleaming brasses. Even if this were not an attractive pub, Brian and Carole, who own the inn, would ensure with their friendly and outgoing personalities, that the White Lion would make you want to come back. Carole's family have been in the pub trade for many years and these two feel they have a great challenge in keeping up the good name of the family. They have no need to worry, they have succeeded. Carole's cooking is of a very high standard and Brian takes enormous pride in his beer. In addition to the normal menu there is a very good value Sunday lunch. The pub is fun, friendly and definitely one to seek out.

USEFUL INFORMATION

OPEN: Mon-Fri: 11-3pm & 7-11pm
  Sat: 11-11pm
  Sun: 12-3pm & 7-11pm
CHILDREN: Very welcome
CREDIT CARDS: None taken
LICENSED: Full Licence
ACCOMMODATION: Not applicable

RESTAURANT: Traditional English. Excellent value
BAR FOOD: Good choice. Good value
VEGETARIAN: Always 2 dishes
ACCESS FOR THE DISABLED: Ideal
GARDEN: Large. Swings etc. Patio. BBQ

THE SWAN INN
Inn

Letton,
Herefordshire

Tel: (0544) 327304

Ten miles out of Hereford, in a truly rural location, on the side of the A438, the main route between Hereford and Brecon, you will find Letton, a charming spot with the 17th-century Swan Inn in a short row of picturesque black and white cottages.

Because of the age of the building, the pub has a wonderfully eccentric floor in the public bar whilst the dining room, a former corn barn, shows the black and white timber frame construction so typical of the area. The exposed oak beams in the lounge bar are in fact 'second hand' having been removed from Kington workhouse, and some external timbers first saw service in the waiting rooms of the now closed, Golden Valley Railway at Dorstone. The main rooms are heated by open log fires or wood burning stoves, which add to the warmth of the hospitality that is outstanding. The owners, Mike and Julia Boardman and her mother, Joyce Chapman, universally known as 'Mother' have that indefinable touch which makes people feel at home.

Simple, reasonably priced food is available throughout opening hours. Specialities include Mike's carefully prepared Indian dishes, a boozy Steak & Kidney Pie, and Tipsy Pork braised in local cider with a hint of sage, to name but a few, or just a pot of tea. Games for children and a Caravan Club CL for 5 caravans are also available.

USEFUL INFORMATION

OPEN: Mon/Tues: 11-3pm & 6-11pm
Wed/Sat: 11-11pm
Sun: 12-3pm & 7-10.30pm
CHILDREN: Welcome. Small portions
CREDIT CARDS: None taken
LICENSED: Full Licence. Tea & Coffee
ACCOMMODATION: Not at present

RESTAURANT: Excellent value
BAR FOOD: Varied, mostly
home-cooked
VEGETARIAN: About 4 choices
daily
ACCESS FOR THE DISABLED:
One low step; double doors
GARDEN: Yes. Tables and benches

THE RED LION
Public House

Madley,
Herefordshire

Tel: (0981) 250292

There are more public houses named Red Lion than any other. Seldom however, will you come across one that dates back in parts to the 11th century and in others to the 15th century. The Red Lion in the small Herefordshire village of Madley is the one. It oozes history, and is full of old heavy beams and brasses with a wonderful flagstone floor in the Public Bar which could tell you a story or two if it could only speak. A modern day curiosity is the 17 foot Python skin in the Lounge Bar which first made its appearance in 1957.

The Red Lion is a family run pub which has recently been taken over completely by Ellie Gallagher, the daughter of the last licensee. She carries on the family tradition of good hospitality, good ale and good food inside the pubs welcoming doors. Ellie is helped frequently by Alex, her oldest son who waits table, and daily by Rose who describes herself as a Jack of all trades and who has been with the family for 12 years; there is little she does not know about the regulars likes and dislikes. It is a comfortable pub with a function room, a small private dining room for meals and meetings and a Pool table set off from the Public Bar. The food is all home-made with casseroles, steak and kidney pie and a super treacle tart on the menu in amongst many delicious dishes. Chips are very popular because they are real home-made ones. There is a children's menu and dishes for Vegetarians. Good value.

USEFUL INFORMATION

OPEN: 12-2.30pm & 7-11pm
CHILDREN: In bar when eating & garden
CREDIT CARDS: None taken
LICENSED: Full Licence
ACCOMMODATION: Not applicable

RESTAURANT: Not applicable
BAR FOOD: Large portions, simple home-made
VEGETARIAN: 5 dishes daily
ACCESS FOR THE DISABLED: Yes, lounge bar
GARDEN: Yes with slides & swings

THE BRIDGE INN

Public House

Michaelchurch,
Escley,
Herefordshire

Tel: (0981) 23646

The Bridge Inn is one of those story book places, situated at the foot of the Black Mountains between Hereford and Hay-on-Wye. It is right by Escley Brook and surrounded by fields, in which cows and sheep graze contentedly. In summer, customers can drink and dine outside the pub watching the trout in the river, and enjoying the company of the Muscovey Ducks and Ducklings who walk freely amongst them.

Some parts of the pub date back to the 14th century. It has been added to over the years but it still has the feel of centuries about it. Once it was used by Drovers who would stop here whilst they were driving their sheep to market in Hereford. Imagine the fun people have on the Sunday of August Bank Holiday weekend when the famous 'Duck Race' takes place. Plastic ducks are released 2 miles away up river and the winning post is The Bridge Inn. It is all for charity and is a yearly favourite with many people.In the pub there is a lounge, a public bar and a restaurant that seats 22. Jean Draper, the owner, does the cooking with the help of Rosie her assistant. She uses many of her own recipes all the year round, vegetarian ones in particular. Her Leek Croustade - leeks in sauce with a crunchie topping - is a mega favourite for which people keep coming back. It really is a super pub.

USEFUL INFORMATION

OPEN: 12-2.30pm & 7-11pm
   Closed Mon lunch
CHILDREN: Yes, well behaved
CREDIT CARDS: None taken
LICENSED: Full Licence
ACCOMMODATION: Not applicable

RESTAURANT: Many home-cooked recipes
BAR FOOD: Grills and home-cooked dishes
VEGETARIAN: Own recipes. Several dishes
ACCESS FOR THE DISABLED: On one level
GARDEN: Large. Lawn & patio for eating etc

THE YEW TREE INN

Public House & Restaurant

Priors Frome,
Hereford.

Tel: (0432) 850467

Priors Frome is a pretty hamlet just off the road between Mordiford and Dormington and only 4½ miles from Hereford. The Yew Tree Inn is about 150 years old and built on two levels with attractive lawns and gardens which lend themselves to the Barbecues that are held there in summer. There is ample car parking and so Trevor and Lynne Marshall, the proprietors are happy to welcome coach parties. They do ask however for a phone call beforehand if food is required.

The two bars are welcoming places and the restaurant on the lower level is an attractive setting in which to have a meal. Apart from enjoying the views over the Black Mountains and the Hay Bluff you can go fishing, hang gliding, walking or horse riding. If you are not an outdoor person then perhaps a visit to Hereford Cathedral would be a good idea. It is famous for Map a Mundi and the world renowned chained library. The pub has Darts and Quoits teams as well as a Quiz team. Visitors are very welcome to join the 'In House' Quiz night. The food is good with a wide range of lunchtime snacks as well as Steaks, Grills, Swordfish and the unusual cutlet of Wild Boar with a Whisky sauce. On Sundays there is a Carvery which is more than generous in its helpings. Whilst there is no fixed Vegetarian menu Trevor Marshall, who is the Chef, will try to accommodate any request. This is a good value for money establishment.

USEFUL INFORMATION

OPEN: Wed-Sun: 12-2.30pm & 6-11pm
Mon-Tues: 7-11pm only
Sun lunch 12-4pm
CHILDREN: Well behaved welcome
CREDIT CARDS: Visa / Access
LICENSED: Full Licence
ACCOMMODATION: Not applicable

RESTAURANT: Full A La Carte menu
BAR FOOD: Traditional home cooked
VEGETARIAN: On request
ACCESS FOR THE DISABLED: Limited in restaurant
GARDEN: Very pleasant garden

CLOISTERS WINE BAR

Wine Bar & Restaurant

24, High Street,
Ross-on-Wye,
Herefordshire

Tel: (0989) 67717

The market town of Ross-on-Wye has remained almost unchanged since the mid 19th century. Its position is superb, standing above the River Wye, one of the most beautiful rivers in Britain and surrounded by the impressive ruins of Tintern Abbey, Symonds Yat and the scenic beauty of the Forest of Dean.

Cloisters Wine Bar, in a building that dates back to the 18th century, stands out in the High Street because of the glory of its stained glass windows. That is enhanced when you enter by the wealth of exposed beams and nooks and crannies that make it a truly secluded and intimate restaurant, full of olde worlde charm. Imagine dining here in winter in front of an open fireplace, surrounded by dried flowers and hops hanging from the ceiling. Suddenly all the winter chills have disappeared and you just know you are going to have a memorable meal accompanied by excellent wine. The small balcony at the rear of the restaurant is ideal for romantic dinners but beware of your head as the sloping ceiling may catch you unawares! Bryan and Anna Harman are the owners of this very special place. With the help of their efficient and friendly staff they create a totally relaxed and informal atmosphere. The menu is full of gastronomic delights including some unusual fish such as Parrot Fish, Sweet Lips, Monkfish and Groupa. If you are not adventurous there are steaks of all kinds with or without sauces. It is sheer pleasure to dine at Cloisters.

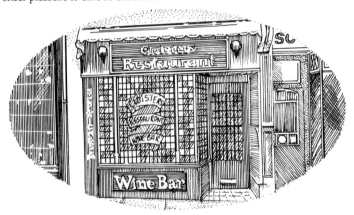

USEFUL INFORMATION

OPEN: Mon-Sun: 6-11pm
Sat/Sun lunchtimes
CHILDREN: Not under the age of 10
CREDIT CARDS: None taken
LICENSED: Wide selections wines,
beers etc
ACCOMMODATION: Not applicable

RESTAURANT: Fresh local
produce. Unusual fish
BAR FOOD: As above
VEGETARIAN: Approx 6 dishes
daily
ACCESS FOR THE DISABLED:
Difficult
GARDEN: No

FRESH GROUNDS AT RAGLAN HOUSE
Restaurant with Rooms

Raglan House,
17, Broad Street,
Ross-on-Wye.

Tel: (0989) 768289

Ross-on-Wye is a delightful place for anyone to visit but recently it has added a jewel to its sparkling crown; Fresh Grounds at Raglan House, in the heart of the main street, is something very special. This Queen Anne and early Georgian building has been superbly renovated recently and made into a delightful restaurant with 7 bedrooms all en-suite and furnished to a very high standard. In addition to being en-suite the bedrooms all have colour TV and tea/coffee making facilities. It is quite unexpected and all the more charming for it.

Fresh Grounds has been described as a club, rather than a restaurant, where old friends meet and newcomers rapidly become part of the scene. People who stay enjoy the wonderful attention they get from the owner, Norma Snook, who genuinely enjoys looking after them. This lady loves cooking and the results are delicious. Homemade soups with freshly baked bread, scrambled egg with Smoked Salmon, mouth watering quiches and pies and succulent braised beef are just some of the dishes available. Norma always uses local vegetables if it is at all possible and everything is cooked on the premises. The afternoon teas are always in demand with light home-made scones, delicious cakes and rich Gateaux that tempt the iron will of any dieter! Dinner is also a meal to be savoured.

USEFUL INFORMATION

OPEN: Mon-Thurs: 9-5pm
Fri/Sat: 9-late
CHILDREN: Welcome, high chairs
CREDIT CARDS: Visa/Mastercard/
Diners
LICENSED: Wines, spirits, lagers etc
ACCOMMODATION: 7 en-suite
rooms

RESTAURANT: Fresh, wonderful
food
BAR FOOD: Not applicable
VEGETARIAN: Always 3 dishes
available
ACCESS FOR THE DISABLED:
Level entrance
GARDEN: No

PHEASANTS
Restaurant

52, Edde Cross Street,
Ross-on-Wye,
Herefordshire.

Tel: (0989) 65751

It is almost impossible to believe that until quite recently Pheasants was just a tiny pub building. Its present owner, a woman of many surprises and talents, Eileen Brunnarius has created a Victorian style dining room with no more than a dozen tables, fronted by a dispense bar and a fireside lounge. She has deliberately made it a 'home from home' atmosphere into which you are not only welcomed by her but also B.B.C the 'Big Black Cat' and the witty, whimsical waiter and wine-buff, Adrian Wells.

Pheasants is all about intimate dining whether at lunch time or in the evening. Eileen's interest in old English recipes and the resulting dishes delight her clientele. Her carefully thought out menus are nicely balanced, beautifully presented and very tasty. At lunchtime there are simple dishes ranging from a Brunch Pancake to Hazelnut and Mushroom Wellington or Old English Duck Pie, followed by Eileen's famous Bread and Butter Pudding'. Dinners are more varied, offering a 'bistro' style menu, as well as the more elaborate 'A la Carte' both offering you the chance to sample some of the international wines - by the glass. In summer the secluded walled courtyard is the most delightful and tranquil place in which to enjoy a meal. Pheasants is 3 minutes from the centre of Ross, and for those who wish to stay there are two attractive bedrooms. A 10% discount on evening meals is offered to those staying. An opportunity not to be missed even if you only have time for a quick lunch. You will want to return.

USEFUL INFORMATION

OPEN: Tues-Sat: 12.30-2pm & 7-10pm
CHILDREN: With well behaved parents
CREDIT CARDS: Amex/Access/Visa
LICENSED: Yes. Fine wines & aperitifs
ACCOMMODATION: 1 twin, 1 double
RESTAURANT: Simple, elegant, delicious

BAR FOOD: Not really but it is flexible
VEGETARIAN: 2 starters & 2 main courses
ACCESS FOR THE DISABLED: Level. Toilet upstairs
GARDEN: Walled courtyard with pond in summer

THE ROSSWYN HOTEL

Hotel

17, High Street,
Ross-on-Wye
Herefordshire

Tel: (0989) 62733

This 15th-century freehouse, conveniently situated off the market square, offers just about everything anyone could wish for. Owned and run by Rose Livesey and her family , the eight well appointed bedrooms are attractively furnished. Some have four poster beds and most a bathroom en suite. Two night 'Bargain Breaks' are available all the year round at a very reasonable fixed rate. Staying here would allow you not only to enjoy the wonderful atmosphere of the hotel with its wealth of exposed beams, fine Jacobean stair case and a superb carved Elizabethan fireplace, you would also have the opportunity to explore Ross, the Wye Valley, Forest of Dean and the Black Mountains, returning to the hospitable welcome of the bar.

During renovations in the early 1970's a small hidden room was discovered in the cellar which is now a wine bar, and it is generally believed that this was a priest hide dating from the Reformation.

The restaurant which is open to non-residents from Monday-Saturday evenings serves delicious and imaginative food from French and English recipes using fresh local produce where possible. The menu is constantly changing. The 2 bars are open all day and a large range of bar meals are served there at lunchtime and in the evenings. All the food is home-cooked and the portions more than generous. A delightful place.

USEFUL INFORMATION

OPEN: All day every day
CHILDREN: Garden & play area
CREDIT CARDS: Access/Visa/Amex
LICENSED: Full on Licence
ACCOMMODATION: 8 doubles

RESTAURANT: High quality
English & French
BAR FOOD: Wide range, substantial
VEGETARIAN: Special menu in
restaurant. Bar 2-3 dishes
ACCESS FOR THE DISABLED:
Not suitable
GARDEN: Sun terrace & lawns with
swings

THE LOUGH POOL INN
Public House & Restaurant

Sellack,
Ross-on-Wye,
Herefordshire.

Tel: (098987) 236

If one wanted to conjure up in ones mind the perfect pub in a wonderful setting, that is what you would find at The Lough Pool Inn at Sellack just 4 miles from Ross and 8 miles from Hereford, close to the River Wye and the Wye Valley. The location is a secluded one, next to the pool from which the pub takes its name. The gardens are delightful, complete with an old cider press. and equipped with tables and chairs for dining outside, when the weather permits.

The pub is a 16th century black and white timbered building which is as delightful inside as out. The unspoilt timbers, the nooks and crannies, the flagstone floors and large open fireplaces just enhance the warm and welcoming atmosphere. Phil Moran with his wife Jan are the owners and he is also the imaginative chef. The menu is exciting and not expensive. In the bar you can choose from a home-made soup or deep fried Brie with Cranberry Sauce for example, and follow it with a number of different dishes including a super Vegetarian Spinach, Cheese and Mushroom Pie. The restaurant has some outstanding dishes but probably the most unusual and popular is Greek style Goat Casserole, tender pieces of local milk-fed Kid casseroled in the Greek way with yoghurt,tomatoes and garlic. For the traditionalist the Herefordshire Beef Steaks are superb.

USEFUL INFORMATION

OPEN: 12-3pm. Eve: 6.30-11pm
Sat: 7-11pm. Sun: 7-10.30pm
CHILDREN: Yes. No children under
14 in bar
CREDIT CARDS: Visa/Access/
Master/Euro/Diner
LICENSED: Wines, spirits, beers/cider
ACCOMMODATION: Not applicable

RESTAURANT: Interesting. Good
quality
BAR FOOD: Wide range. Value for
money
VEGETARIAN: Always some dishes
ACCESS FOR THE DISABLED:
Easy access
GARDEN: Yes with tables/benches for
30/40

THE LAMB INN

Public House

Stoke Prior,
Leominster,
Herefordshire.

Tel: (0568) 82308

Herefordshire has many wonderfully laid back villages and Stoke Prior, near Leominster, must come high on the list. Once upon a time it would not have been so restful; the Romans had an encampment, and there is more evidence of activity in the Middle Ages. It is sleepy, picturesque and its residents revel in the quality of their lives. When they want to shop or feel like a little hustle and bustle they set off for Leominster, an old market town, which is just three miles away, or perhaps they will drive the ten miles to historic Ludlow. Most times however, they are happy to enjoy the social life that The Lamb Inn provides. Some two hundred years old, it has been refurbished recently, but it still remains a good country pub.

During the summer, the pub is visited fortnightly by Morris Dancers, and in the winter it is the home of two Darts Teams and the local Football side. Shooting Dinners are another feature in the winter time. Bed and Breakfast is available here with one of the three rooms furnished as a Family room.

There is no separate restaurant but the food served in the dining area, separated from the bar, is home-made and has many Daily Specials. Children have their own menu and there are always three dishes for Vegetarians. You should try 'Hereford Bull' - a hot beef roll which is delicious and one of the tastiest items on this wholesome menu.

USEFUL INFORMATION

OPEN: 12-3pm & 7-11pm
CHILDREN: Always welcome
CREDIT CARDS: None taken
LICENSED: Full Licence
ACCOMMODATION: 3 doubles.
    Family room

RESTAURANT: Not applicable
BAR FOOD: Varied with
    home-made dishes
VEGETARIAN: Always 3 dishes
ACCESS FOR THE DISABLED
    Ramp to entrance
GARDEN: Large with swings etc.
    Tables & benches

THE CADMORE LODGE HOTEL

Hotel, Restaurant & Country Club

Berrington Green,
Tenbury Wells,
Worcestershire.

Tel: (0584) 810044

Cadmore Lodge is a new hotel offering excellent sporting opportunities together with super cuisine, accommodation, conference and function facilities. John Weston a civil engineer, designed and created the whole venture with his wife Elizabeth, a wild life expert and keen sportswoman. The hotel has a very pleasant and welcoming atmosphere.

Cadmore Lodge is situated 2 miles west of the market town, Tenbury Wells, and lies in its own secluded valley with 60 acres of woodland, a nine hole golf course and 2 shimmering lakes. The Estate with its wealth of wild life offers an ideal country holiday to the naturalist. In addition to golf there is good fishing on the estate lakes and streams. The River Tene offers Salmon, grayling and coarse fishing. For those who want something other than sporting pursuits the historic town of Ludlow is only 7 miles away and both Cathedral cities of Hereford and Worcester just 20 miles off.

The accommodation has a Three Crown rating and comprises 8 well appointed en-suite double rooms. There is a comfortable lounge, a function room and an attractive dining room. The bars are welcoming and the skilled chef offers a tempting menu whether it is the set price dinner or dishes taken from the A La Carte selection.

USEFUL INFORMATION

OPEN: 8am until after midnight
CHILDREN: Welcome
CREDIT CARDS: Access/Visa/ Mastercard
LICENSED: Full & Supper Licence
ACCOMMODATION: 8 doubles en-suite 3 Crowns

RESTAURANT: High quality, fresh produce
BAR FOOD: Good selection, good value
VEGETARIAN: Yes. 5/6 dishes daily
ACCESS FOR THE DISABLED: Yes
GARDEN: 60 acres, walks, patio by lake

THE ROYAL OAK HOTEL
Hotel

Market Street,
Tenbury Wells,
Worcestershire.

Tel: (0584) 810417

Tenbury Wells is blessed with many beautiful buildings and one of them is the 15th-century Royal Oak standing in Market Street, one of the main streets of this busy market town. Beautiful in its own right, Tenbury Wells has the added good fortune of being surrounded by glorious countryside.

If you are seeking somewhere to visit, you will do no better than walk in the countryside, explore the town and then find your way to the welcoming hospitality of The Royal Oak. It must have looked in the 15th century, much as it does today, with low ceilings and the original beams gracing the bars and dining room. The six bedrooms make the hotel a good place to stay especially if you have a family, for Terry and Heather Cooper, the owners, have children of their own and are very conversant with their needs. The beer garden is popular in summer both to sit in and to enjoy the fun of the barbecues which are held regularly, weather permitting. The Royal Oak is blessed with an experienced chef, who loves his work and produces some superb dishes. A grilled Lamb Steak in Orange and Rosemary Sauce is one of them. A delicate Cucumber Sauce accompanies fresh Salmon. He is imaginative but equally aware that healthy eating is important. A selection of Bar Meals is available if you have not the time for indulging in a wonderful meal in the restaurant. Morning coffee is available from 10-11am.

USEFUL INFORMATION

OPEN: Coffee 10-11am. Bar 11-3pm
CHILDREN: In family room & garden
CREDIT CARDS: Visa / Access / Amex
LICENSED: Full Licence
ACCOM MODATION: 6 bedrooms

RESTAURANT: Imaginative menu
BAR FOOD: Excellent bar meals
VEGETARIAN: Always 6 dishes
ACCESS FOR THE DISABLED: Yes
GARDEN: Beer garden & barbecue

YE OLDE SALUTATION INN

Inn

Market Pitch,
Weobley,
Herefordshire.

Tel: (0544) 318443

You take one look at Ye Olde Salutation Inn, in one of the best examples of a medieval village in the country, Weobley, and you think 'that is the place for me to stay'. It has a charm all of its own on the outside with its black and white timber-framed building dating back over 500 years. Inside it is just as delightful with a large Inglenook fireplace in the comfortable lounge bar, which leads into the 40 seater Oak Room Restaurant.

Chris and Frances Anthony are mine hosts in this former Ale and Cider House which, with an adjoining cottage, makes up the Salutation. The Anthonys endeavour, most successfully, to maintain the traditions of village life throughout the Inn. The 5 letting rooms, three of which are en-suite have tea/coffee making facilities. One of the bedrooms boasts a luxury four-poster bed. The guest bathroom has been furnished in the Victorian style and there is also a lounge with TV. The inn has full central heating. Many people come to the Salutation to lunch or dine after exploring the Herefordshire countryside. You can walk through the Castle Green with its impressive earthworks leading to the open countryside of the Garnstone Estate. The food that will be served, before or after your walk, will be expertly cooked and a meal to be savoured.

USEFUL INFORMATION

OPEN: 11-3pm & 7-11pm
CHILDREN: Eating area, lounge
conservatory
CREDIT CARDS: Mastercard/Visa
LICENSED: Full Licence
ACCOMMODATION: 5 bedrooms,
3 Crowns commended

RESTAURANT: High quality,
interesting menu
BAR FOOD: Wide choice
VEGETARIAN: 3/4 dishes daily
ACCESS FOR THE DISABLED:
From car park. Lounge, rest. only
GARDEN: Patio style with seating
for 28

Stokesay Castle, viewed from the north

INCLUDES:

The Carpenters Arms	*Bridgnorth*	p. 235
The Falcon Hotel	*Bridgnorth*	p. 236
The Feathers	*Brockton*	p. 237
The Forester Arms	*Broseley*	p. 238
The Woodcock Inn	*Castle Pulverbach*	p. 239
Acorn Restaurant	*Church Stretton*	p. 240
The Plough Inn	*Claverley*	p. 241
The Crown Inn	*Clunton*	p. 242
Stokesay Castle Hotel	*Craven Arms*	p. 243
The Champion Jockey	*Donnington*	p. 244
Bache Arms	*Highley*	p. 245
The Coracle	*Ironbridge*	p. 246
The Bennetts End Inn	*Knowbury*	p. 247
The Red Lion	*Little Dawley*	p. 248
The Green Dragon	*Little Stretton*	p. 249
Charlton Arms Hotel	*Ludford*	p. 250
Wingfield Arms Hotel	*Montford Bridge*	p. 251
Pheasant Inn	*Newport*	p. 252
The Miners Arms	*Priest Weston*	p. 253
The Lion Inn	*Priorslee*	p. 254
The Nell Gwynn	*Shifnal*	p. 255
The Cornhouse Restaurant	*Shrewsbury*	p. 256
Carols	*Telford*	p. 257
The Sutherland Arms	*Tibberton*	p. 258
The Plough	*Wall under Heywood*	p. 259

'A man hath no better thing under the sun,
than to eat, and to drink, and to be merry.'
Ecclesiastes

SOUTH SHROPSHIRE

The temptation, when you decide to visit South Shropshire, is to seek out immediately places like Ludlow, a place of historical romance and one of the most beautiful country towns in England. This is what I have always done in the past but this time I was asked to stay with friends in **Telford,** a new town that is light years ahead. My friends had moved there with reluctance when a new posting for the husband made it imperative. To their surprise they have found living in this new town a good experience. Some of their enthusiasm rubbed off on me and I too was agreeably surprised at the great effort that has been made to make it a 'green and pleasant land'. Over a million trees, plants and shrubs have been planted throughout the town. TELFORD TOWN PARK is a massive area of attractive open countryside in the very heart. I watched children revelling in the little steam miniature railway, people venturing out onto the lake in paddle boats and families sitting contentedly on the grass. The park is a mixture of landscaped and natural scenery complete with a lake at the side of which is an amphitheatre and a sports arena. The town offers all sorts of facilities and seems to me to be full of young and enthusiastic people who enjoy what it has to offer.

Pitchford Hall

Having been shown the town shopping centre I was taken to the Meeting Point House, in Southwater Square, a building overlooking the lake, home to swans and ducks living in harmony, which is an inter-denominational Charity building used by every religious body in Telford. It is a bright, cheerful place and in part of it is a Restaurant and Cafe owned by Carol Dixon who operates it with her son, Gary. The food is all home-cooked and quite delicious but be warned - there are no chips on the menu! It was the Dixon's who told me that in summer all sorts of events take place in the park including colourful Morris Dancing.

One of the reasons that made my friends happy with Telford was the unique range of top class sporting facilities, with everything from golf and tennis to skiing provided in a range of superb modern sports centres. In addition to the National Sports Centre at nearby Lilleshall, Telford has six fully equipped sports and leisure centres of its own. The Telford Ice Rink is one of the finest in the Midlands, and it is the home of one of the country's top ice hockey teams. Ice Skating has always thrilled me and I enjoyed watching the skaters of all ages gliding their way across the rink, with the occasional fall or two of course.

*A visit to **Lilleshall** allowed me to see the imposing ruin of the Abbey which makes an unforgettable picture as you approach it from the west. The view looks through the monumental gateway along the Abbey's full 228 foot length, with the leafy countryside beyond framed in the great east window. It is breathtaking. The abbey dates from the 12th century and there are extensive remains of its impressive masonry still standing. It is open to the public daily.*

You will find LILLESHALL HALL NATIONAL SPORTS CENTRE just off the Newport to Telford road. It was built originally in 1829 for the 1st Duke of Sutherland whose claim to fame was as a great road builder. He is commemorated today with a towering 70ft obelisk which stands on a hill overlooking the village. One wonders what he would make of to-days's roads!

The National Sports Centre is a training ground for many of our international sports stars. It has facilities for a wide range of sports open to local people who do stay here. It can accommodate 185 and has good Lecture and Seminar facilities with Audio/Visual Aid equipment. It is a popular choice for Conferences and Seminars for those who have the taste for sport. If you want any further information do ring (0952) 603003.

Whilst I was this far up the road I decided to carry on to **Newport** before returning to meet my friends in the evening. It is only eight miles to the north-east of Telford and is as different as chalk and cheese. Here I found a pleasant, unspoilt market town, centred around the broad, elegant High Street; a street just asking to be explored. At number 68 High Street, I discovered the PHEASANT INN, a hostelry that has been dispensing hospitality for 250 years or more. Had I realised what a welcoming place it was beforehand, I would have stayed a night or two. The accommodation on offer is unpretentious but comfortable and mine hosts, Philip and Lyn Collins have a nice brand of humour and a great understanding of people's needs. I lunched on one of the specialities of the house, Fish Pie and very good it was.

Strolling along after lunch I took a look at the several fine Georgian and Victorian buildings which were built long after a disastrous fire in 1665 almost destroyed the town. For those who love exploring churches, the large and graceful church of ST NICHOLAS, standing on an island site in the middle of the road in the High Street, is one you will want to see. There is a font from the year of the Restoration, a coffin lid carved quite wonderfully 700 years ago, and a list of rectors going back to the Normans.

The other buildings I enjoyed were THE JACOBEAN GUILDHALL and ADAM'S GRAMMAR SCHOOL, founded in Cromwell's time by William Adam. It is a charming building with a cupola and its original clock, set behind a small courtyard with almshouses on each side of the gates.

The most famous boy of Newport school was the wise and extraordinary man, Sir Oliver Lodge who experimented in wireless and sent wireless telegrams long before Marconi. He interested himself in all sorts of things from the mysterious problems of telepathy to the conquering of fog. Another famous man of Newport was the satirical poet of Shakespeare's day who wrote lines we have all heard at some time or another:

I do not love thee, Dr Fell,
The reason why I cannot tell,
But this I know, and know full well,
I do not love thee, Dr Fell.

Within the postal address of Newport is the pretty, rural village of **Tibberton,** *once part of the land belonging to the Duke of Sutherland, hence the name of the village pub, THE SUTHERLAND ARMS where Jonathan Morris and his wife Sheila are the owners. They run an excellent business and all the time look for ways in which to improve. When I popped in they were in the throes of making a better entrance for wheelchairs and enhancing the kitchens to allow food to be served in the evenings as well as at lunch time. You will find them interesting to talk to. Jonathan was once the lockkeeper on the Shropshire Union Canal and with Sheila, he ran horse drawn trips in his boat, the Iona, from Norbury Junction.*

Before you get back into the centre of Telford you come to **Donnington** *where, in Wrekin Drive, there is a very lively pub, THE CHAMPION JOCKEY, which seems to have something going on all day long. I popped in early one evening and saw people already settling down for an evening of live entertainment, which is a regular feature. Locals told me that Pauline Thompson, who with her husband Peter, are the proprietors, makes one of the best Cottage Pies in the county.*

I was introduced to another nice pub in the attractive village of **Priorslee** *which is just on the outskirts of Telford. THE LION INN is less than five minutes from Junction 4 or 5 off the M54, yet it has little to do with the 1990s, apart from its modern amenities. It is a 16th-century coaching inn, with oak beams, shining brass and a vast Inglenook fireplace which houses a roaring log fire. I arrived there having spent a fascinating but tiring time at COSFORD AEROSPACE MUSEUM which is just 15 minutes away.*

This is one of the world's most spectacular collections of civil and military aircraft, with more than 70 aircraft, missiles and engines on display. For me a feeling of nostalgia appeared when I saw the famous fighting machines of World War II - at least those that belonged to the Allied Airforces. There was the legendary Spitfire, the Mosquito and the vast American Liberator bomber. You can see inside the interiors of the JU52 and Field Marshal Montgomery's personal Dakota DC3.

I was none too happy to be reminded of the German missiles of the War especially the dreaded 'Doodlebug' which used to be far more frightening than the nightly bombing. We should be thankful though that the chilling collection of experimental weapons were never launched. Perhaps it is good for us to be reminded of what might have been and what could be again if we do not keep a strong Armed Service.

The Aerospace Museum at Cosford

The Museum has a post war Canberra, a Lincoln and a Javelin - the world's first delta-wing fighter. The massive Thor, Bloodhound and Blue Steel missiles bring back memories of the Gulf. One special display I enjoyed allows vistors to see the inside nose section of a Vulcan bomber.

Cosford has the largest collection of research and development aircraft, including the TSR2, the Fairey Delta 2, the Gloster Meteor and Neville Duke's famous Hunter.

The world of civil aviation is represented by The British Airway's Collection - a superb range of majestic airlines from the 1950s and 1960s that includes the Comet, Britannia, Viscount, the VC10 and the Boeing 707. There is a walk through display inside a Trident airliner. That brought back memories too of one awful flight to Geneva when shortly after take off one engine went hurtling to the ground and we had to limp back to the airport. The pilot was brilliant but it was none too encouraging to look out of the window and see the crash tenders, ambulances and fire engines waiting to greet us. All was well - I am still here to tell the tale and have flown many thousands of miles with British Airways since then.

Inside the British Airways Exhibition Hall, models and airliners trace the history of Britain's civil aviation history but that is only part of what there is to see. A remarkable collection of models includes a 22ft replica of Concorde, and there is a complete exhibition of aircraft engines, from the early piston engine to the colossal power of modern jet flight.

I have probably rambled on about this Aerospace Museum but it is outstanding and for anyone with a feel for aircraft, Cosford has to be seen. Allow plenty of time, one afternoon is hardly sufficient.

The Museum is open daily from 10am-4pm and you will find it on the A41 1 Mile from Junction 3 on the M54.

The official address is Cosford, Shifnal and it is to **Shifnal** *I will take you next. Dickens would not be pleased if he were to visit the town today. He mentioned the place in the Old Curiosity Shop; it was an important coaching-stop on the Holyhead Road and he thought of it as a pleasant village. This is no longer so, it has been industrialised but there are still delightful buildings including THE NELL GWYNN, a restaurant, in Park Street, which must be one of the most beautiful timbered buildings in the whole of Shropshire. The moment you step inside its welcoming doors you are filled with a sense of history. People come from miles around to eat in this wonderful atmosphere. Next door is the equally interesting old pub, The Charles II which is part of the Nell Gwynn.*

Market days are good fun and very lively, held on Wednesdays and apart from that you can just imagine you are walking with Dickens when you see some of the narrow streets, under timbered eaves and gables burdened with age. In a quiet corner of the town the 750 year old tower of the parish church rises in glory, unperturbed by the twentieth century activity below. The church's two-storeyed porch, with its graceful trefoiled arch and vaulted roof, is 13th century. In the nave there is a curious stone which tells of the remarkable story of two local people whose ages totalled 251 years. William Wakeley is said to have died in 1714 at 124 and Mary Yates to have died later in the century at 127. William lived through eight reigns and the intrepid Mary walked to London after the Great Fire in

1666 when she was in her teens, and married her third husband in her nineties. All quite useless information, as my son would tell me, but I find such things fascinating.

Within easy reach of Telford and Shifnal are so many wonderful places to visit. Just 3 miles north of Junction 3 of the M54 is WESTON PARK, on the A5 at **Weston-under-Lizard.** *This classic 17th-century stately home is open from Easter to the end of September to the General Public but all the year round for Conferences, Product launches, Banquets Wedding Receptions and for very special gourmet 'Dine and Stay' evenings which are open to the public. These are truly wonderful occasions and will long stay in your memory. If you are interested do ring (0952) 76207 and enquire for dates.*

Weston Park, the historic home of the Earls of Bradford, is one of Britain's most popular stately homes. The interior has been superbly restored and holds one of the country's finest private collections of paintings, with originals by many of the great masters. There are fine tapestries from the famous 18th-century makers Gobelin and Aubusson, and letters from Disraeli which provide a fascinating commentary on Victorian history. It is quite wonderful.

No less remarkable are the grounds. The park was one of Capability Brown's masterpieces of landscape and architecture, with fallow deer and rare breeds of sheep grazing the pastures. Each successive generation of the family has done something to enhance their heritage. Today the woods are at their loveliest in spring and early summer, colourful displays of daffodils giving way to rhododendrons and azaleas. The park has some splendid architectural features including the Roman Bridge and Temple of Diana, both designed and built by James Paine for Sir Henry Bridgeman around 1760. Children relish the Woodlands Adventure Playground with its wide range of exciting obstacles. The little Weston Park railway made it simple for me to see Temple Wood, as it wandered its way along 1½ miles of track.

The Old Stables is the setting for the tearooms in which you can get good country cooking at sensible prices. If you prefer to picnic you are welcome to do so in an area set aside which is situated in the shade of trees beside a stream. Definitely the thing to do on a balmy summer's day.

Weston Park at Weston under Lizard

From Weston Park it is only a short distance to BOSCOBEL HOUSE, in which Charles Stuart sought sanctuary after his defeat at Worcester. As I drove along the quiet road I wondered if the King had wished he was just a simple Shropshire man, secure in his everyday life rather than a royal. The Giffords of Chillington owned Boscobel and as staunch catholics they had honeycombed the house with hiding-places for priests. If you see the house today many of them still exist. One will be pointed out to you as the kings, which is reached by a short flight of stairs leading to the cheese room. On one landing is a trapdoor which leads down to a hiding-place, lined to deaden the sound. At this time however the house was tenanted by William Penderel, one of six brothers who were loyal supporters of the Stuart cause.

It was not to Boscobel but to WHITELADIES, nearby where Humphrey Penderel lived that Charles first looked for a safe hiding place. Here he left all his retinue but Lord Wilmot and became a countryman wearing a coarse shirt, darned stockings, a leather doublet with pewter buttons, a ragged coat and breeches, a battered old hat and rough boots. He darkened his face and his hands with soot and accompanied only by Richard, he crept out, avoiding the troops that he knew to be in the neighbourhood. He was attempting to make his way over the Severn and into Wales, stopping at Madeley, the

211

home of Francis Woolf. The journey was fraught with danger and at one stage he and Richard were chased by a miller and a number of soldiers. They ran until they could go no further and simply fell in the mud. It was not until all was quiet again that they continued their journey. They must have looked awful. When they reached Madeley they were housed in a barn for the rest of the night and the next day but they were never to continue their journey.

The countryside was full of soldiers and they learnt that all the ways over the Severn were guarded. The only thing to do was to make their way back to Boscobel by the same route that they had come, avoiding the mill where they had run into trouble before. The only way to do this was to swim across a river but Richard could not swim. Charles helped him over but by this time the King's feet were so blistered and torn and his boots full of grit, that he felt he could not go on. It was Richard Penderel who kept him going and at last they reached the safety of Boscobel where the Royalist, Colonel Carlos, greeted him. Charles's aching feet were doctored, his boots dried and he was given a change of stockings. Outside the house was a great oak and into this Charles and the Colonel climbed. They slept during the day but woke to the sound of Cromwell's men hunting in the wood searching for the King. There was a price of £1,000 on the King's head; something all the Penderels knew about but such was their loyalty that no one even thought of betraying him. They would have died in his cause if need be. For two more days and nights Charles stayed at Boscobel, sleeping in the hole beneath the trapdoor in the cheese room until finally it was thought safe enough for him to set out on the long journey which would eventually end in France.

Boscobel House opens daily from Good Friday to the end of September; Tuesday to Sunday during the rest of the year; closed December 24-26 and January 1st.

A track leading off the road, about a mile from Boscobel House will lead you to the ruins of WHITE LADIES PRIORY, a 12th-century nunnery. Although much of the original building has disappeared, the walls of the Priory church are still standing. It is open daily.

You must visit **Tong** whilst you are in this area. It is only a small village but the magnificent church of ST BARTHOLOMEW would not be out of place in a city. It is frequently referred to as 'The *cathedral of the West Midlands'. Built in the 14th century, it is Perpendicular and has a tower which is not square in shape but is that of an octagon with flourishing pinnacles, battlements and a spirelet above it all. The Golden Chapel, has a gilt fan-vault and the nave a lovely timber roof ornamented with bosses. In the porch is a curious board which lists the various occasions when the Great Bell is to be rung. Dickens would have you believe that the porch was a resting place for Little Nell and her grandfather during their flight from London and she is reputedly buried in the churchyard. The choir stalls deserve inspection because of their superb carvings, but you will find it hard to ignore the demand that the effigies make for your attention; they are many but my favourites are the serene ones of Sir Richard Vernon who died in 1451 and his wife, who is dressed in beautiful robes and a headdress whilst he wears armour. The church is open daily from 9am until dusk and from 10 until 7.30pm on Sundays.*

Just north of the village, off the A41, you can see a peculiar, pyramid-shaped building set back a few hundred yards from the road. It's called the EGYPTIAN AVIARY, and it's a bizarre hen-house designed by a celebrated local eccentric called George Durant in the early 19th century.

*The mention of **Madeley** took me to there just off the A442 between Telford and Bridgnorth. It has nothing of especial interest but I wanted to see for myself, the church where 'Fletcher of Madeley', a great friend of John and Charles Wesley, ministered to his flock for 25 years. He arrived in 1760 and set about reforming his unruly parishioners. If they did not come to church he went looking for them either in their homes or the inn. On Sunday mornings he went round with his bell at 5 o'clock to wake them up. I can just imagine how popular that was! He was a truly good man, caring deeply for the poor. He taught children at school and started a Sunday School for them. When he died John Wesley preached the sermon at his funeral and told the full church that he had never met so holy a man.*

I must mention a superb country house hotel here, MADELEY COURT, once the home of Abraham Darby. This was a house that at one time had lost its way and was in need of extensive repairs. When I visited it this time I found it to have been sympathetically and beautifully restored. It offers comfort, a high standard of service and superb food served in the original 13th-century hall. A place you will enjoy staying in, it is quite unique. When you go there you will see that it stands between two lovely, green, wooded hills. It is hard to believe that a hundred years ago these hills were a scar on the countryside with not a tree in sight. They were rubbish heaps from the mines, of such a size that they blocked out the windows of the house. Someone with a feel for the environment started the planting process and so today they are places of beauty.

On my way to Madeley I stopped for a meal at THE RED LION in **Little Dawley** which is really part of Telford. The pub has been there for three hundred years and is definitely a country inn even if it is in the heart of Telford. It is wonderfully situated for a visit to **Ironbridge** which was my destination after Madeley. The food is good, fresh pub fare at sensible prices. You can get breakfast from 10am and scrumptious cream teas in the afternoons.

The whole of THE IRONBRIDGE GORGE is one big real-life museum that tells you every chapter of the fascinating story, on the spot, where it happened. There is no other place anywhere in the world like the Ironbridge Gorge. Make sure you allow yourself plenty of time to enjoy it.

The Severn flows through this deep gorge and the houses cling to the hillsides, looking as though a puff of wind would blow them into the swirling river, but they have been there for hundreds of years and are as much a part of this incredible place as the Museums. The chief distinction is, of course, the bridge, believed to be the first iron bridge ever built. It was built by Abraham Darby of Coalbrookdale in 1777. It is 196 feet long with one span of 100 feet and two smaller ones, the total weight of iron being about 380tons. So much for the statistics, worth knowing but fading almost into insignificance alongside the many things one has to see.

Over 250 years ago the Severn Gorge witnessed momentous events which culminated in the Industrial Revolution and it was the fortunate combination of coal, iron, water power and transport, all concentrated in this Shropshire Valley, which sparked off the series of events which affected all of us.

Finding somewhere to stay is not a problem at Ironbridge. I have stayed in the past at THE LIBRARY HOUSE, a fascinating 18th-century house near the Iron Bridge. It is reasonably priced, all the rooms are en-suite and the food is all home- cooked. It is somewhere I would be happy to visit again. George and Chris Maddocks are the owners and if you would like details ring them on (0952) 432299.

The Severn at Ironbridge

For a restaurant you will not do better than to climb the stairs of 33a High Street ,to THE CORACLE RESTAURANT. The setting is perfect, it is just 50 yards from the Iron Bridge in a Grade 2 Listed Building dating back to 1779. I enjoyed the intimacy of the place with just 24 covers. It still has the original oak beams and nice pine furniture. The name stems from the small craft used on the river for fishing and poaching. Coracles are still made by Eustace Rogers who lives nearby.

Abraham Darby is very important to Ironbridge obviously, and just a short walk from the Gorge is ROSEHILL HOUSE, one of the elegant mansions where the Darby family lived in the 18th and 19th centuries. It is sheer pleasure to wander through the beautifully restored rooms with original period furniture. It gives you an understanding of how a wealthy ironmaster would have lived in the early 1800s.

In total contrast is CARPENTERS' ROW, a terrace of workers' houses built by the company in the late 18th century. There is *nothing grand about them. Four cottages have been restored and furnished to recreate a home from different periods between 1780 and 1930. Carpenters' Row is open to small groups by special appointment only.*

The six major attraction sites of the IRONBRIDGE GORGE MUSEUM really bring the story to life. It is truly remarkable and without doubt deserves the many national and international awards it has won including 'Museum of the Year', 'European Museum of the Year' and 'AA Best Museum 1987'.

The greatest accolade came in 1986 when the Gorge was recognised internationally, with its designation as a World Heritage Site - the first British site to receive this honour - ranking Ironbridge Gorge alongside the Pyramids, the Grand Canyon and the Taj Mahal, in an elite group of less than 250 sites worldwide. World Heritage Sites are designated by the United Nations; they are defined as places of such exceptional interest and value that their protection is a concern for all nations.

THE MUSEUM OF IRON is where it all began. At **Coalbrookdale** *Abraham Darby began to smelt iron ore using coke, instead of the traditional charcoal, much to the amazement of his fellow ironmasters. It was this one action that started the industrial revolution. Darby's discovery gave man the power to mass- produce cheap iron for the first time, paving the way for the rise of large-scale industry. The furnace that Darby used in 709 is still here. It is probably the most important industrial history monument in the world, and it is the centrepiece of this remarkable collection that traces the history of iron in a series of informative displays, models and exhibits. Darby's furnace is housed in its own special building. Climb up and you can look down into the heart of the furnace with an exciting sound, light and smoke display that is very real.*

Nearby is the Great Warehouse built by Darby's Coalbrookdale Company in 1838 which contains the Museum's main collection. In here you will discover the whole story of this great man and the history of iron from the earliest times - including a full size reconstruction of an Iron Age furnace and a working scale model of a charcoal blast furnace.

Darby's discovery in 1709 opened the way for momentous developments at Coalbrookdale - the cylinders for the first steam engine; the first iron wheels; the first iron rails; the first iron-framed building.

In 1777, Abraham Darby III enlarged his grandfather's first blast furnace to cast the massive ribs for the Iron Bridge. The building of the bridge in 1779 turned the Gorge into one of the world's major iron centres.

These tremendous years have been recreated at the Museum with a series of displays leading you through the achievements of the Darby family.

It also tells the story of the Coalbrookdale community. The Darby dynasty and the impact of their Quaker beliefs - and the men who worked for them, with sections of their housing and their arduous working conditions, often labouring for up to a 24 hour stretch.

*When Ironbridge began to decline as a centre of the industrial revolution after 1810, it entered a new period of prosperity as a centre for art and design, with the emergence of the fine porcelain and decorative tile industries at nearby **Coalport** and **Jackfield,** and the development of Coalbrookdale as a world renowned centre for fine art castings.*

Probably the greatest claim to fame was the Great Exhibition of 1851 for which the company produced the huge ceremonial gates for the Crystal Palace site and a series of major design commissions for the exhibition - including the magnificent 'Cupid and Swan' fountain, which you can still see at the Museum of Iron. There is also a superb collection of Victorian art castings, together with a series of displays illustrating the spectacular process of producing cast iron.

An unusual shop specialises in cast iron products while next to the Museum is the ELTON GALLERY and the IRONBRIDGE INSTITUTE, one of the country's most important centres for the study of industrial history. There are regular exhibitions of paintings, drawings, prints and commemorative pieces tracing the development of industry and technology.

The Museum is open from March to early November from 10am-6pm- The Coalbrookdale Furnace and Elton Collection remain open in winter from 10am-5pm.

The highlight of the Gorge for me is the amazing open air museum at BLISTS HILL. Here you can experience the way of life and the atmosphere of nearly 100 years ago, as you wander through a living, working, industrial community of the 1890s.

Blists Hill is a living museum, there are no glass display cases or historical notes to study. You can see the past at work. The blacksmith, the cobbler, the locksmith and the plasterer still carry on their traditional crafts, using the tools and the equipment of a hundred years ago. At the sawmill you can watch gates, wheelbarrows and coffins being made, while the printer still produces handbills, tickets and posters for the local community.

A full, working candle factory from nearby Madeley has been rebuilt here and a foundry restored to its original condition. In the 19th century, Blists Hill was part of an important coal mining area; you can still visit the pithead at the Blists Hill mine and watch the massive winding engine that used to lower the miners 600 foot underground.

The Shelton Tollhouse and the Squatter's Cottage have been rebuilt and furnished to show exactly how the ordinary people of the 1890s would have lived. The tollhouse was designed by the great roadbuilder, Thomas Telford, as ideal accommodation for a working man while in 1861, the tiny squatter's cottage housed a family of nine.

In the main street you can browse through a row of Victorian shops, complete with the butcher's, the sweetshop, the chemist and the local inn, where you can stop for a drink.

The bank and the doctor's surgery have been reconstructed too, together with the little iron mission church - and in the curious gospel car and the tiny tin chapel you can see the peculiar meeting places of the smaller religious groups.

The past surrounds you, with railway sidings, a canal wharf with its 19th-century tub boats; an early Victorian road, built to Thomas Telford's exact specifications; the primitive mining conditions at the footrid and the fireclay mine.

One of the features is the remarkable HAY INCLINED PLANE, designed to lift canal boats up the steep banks of the Gorge from the River Severn to the Shropshire Canal. Its 207 foot rise is equivalent to more than 27 conventional locks, and in its heyday it could lift a five-ton tub boat in three and a half minutes.

Boats were normally passed over the incline in pairs, with a loaded boat at the top pulling up an empty vessel from below- loaded boats would have been raised from the bottom by a huge steam winding engine at the head of the incline.

The Museum is open mid-February until the end of October from 10-5pm.

THE MUSEUM OF THE RIVER was formerly the Severn Warehouse, built in the 1840s to house the iron products of the Coalbrookdale Company prior to shipment down the River and onto the world's markets. This Museum has a spectacular 40 foot model of the Gorge as it was in 1796. There are displays on the way the River is managed now compared with the time of the Industrial Revolution.

It helped me to understand the methods by which the modern western world takes for granted fresh water at the turn of a tap. A dramatic audio-visual show about the history of the Gorge and its Museums gives a fascinating presentation of industry's uses and abuses of water.

The Museum is open all year from 10am-6pm in summer and 10am-5pm in winter.

Whilst we are talking about the River it is worth mentioning that the cruiser 'Lady Catherine' offers visitors a unique view of the Gorge on its regular hourly trips, complete with commentary, up and down the River Severn. The cruiser operates from 11am to dusk daily from the second week of March to the end of October.

Underneath Blists Hill is THE TAR TUNNEL, the entrance to which is in Coalport village. The Tunnel was one of the great natural curiosities of the 18th century - a gushing spring of natural bitumen which miners discovered more than 300 yards underground. You can explore part of the 1,000 yard tunnel which still oozes tar through the joints in the brick lining of the tunnel, but when it was first opened it channelled as much as 4,500 gallons a week.

For more than a hundred years **Coalport** *was the home of some of the most beautiful porcelain ever made. By the mid-19th century, the Coalport works had become one of Britain's largest porcelain manufacturers and the Coalport name was famous across the world for its fine china.*

Today the buildings house a dazzling display of china from the Victorian era, together with a lively, informative tour through the history of the Coalport porcelain industry. The visit starts with a colourful display of porcelain-making techniques, including a cutaway scale model of a bottle kiln and an illustrated guide to the curious words and phrases used by the craftsmen who seem to have invented a language all their own.

You walk through a reconstruction of the Coalport workshops, showing the intricate processes used in the creation of delicate porcelain - throwing, slip-casting, transfer printing, painting and gilding. Frequently there are live demonstrations of these traditional skills.

The history of Coalport is told in a vivid audio-visual programme, complete with authentic recorded commentary by people who worked at Coalport in the early 1900s.

The centrepiece of the Coalport display is a superb exhibition of 19th century Coalport china, housed in one of the Museums's distinctive bottle shaped kilns. Here you'll find examples from many of the famous artists who came to work at Coalport, and some of the celebrated special pieces made by the company for Victorian state occasions.

In another disused bottle oven is a full-size reconstructed kiln showing exactly how the china was stacked and fired. There are also opportunities for visitors to try their hand at pottery making of various kinds.

Coalport is still famous for fine china but since 1926 the Coalport tradition has been carried on at Stoke-on-Trent, where the company operates as part of the Wedgwood group. The collection of present-day Coalport china is stunning and available, for sale in the Museum Shop.

The Museum is open from March to November, 10am-6pm and during the winter from 10am-5pm.

I know from the attractive tiles on the side of my big Victorian fireplaces that it was in this era this distinctive art form reached its peak. At THE JACKFIELD MUSEUM you can see a rich variety of superb wall and floor tiles. Probably the highlight of your visit will be the brilliant colours and eye catching designs of glazed tiles used for walls, porches, fireplaces and washstands. These were decorated by hand- painting, transfer printing and stencilling, using an amazing range of brightly coloured glazes. Special effects included embossed designs and the unique Jackfield patent mosaic effect.

This collection features a full range of glazed tile designs, including large scale hand-painted pictorial designs produced for special commissions. You can trace the development of tile decoration from the Victorian era, through the art nouveau and art deco period, to a range of attractive, silk- screened designs from the 1950s.

The museum is open from March to November 10am-6pm and in winter from 10am to 5pm.

From The Coracle Restaurant you can see THE IRONBRIDGE TOY MUSEUM, in The Square, a collection that will delight all ages. It overflows with toys, games and childhood memorabilia ranging from magic lanterns to Bayko building sets, clockwork trains to Rupert Bear.

It impresses for several reasons but left me full of nostalgia for what had been and delighted by the reacquaintance of some of the characters still beloved today. You can see the influence of film and television culture which is demonstrated by the wealth of well-known characters from Disney, Tom and Jerry, Popeye and Charlie Chaplin.

There is a changing display of Meccano and other construction and scientific toys, while the role of the local toy industry is represented by dolls, teddies and soft toys from the Merrythought, Chad Valley and Norah Wellings factories.

The Museum is open from 10am daily.

Whilst we are talking about toys, THE TEDDY BEAR SHOP AND MUSEUM, which opens 7 days a week from 10am, will appeal to anyone who is a lover of bears. You will find the Museum just a little way from the Museum of the River, run jointly by Merrythought Toys and the Ironbridge Gorge Museum Trust.

Merrythought means wishbone and how many of us have made wishes this way from our childhood onwards - I still do today. You could not wish to see a better collection of bears and soft toys. I am pretty sure you will be tempted to ensure your wish is granted and part with some money to take one home as a souvenir of Ironbridge.

The places to visit in Ironbridge are too many to mention but do try and include THE OPEN AIR MUSEUM OF STEEL SCULPTURE, on an open site at the top of Cherry Tree Hill next to the Ironbridge bypass. There are more than 40 steel sculptures to be seen.

The Museum Park is open from 1Oam-5pm daily, except Monday, from March to November.

DALE END PARK is a superb example of riverside landscaping, which has created a well loved picnic and recreation area out of what was once an unused piece of land. The very attractive garden at its eastern end was based on the arboretum of nearby Eastfield House whose owner, at the turn of the century planted the remarkable display of specimen trees which were added to in the 1970s.

Dale End Park is open all the year, admission free.

On the edge of Dale Park is UNDERWATER WORLD in which you can discover the life that lies below the River Severn. You can see the fish and other creatures from all parts of England's longest river in landscaped displays designed to recreate their natural habitats.

For opening times please ring (0952) 432484.

After the strenuous activity in Ironbridge it might be as well to take a look at **Broseley** across the Gorge. This was the great urban centre of the Coalbrookdale coalfield during the Industrial revolution. The ironmaster, John Wilkinson, built his furnace here, and in its heyday it was a rival to Coalbrookdale itself as a centre of the iron *industry. John Wilkinson was the man who had the idea of building iron barges. He persevered in spite of being laughed at and he had the last laugh when, on one summer's day in 1787, the first iron barge was launched on the Severn. From this the idea of the iron ship was born, and Broseley was its birthplace. John Wilkinson was so dedicated to the use of iron that he asked to be buried in an iron coffin!*

I had two reasons for coming here firstly because I had been told that THE FORESTER ARMS in Avenue Road was something special. It sits on the edge of this small town and has nothing but fields and a small colourful copse on one side of it. The oak trees have a beauty of their own particularly when they first come into leaf, and in the Autumn when their leaves take on a golden reddish hue.

The pub is over 200 years old and the owners, Keith and Jenny Langton describe it as a country pub run by country people. It is an apt description.

The second reason was to visit BENTHALL HALL, a mile away to the north-west. It belongs to the National Trust who have made sure that it remains as it would have been when it was built in the 16th century. It really is an excellent example of domestic architecture of that period. Built of local sandstone, the interior contains a magnificent oak staircase of 1618, wonderfully ornate plaster ceilings, and a charming white panelled drawing room. The Gardens are beautiful and to go there is sheer pleasure.

Benthall Hall is open from April 1st until the end of September, Wednesdays, Sundays and Bank Holiday Mondays from 1.30pm-5.30pm. The House and/or Garden is available for parties at other times by arrangement with the Custodian who can be contacted on 0952 882159..

Much Wenlock *cries out to be visited; it is a lovely old market town full of history. Arthur Mee described it as somewhere that 'sleeps in the hills, dreaming of all that has been, stirring with the memory of warrior kings and the ancient strife of the Border valleys,and inspired by the natural spectacle from Wenlock Edge'.*

The ancient Tudor Guildhall is still in use as a court house and council chamber. There are charming timber-framed buildings in the

223

BULL RING. You will find picturesque half- timbered cottages, a wealth of graceful Georgian houses and a 15th-century house near St Owen's Well, which features an archway made from oak boughs.

MUCH WENLOCK MUSEUM brings alive the social history of the area with a series of special displays on local trades and crafts but it is the ruined Priory, which was founded as long ago as the 7th century, that excites most people. This is one of the region's most ancient religious foundations, founded by the granddaughter of King Penda of Mercia, destroyed by the Danes and restored by Lady Godiva. Most of the tall, imposing ruins you can see today date from the Norman period, including the church and cloisters, the prior's lodge and the chapter house - which features a remarkable pattern of interlaced arches.

Wenlock Priory is open daily except Mondays.

The steep wooded escarpment, known as WENLOCK EDGE, runs for 16 miles and provides a series of spectacular viewpoints across to the Stretton Hills and the Long Mynd. It is essentially a geological phenomenon; the rock, Wenlock limestone, was formed more then 400 million years ago in a tropical sea. It developed as a barrier reef built up largely from the skeletons and shells of sea creatures.

Three miles north-east of Much Wenlock on the B4378 you will come to BUILDWAS ABBEY. Standing in a beautiful situation on the banks of the River Severn quite close to Ironbridge Gorge, it is a worthwhile place to visit. It must be one of the country's finest ruined abbeys. Dating back over 800 years to Norman times it is surprising that so much is still standing today. The imposing walls of the abbey church with 14 wonderful Norman arches remain. It was probably completed in 1200 with the Norman and Early English architecture remaining virtually unaltered until the Dissolution in the 1530s.

Buildwas Abbey is open daily from Good Friday to the end of September. During the rest of the year it is closed on Mondays.

If you want to find a good pub just outside Much Wenlock then I suggest you take the B 4378. Four miles along the road you will come to **Brockton,** a tiny place but what it does have is an exceptional, characterful country inn, THE FEATHERS which *concentrates on food. It has a substantial and very complimentary entry into the 1992 Egon Ronay Pub Guide and in my opinion it is one that should definitely be put on your visiting list.*

Whether you are in Telford, Wellington, Ironbridge or Much Wenlock, you should make the effort to reach the summit of THE WREKIN. It is a curiosity and one of the most distinctive landmarks in the Shropshire Hills. The Wrekin is 1335 foot high, rising sharply from the flatness of the surrounding countryside. It is the site of an ancient Iron Age hill fort and it has been the focus of local legends and superstitions for hundreds of years. My favourite is that the hill was formed by a giant who had quarrelled with the people of Shrewsbury. The giant was determined to punish the townsfolk and set off with a huge spadeful of earth to bury the whole town. On the way he met a cobbler by the roadside carrying a sack of shoes to be mended. The cobbler thought the giant was up to no good so he persuaded him that Shrewsbury was too far to walk, showing him the whole bag of shoes he had worn out walking the enormous distance from the town. The giant decided the cobbler was right; he ditched the spadeful of earth on the spot - and the Wrekin was formed.

Bridgnorth *is two towns in one perched dramatically on a steep cliff above the River Severn. It is naturally beautiful and quite unlike anywhere else in England. This picturesque market town has High Town and Low Town linked by the famous Cliff Railway, which climbs up a hair raising incline. The only other one I know like it, is the Cliff Railway which joins Lynton and Lynmouth in Devon.*

Knowing I would find much to see and do here I had arranged to stay in the 17th-century FALCON HOTEL, in St John Street, Low Town. I could not have made a better choice. The 15 bedrooms are all ensuite and it is the epitome of comfort and good service. Just 15 minutes from the M54 it is an ideal base for business trips in the West Midlands or for a family holiday or mini-break.

There is something reminiscent of old Italian towns as you climb the Stoneway Steps cut sheer through the rocks, or wander about the maze of old half-timbered buildings and elegant 18th-century houses. One of these is the curious 17th century Town Hall. This timber framed building is built on an arched sandstone base partly across the roadway in the middle of the High Street. At the east end of the street is The North Gate, the only remaining one of five gates in the town's fortifications. There is a Museum over the arches.

BRIDGNORTH CASTLE is famous for its leaning tower which is 17 degrees out of straight. The leaning tower of Pisa is only 5 degrees! Looking at it you wonder how on earth it could have survived for 850 years but it has and is perfectly safe. Built in the 12th century, the castle was attacked by Parliamentary troops in the Civil War and the bombardment left the keep inclined. The Castle grounds are now a public park where you can admire a splendid view over the river and Low Town.

If you are Irish you will think you have walked into a piece of Ireland when you enter the doors of the 300 year old CARPENTERS ARMS in Whitburn Street, High Town. Adjacent to the new Smithfield Shopping Complex it is a busy pub to which people come for the good hospitality dispensed with such good humour by Sean Traynor. The whole atmosphere is Irish including the food and the music and a ceilidh thrown in for good measure from time to time.

East Castle Street is an elegant Georgian cul-de-sac in which the CHURCH OF ST MARY MAGDALENE designed by the great engineer Thomas Telford rises gracefully with its domed tower; Bridgnorth's most well known landmark.

If you are looking for the town's oldest house you will need to follow Cartway from High Town to the river, and here you will find BISHOP PERCY'S HOUSE, a superb black and white Elizabethan building which is open to the public by appointment.

Apart from the museum over the arches of the North Gate you should also take a look at BRIDGNORTH COSTUME AND CHILDHOOD MUSEUM situated in the Italianate-style New Market Building at Postern Gate. It houses galleries containing fascinating costume displays and a Victorian nursery which gives you a glimpse of the sort of life and playthings Victorian children had. The Museum has a tea shop and a gift shop.

Bridgnorth Costume and Childhood Museum opens daily except Tuesdays.

I would think almost everyone would be enchanted by the long established MIDLAND MOTOR MUSEUM, the only one of its kind in Europe. Added to the collection of some of the world's fastest cars and motorcycles are the more laborious but equally absorbing relics of the steam era - including an early traction engine. I am told that the Museum is to have even more additions in the next twelve months. It has 100 superbly restored and maintained vehicles, from the classics of the 1920s and 1930s, Rolls Royce, Bugatti and Bentley among them, to the glamourous Aston Martin, Ferrari, Jaguar, Lotus and Porsche.

The exhibition covers a 25 acre site in the converted stable area of Stanmore Hall, an historic house on the outskirts of Bridgnorth.

To the east of Bridgnorth is **Claverley,** a pretty village with black and white houses and a fine Norman church. There is a nice story told about a friend of this village who left eight shillings a year for a man to drive dogs out of the church and wake up sleeping people. The man was given a long rod with a knob at one end and a fox's brush at the other. He would tap the heads of sleeping men with the knob and touch the faces of sleeping women with the tail. THE PLOUGH INN is the place to meet. It is quite charming and welcoming, serving good ale and good food.

Just down the A 458 you will come to **Quatt,** a village like its neighbours, **Badger** and **Birdsgreen,** which has become commuter housing land and lost much of its village community. What it does have though is DUDMASTON HALL, now in the care of the National Trust but still the home of Sir George and Lady Labouchere. Their rooms in the main house are small on the whole and filled with Sir George and Lady Labouchere's personal possessions and it is this intimacy that makes the house so good to visit.

The Laboucheres have done so much for Dudmaston which, for the last 850 years, has always passed by descent or devise and has never been offered for sale. It has seen bad times when the money ran out and it was stripped of all its furniture and pictures, but it is the present incumbents who have given it a period of unusual enrichment. Sir George and Lady Labouchere have introduced wonderful 18th-century Dutch flower pictures, fine Continental and English furniture and an important collection of contemporary paintings and sculpture.

Dudmaston Hall is open from April to September from 2.30-6pm on Wednesday and Sunday afternoons.

*I made my way a little further south stopping at **Highley** where there is a station for the SEVERN VALLEY RAILWAY and a good pub, THE BACHE ARMS, pleasantly situated near the river.*

There are few better ways of seeing the Shropshire countryside with its wooded valleys and changeable moods, than from the Severn Valley Steam Railway which runs from Shrewsbury to Hartlebury, north of Worcester. It is designed to capture the atmosphere of railway history to the last detail with captivating, evocative little stations like Highley, Hampton Loade and Arley, signal boxes and railway inns. Some two hundred thousand people, many of whom come from overseas, travel on the Railway each year, making it one of the most popular tourist attractions in the Midlands. It has become the home of the largest collection of working steam locomotives and restored railway coaches and wagons in Britain.

For information and times call the 24 hour talking timetable on 0299 401001. Trains run from March until November.

***Ludlow** beckoned and I happily answered its call, first having ensured that I could stay at one of my favourite places THE CHARLTON ARMS HOTEL at **Ludford Bridge,** a fine and early medieval packhorse bridge just outside Ludlow alongside the River Teme. It is only ten minutes walk from the Castle. Apart from the hospitality it is such a pleasure to wake up in the morning and hear the sound of the river flowing almost beneath your bedroom window.*

The Inner Bailey at Ludlow Castle

Here is a town that has few equals. Its river rings it like a moat and to walk about its castle and streets is quite thrilling. We are lucky to claim it as a part of England because it is almost on the Welsh border. It became a fortress from which Wales's unruly and mutinous tribes were eventually knocked into submission.

The church of ST LAURENCE soars upwards and vies with the castle for supremacy. It is an outstandingly beautiful Perpendicular church with an earlier foundation, twice restored in the 19th century. The church is open in the summer from 9- 5pm and in winter until 4pm.

I would happily linger in Ludlow however this time I must move on but first I went for lunch at THE BENNETTS END INN at **Knowbury.** *Not the easiest place to find, yet it is only 5 miles from Ludlow or Tenbury Wells and one mile from the A4117. When you reach the centre of the village you will see a crossroad, turn left where it is signposted Hope Bagot, and half a mile down this narrow lane you will come to the pub. Well worthwhile seeking out.*

There are some beautiful places to visit between Ludlow and Shrewsbury, some of which I want to tell you about now. I decided to stay at THE STOKESAY HOTEL in School Road, **Craven Arms,** *just off the A49. It is a comfortable, friendly place where you are well looked after.*

It gave me a base to rediscover some of my favourite haunts like STOKESAY CASTLE. It stands just off the Ludlow-Shrewsbury Road, half a mile south of Craven Arms. There is a car park up the signposted lane and past the church, only a few yards from this romantic ruin.

The marvellous state of preservation does give a very clear idea of the conditions in which well-to-do medieval families lived. It is one of the earliest fortified manor houses in England with the oldest parts dating from the 12th century and the Great Hall from the 13th. It is an extraordinary structure with massive stone towers topped with a timber-framed house.

There are several legends about Stokesay one of which particularly appeals to me. Two giants, who owned much land hereabouts, kept their great wealth in a chest below the vaults of the castle, but one day the key of the vault was dropped into the moat and in spite of endless searching it was never found. Legend has it that the treasure remains in the vault today, guarded by a raven. The raven is seldom seen but the ground floor of the south tower, where the entrance to the secret chamber must be, is always locked. No doubt the search is still on for the key!

Stokesay Castle

Opening times are from the first Wednesday in March daily except Tuesday from 10-5pm. April to September daily except Tuesday from 10-6pm. October, daily except Tuesday from 10-5pm and November, weekends only 10-3pm.

If you have ever read A.E. Housman's 'A Shropshire Lad' you will know his description of the Cluns. He thought it a quiet area:

> *Clunton and Clunbury,*
> *Clungunford and Clun,*
> *Are the quietest places*
> *Under the sun.'*

He is quite right, it is an area of peace and tranquillity and certainly quieter than the olden days, when border warfare made it a strategic point. In **Clunton,** *which lies between Craven Arms and Clun there is a friendly country pub, THE CROWN INN, which is* just the place to visit if you want to walk and seek out the history of a Roman Fortress and Bury Ditches. You will also get one of the best steak and kidney pies in Shropshire here.

The A49 going towards Shrewsbury will take you to **Little Stretton** which must be one of the most beautiful villages in Shropshire complete with a little thatched church and a village inn that is 250 years old. THE GREEN DRAGON is a real village inn with no juke boxes and no gaming machines but fine ale and freshly cooked food. The pub is a popular haunt of walkers on the LONG MYND HILLS and ASHERS HOLLOW.

The rare thatched church - Little Stretton

Little Stretton's big neighbour, **Church Stretton** is somewhere else you should visit. Houses dot the valley and climb the slopes. To the west is the great moorland ridge of the Longmynd rising nearly 1700feet, with the beautiful Cardingmill Valley below and the prehistoric Portway running along the top. To the east are the rugged Caradoc Hills with Watling Street at the foot, and the banks and trenches of Caer Caradoc's stronghold 1500ft up.

The strange cross-shaped church goes back 850 years and in the old churchyard is a stone of 1814 to Ann Cook which says:

On a Thursday she was born
On a Thursday made a bride
On a Thursday broke a leg
And on a Thursday died.

Thursday was obviously not a lucky day for Ann Cook!.

For somewhere different for a meal and somewhere that is excellent, visit THE ACORN WHOLEFOOD RESTAURANT, in Sandford Avenue, where wholefood is of the greatest importance. The wholefood cakes are better than anything I have ever tasted before.

Along the B4371 you will come to **Wall under Heywood** situated in the outstandingly beautiful Apedale. It is somewhere you will want to see and the bonus is a first class pub, THE PLOUGH. The food is excellent and the Dining Room is strictly non-smoking!

I was recommended to another excellent pub and found it well worth the effort of going out of my way. It is at **Priestweston,** just inside the Powys border to the northwest of **Bishops Castle.** The pub is THE MINERS ARMS. An old 16th- century building that was rescued from total ruin by Eddie and Glenda Edwards in 1987. They knew it was a special place when they bought it and now after careful restoration it is super. In September there is a Folk Festival complete with Morris Dancers. The old church at Middleton just 1½ miles away is worth seeing and it is ideal for walkers.

And finally to **Shrewsbury,** where once again A.E. Housman says it all:

High the vanes of Shrewsbury gleam
Islanded in Severn stream;
The bridges from the steepled crest
Cross the water east to west.

It is almost an island with its castle standing in a narrow strait and more than half a dozen bridges crossing to and fro. It has old black and white houses, half-timbered of the Elizabethan era, fine brick buildings of the 17th century and wonderfully elegant Queen Anne and Georgian town houses, narrow streets and alleyways with strange names - Grope Lane, Shoplatch, Dogpole, Wyle Cop and Pride Hill. Everywhere oozes history and clamours for your attention.

The Old School - Shrewsbury

You will want to visit ROWLEY'S HOUSE in Barker Street which is set in a magnificent timber-framed building of the late 16th century. Housed here is the largest collection of material from the Roman city of Viroconium at Wroxeter including the silver mirror unique to Roman Britain.

It is open all the year. Monday-Saturday from 10-5pm. Sundays, Easter to late September from 12-5pm.

On College Hill is CLIVE HOUSE, just five minutes from Rowley's House. Clive of India lived here in 1762 when he was Mayor of Shrewsbury and one or two momentoes of this great man remain. Several rooms have period settings and a magnificent collection of Shropshire ceramics. The gardens are open to visitors.

It is open all year. Monday from 2-5pm. Tuesday-Saturday 10-lpm and 2-5pm.

In THE CASTLE you will find THE SHROPSHIRE REGIMENTAL MUSEUM with wonderful displays of all things military, even a lock of Napoleon's hair. The Castle dates back to 1083 but last saw service during the Civil War when Charles I is reputed to have stayed there for a short period. Thomas Telford later remodelled the interior as a private house in the late 18th century.

It is open all year. Monday-Saturday from 10-5pm and Sundays from Easter to October 10-5pm.

Where do you stay and where do you eat. The choice is huge but I can recommend THE CORN HOUSE RESTAURANT in Wyle Cop, where Pat Pennington and her son Grant run an establishment that is a Mecca for many people who live in and around Shrewsbury. It has a wine bar on the ground floor which is a very popular meeting place.

*For somewhere to have a drink and a good meal just four miles west of Shrewsbury, then THE WINGFIELD ARMS at **Montford Bridge,** is a good idea. Parking is easy which is always a bonus after the difficulties one encounters in Shrewsbury. If you have a Caravan you may find it ideal because there are 6 acres of park running right down to the water's edge from which there is some very good fishing.*

*Then there is THE WOODCOCK INN in the little village of **Castle Pulverbach,** eight miles to the south of Shrewsbury just off the A5. It is unusual inasmuch as it is also the village Post Office. It is only open in the evenings from Monday to Friday but on Saturdays and Sunday it does open at lunchtime as well.*

I stayed in THE TUDOR HOUSE in Fish Street, Shrewsbury, built in 1460. It is charming, warm and comfortable and full of character. There are many more places of course.

Your time will be wonderfully spent just exploring this wonderful town but you may want to visit ATTINGHAM PARK, bequeathed to the National Trust by the 8th Lord Berwick in 1947. In the Mansion, the splendid Regency State Rooms are open to the public which are full of superb silver, much of it collected by the 3rd Lord Berwick when he was Ambassador to Italy in 1807-1832. There is also a fine collection of French and Italian paintings and furniture, brought to England by the 2nd Lord Berwick and his brother, the 3rd Lord Berwick.

The Park is open every day throughout the year except Christmas Day. The Mansion is open from April 1st until 30th September, or Easter if it is earlier, on Saturday-Wednesday inclusive from 2-5pm and Bank Holiday Mondays from 11.30-5pm. From October lst- 30th October on Saturday and Sunday only from 2.

THE CARPENTERS
Public House

55, Whitburn Street,
Hightown,
Bridgnorth, Shropshire.

Tel: (0746) 761001

This is an interesting pub which in its time has been dwelling houses and there is evidence that it was also a slaughter house. Today it is a comfortable hostelry still with the original oak beams that probably came from an old 'man of war' ship about three hundred years ago.

The Carpenters Arms is adjacent to the new Smithfield Shopping Complex where there was once a busy cattle market. You can just imagine how busy the pub would have been with people attending the market. It is just as busy now but with a different clientele drawn from shoppers, visitors and business people. They come here for good food and hospitality dispensed with such goodwill by Sean Traynor and Rosemary and his mother, Molly, who is in charge of the food. Sean's name will tell you that he is Irish, and he brings to the Carpenters a touch of the old country and its delightul music. There are two bars in the Carpenters as well as a lean-to barn used for Folk and Jazz events which have all the hallmarks of a good ceilidh. The whole atmosphere is intimate and Irish including the menu. Irish Stew and Irish Soda Bread are firm favourites as well as the famous Ulster Fry, a gargantuan breakfast. The whole menu is interesting, home cooked and good value.

USEFUL INFORMATION

OPEN: Mon-Sat: all day from 10am
Sun: 12-3pm & 7-10.30pm
CHILDREN: With diners
CREDIT CARDS: None taken
LICENSED: Full Licence, Irish
whiskies
ACCOMMODATION: Not applicable

RESTAURANT: Not applicable
BAR FOOD: Home-made Irish
traditional
VEGETARIAN: Always 3 on
offer
ACCESS FOR THE DISABLED:
Limited but welcome
GARDEN: No - but outdoor
facility room

THE FALCON HOTEL

Hotel

St John Street,
Lowtown, Bridgnorth
Shropshire

Tel: (0746) 763134

The 17th century Coaching House, The Falcon Hotel, stands for all that is good about historic Bridgnorth. The town is in effect two towns - High Town with its multitude of interesting shops and the Saturday market, and Lowtown on the banks of the River Severn. It is in this delightful, latter area that you will find the hotel in St John Street. As it has done for centuries, it provides the sort of hospitality typical of the best of English Rural Inns. With the M54 only 15 minutes away it is an ideal base for business trips in the West Midlands or for a pleasant family holiday or mini break.

The Falcon has 15 individually designed bedrooms all with private bathrooms, direct dial telephone, hospitality trays, colour TV; many rooms have video players. The Resident Proprietor and his staff offer all visitors a personal welcome and will provide any information that is required, especially about all the interesting places there are to visit.

There is the excellent self contained Falcon Suite, which is ideal for private or business functions and would be delightful for wedding receptions. The bar/restaurant, which is open to non-residents, is a perfect combination of 17th century character and modern day comfort. The oak beams, interesting curios and open fireplaces, provide a perfect setting for a relaxing drink or meal. Fresh produce is always used in a wide range of dishes from traditional English to the more unusual.

USEFUL INFORMATION

OPEN: All year round
CHILDREN: Welcome
CREDIT CARDS: Amex/Visa/
  Master/Switch
LICENSED: Full on Licence
ACCOMMODATION: 15 bedrooms
  en-suite

RESTAURANT: Traditional
  English. Fresh produce
BAR FOOD: Wide range
VEGETARIAN: Always 5 dishes
ACCESS FOR THE DISABLED: Yes
GARDEN: No

THE FEATHERS
Public House

Brockton,
Nr. Much Wenlock
Shropshire

Tel: (074 636) 202

Four miles outside Much Wenlock on the road to Ludlow is The Feathers, a pub that defies you to pass it by. It has charm and character and has deservedly won high praise from Egon Ronay. The pub is owner operated by Martin and Andrea Hayward, a delightful couple, who make food the priority in all four areas of the establishment. 80% of the trade is food with restaurant standard menus on offer, yet it has the informal ambience of a country pub.

Everything about The Feathers speaks of a house that is run with professionalism yet with an underlying love of the place and the business that shines through in the sparkling cleanliness and the nice touches in the decor. For example a massive pair of bellows, rescued from an old smithy, is now used as a table in the public bar. One menu only is operated wherever you eat at lunch and in the evening. Starters can be chosen as light snacks but in the main the Haywards cater for people requiring a meal. They do not provide sandwiches.

Andrea Hayward is responsible for the production of the menu and uses a lot of her own recipes. The choice covers a wide spectrum supported by a large blackboard in the main lounge which details house specialities. There are seasonal game and fish dishes such as Pheasant in port Wine, and a wonderful dish of Mussels sauteed in White Wine. The wine list is well chosen and the service excellent. It is a venue you must try.

USEFUL INFORMATION

OPEN: Tues-Sun: 12-2.30pm & 6.30-11pm
CHILDREN: Yes. Childrens menu
CREDIT CARDS: None taken
LICENSED: Full with extensive wine list
ACCOMMODATION: Not at present

RESTAURANT: Not applicable
BAR FOOD: Superb menu. House specialities
VEGETARIAN: At least 2 always
ACCESS FOR THE DISABLED: Reasonable
GARDEN: Tables for drinking not eating

FORESTER ARMS

Public House

Avenue Road,
Broseley,
Shropshire

Tel: (0952) 884088

Country people running a country pub is how Keith and Jenny Langton, the likeable owners of the Forester Arms at Broseley, would describe themselves. This friendly establishment is on the outskirts of this small town and has nothing but fields and a small colourful copse on one side of it. The oak trees have a beauty of their own especially when they first come into leaf and in the Autumn when their leaves take on a golden reddish hue.

The pub is over 200 years old and once used for coaching. The stables now form part of the bar. It was used by the Lord of the Manor in times past for collecting his rents and the annual 'Rent Dinners' were held in the pub. Although the rent days have gone not much else has changed and you are just as likely to find yourself standing at the bar with a local landowner as you are the local poacher. It is an enjoyable experience visiting The Foresters and you will be reminded that once Broseley was the centre of the Coalbrookdale Coalfield during the Industrial Revolution and the famous Ironmaster, John Wilkinson lived in the town. There is plenty to do and see before or after a visit to the pub but you may be tempted to stay longer than you intended within its four walls enjoying the excellent food and the warmth of the hospitality.

USEFUL INFORMATION

OPEN: 12-3pm & 7-11pm
CHILDREN: Yes. Large outside play area
CREDIT CARDS: None taken
LICENSED: Full Licence
ACCOMMODATION: Not applicable

RESTAURANT: Not applicable
BAR FOOD: Good range. Freshly cooked
VEGETARIAN: Always 4 dishes
ACCESS FOR THE DISABLED: Yes. Very welcome
GARDEN: Large lawned area & patio

THE WOODCOCK INN

Public House & Restaurant

Castle Pulverbach,
Shrewsbury, Shropshire.

Tel: (0743) 73200

Castle Pulverbach is a small village just 8 miles south of Shrewsbury off the A5. The outside of the Woodcock Inn stands out because of the gleaming whiteness of the walls. Inside it is a traditional mid-Victorian pub with open fires and beams and a nice, friendly, welcoming atmosphere.

The Woodcock is unusual in as much as two days a week it is also the village Post Office. It has one large bar and a games room in which you can play pool, darts or dominoes. With plenty of room in the two large car parks, John and Pat Parker, the proprietors are quite happy to welcome coach parties although they do like some prior warning especially if food is required.

The Woodcock is only open in the evenings from Monday to Friday but on Saturday and Sunday it opens at lunchtime as well. Indeed on Sundays there is an excellent traditional roast lunch. The menu offers a good selection of traditional food and is especially well known for the mammoth Mixed Grills and for the delicious and tender Beef in Beer or mushrooms. Fish, chicken and curries also form part of the menu as well as perfectly cooked steaks. Vegetarians are offered the choice of never less than four dishes on any day, and children are very welcome. In the summer many people enjoy the picnic tables outside where they can sit and enjoy a meal or a drink in the sun.

USEFUL INFORMATION

OPEN: Eve: 7pm-11pm
   Sat: 12-4pm & 7-11pm
   Sun: 12-3pm & 7-11pm
CHILDREN: Welcome
CREDIT CARDS: None taken
LICENSED: Full Licence
ACCOMMODATION: Not applicable

RESTAURANT: Varied, good
   traditional
BAR FOOD: Good value, wide
   range
VEGETARIAN: Always 4 dishes
ACCESS FOR THE DISABLED:
   Easy & welcome
GARDEN: Picnic tables outside

ACORN WHOLEFOOD CAFE

Wholefood Restaurant &
Coffee Shop

26, Sandford Avenue,
Church Stretton,
Shropshire.

Tel: (0694) 722495

If you ever thought that wholefood was boring all you need do to erase that idea forever is to visit Chris Bland's delightful first floor establishment. You will find it tucked away off the main Sandford Avenue, down a plant lined passageway. You climb up some solid bannister railed stairs and are welcomed into an experience. It is one that regulars have known about for sometime but it has taken a while for the word to spread further afield.

Every day Chris cooks a range of mouth-watering, hot dishes, Nut Roast, Jacket Potatoes and Pizza's being some of her specialities, to go with an excellent cold range of salads. Her unusual soups are always popular, and ideal for both vegetarians and meat eaters. Her wholefood cakes are equally fabulous; Carrot and Cinnamon, Teabread and Belgian Cake just some of the many choices. Wholemeal scones with home-made jam tempt many people and once having tried them they wonder why they had rejected them before in favour of white. Different flavour teas line the shelves, with a choice of normal or decaffinated coffee. Chris will tell you that her philosophy is to simply swap traditional ingredients and substitute them for healthier alternatives. The results speak for themselves. A bonus at Acorns is the flowering, suntrapped tea garden; a wonderful place in which to enjoy this delcious food. The restaurant is unlicensed but you may bring your own. Corkage 99p per bottle.

USEFUL INFORMATION

OPEN: 10-6pm Summer, Sun & Bank Hols. 9.30-5.30pm Winter
CHILDREN: Yes. High chairs
CREDIT CARDS: None taken
LICENSED: No. Bring your own
ACCOMMODATION: Not applicable

RESRAURANT: Home-made wholefood
BAR FOOD: Not applicable
VEGETARIAN: All except a meat/fish dish
ACCESS FOR THE DISABLED: Only in tea garden
GARDEN: Tea garden. Perfect suntrap

THE PLOUGH AT CLAVERLEY
Inn & Restaurant

Aston Lane,
Claverley,
Nr. Wolverhampton

Tel: (07466) 365

Sometimes it is hard to realise that the busy, industrial Wolverhampton is only a little way from the delightful village of Claverley, surrounded by beautiful Shropshire countryside and home to a host of charming half-timbered cottages as well as the excellent Plough Inn. It is a marvellous centre for those who enjoy walking. The River Severn flows its majestic way through picturesque Bridgnorth just 4 miles away.

The Plough was constructed in the 18th century largely from reclaimed ships timbers. It has a superb open fire with a heavy copper canopy and many brasses which catch the reflection of the roaring fire whichever way you turn. Someone here at sometime must have had a keen interest in foreign travel for there is one of the biggest collections of foreign currency that you will see in the county. The Plough is a happy pub owned and run by David and Irene O'Gorman. Their pleasant personalities are echoed by the friendliness of the well trained staff. The large lounge bar has cosy alcoves and a special dining area where you can enjoy the various tempting dishes on the menu. Adjoining this is a Children's room. The ever changing menu has many favourite dishes on it including a super Beef and Guinness Pie. There are tender steaks, a Cold Table and several Vegetarian dishes. Daily Specials are very popular and so are the home-made sweets which will tempt those with a sweet tooth.

USEFUL INFORMATION

OPEN: 12-3pm & 7-11pm
  Sun: 7-10.30pm
CHILDREN: Childrens room
CREDIT CARDS: Access/Visa
LICENSED: Full Licence
ACCOMMODATION: Not applicable

RESTAURANT: Imaginative menu
BAR FOOD: Varied menu. Freshly
  prepared
VEGETARIAN: Usually at least 2
  original dishes
ACCESS FOR THE DISABLED:
  Easy access
GARDEN: Large garden with
  swings & seats

THE CROWN INN

Public House

25, Clunton,
Nr. Craven Arms,
Shropshire.

Tel: (05887) 265

You will find this comfortable and friendly country pub in Clunton, on the Newtown road between Craven Arms and Clun. Just the place to visit if you want to walk and seek out the history of the Roman Fortress at Bury Ditches. It is also close enough to the Long Mynd Hills to attract those who want something a little more strenuous in the way of exercise. The situation could not be better with the popular market town of Church Stretton 14 miles off and two castles, Stokesay Castle and Clun Castle - right on the doorstep. For those who are having a caravanning holiday the Crown is ideal; there is a holiday trailer park close by.

Within the pub you will find Peter and Suzanne Wheatley waiting to give you a cheery welcome. Peter keeps an excellent cellar whilst Suzanne attends to the catering. Her food is always home-cooked with generous portions at reasonable prices, her steak and kidney pie being a favourite of visitors and locals alike. Being a wise lady she recognises that both vegetarians and children need special attention and has devised several delicious dishes for the former and made sure the children are able to order their favourites. On Sunday Suzanne produces a traditional lunch of Roast Beef and Yorkshire Pudding with crisp roast potatoes and whatever fresh vegetables are in season. This is a happy and contented local which is a pleasure to visit.

USEFUL INFORMATION

OPEN: 12-5pm & 7-11pm
Normal Sunday hours
CHILDREN: Well behaved welcome
CREDIT CARDS: None taken
LICENSED: Full Licence
ACCOMMODATION: Not applicable

RESTAURANT: Dining room
BAR FOOD: Home-cooked. Good
selection. Childrens menu
VEGETARIAN: 3 plus always
available
ACCESS FOR THE DISABLED:
Easy access
GARDEN: No outside facilities

THE STOKESAY CASTLE HOTEL
Hotel

School Road,
Craven Arms,
Shropshire.

Tel: (0588) 672304

Just off the main A49 at Craven Arms between Ludlow and Church Stretton and close to Stokesay Castle which is open to the public, is the Stokesay Castle Hotel. This friendly hotel offers comfortable accommodation at sensible prices for those who want to stay awhile in this wonderful countryside and explore the Shropshire Hills or take advantage of the excellent fishing available locally. It is not a big hotel but is ideally suited to children, with family rooms and cots available if they are required.

Peter and Caroline Thomas have been mine hosts since October 1991 and have the happy knack of making everyone feel welcome and busy as they may be, for they do all the cooking themselves, they always find time to chat to locals and visitors. The Stokesay Castle is a true local pub in one sense inasmuch as it has a very competitive darts team and a games room which includes a pool table. During the summer the large garden is used for barbecues which are very popular. Children also have their own play area there. Throughout the year there is regular live entertainment which attracts people from quite a distance including the odd coach party or two who are more than welcome. It is as well to remember that if you are coming in a party and want to eat, it would be advisable to book. The food is simple, straightforward, wholesome pub fare which includes a variety of succulent steaks or the ever popular jacket potato with a selection of fillings. Good value.

USEFUL INFORMATION

OPEN: 11-3pm& 7-11pm
   Earlier May-Sept
CHILDREN: Welcome
CREDIT CARDS: None taken
LICENSED: Full Licence. Guest beers
ACCOMMODATION: Single, double,
   family

RESTAURANT: Traditional
   English fare
BAR FOOD: Wide range & snacks
   at all times
VEGETARIAN: At least 4 dishes
ACCESS FOR THE DISABLED:
   Easy access
GARDEN: Yes. Barbecues.
   Childrens area

THE CHAMPION JOCKEY

Inn

Wrekin Drive,
Donnington,
Telford, Shropshire.

Tel: (0952) 608133

The Champion Jockey is a relatively new building in Donnington and quite easy to find on the right hand side of the road if you enter the town from Telford Town Centre. It is a lively, happy pub used by people of all ages. There seems to be something going on all day long whether it is darts, pool or dominoes, or the live entertainment that is part of the fun on Saturday and Sunday evenings. Wednesday evenings are very popular, and give the extroverts a chance at Karaoke.

In the summer there are barbecues outside and recently a splendid children's adventure playground has been added to the garden. There are four double letting rooms, two of which have showers and for the keep-fit addicts there is a special lounge with a sauna and a shower. Peter and Pauline Thompson are the energetic proprietors who keep the whole place running smoothly, and with an informality that does not in the least detract from their professional approach. It is fun and different. The menu offers good food at sensible prices which which will not damage anyone's pocket. You can get a sizeable steak with mushrooms, onion rings, chips, peas and salad for somewhere around the £5 mark. One of the most popular dishes on the daily menu is an excellent Cottage Pie. Pauline has a very light hand with omelettes and her Chilli Con Carne is known quite widely. Sandwiches, Ploughman's etc. are also available. Open all day.

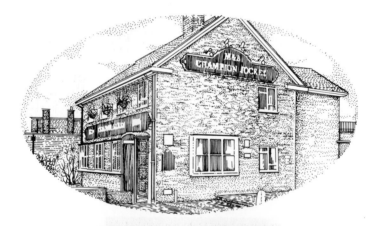

USEFUL INFORMATION

OPEN: All day 10-11pm
Sun: 12-3pm & 7-10.30pm
CHILDREN: During day & early
evening
CREDIT CARDS: None taken
LICENSED: Full Licence, trad. ales
ACCOMMODATION: 4 doubles,
sauna/shower

RESTAURANT: Not applicable
BAR FOOD: Wide choice.
Home-cooked
VEGETARIAN: Yes, varied
ACCESS FOR THE DISABLED:
Easy access
GARDEN: Yes & adventure
playground

THE BACHE ARMS
Public House

High Street, Highley,
Nr. Bridgnorth,
Shropshire.

Tel: (0746) 861266

The Bache Arms is not an old building but in the hundred years of its existence it has become a focal point in the small village of Highley. Imagine the setting; the pub has its own bowling green where you can roll a wood if you wish or sit and watch others do so. The riverside is only three minutes away, there is good fishing closeby, the village has its own open air swimming pool, and for golfers there is an excellent course nearby just asking to be played. Highley is only 7 miles South West of Bridgnorth and within easy reach of the pretty town of Bewdley on the River Severn.

Children love the freedom of the Bache Arms. They are allowed to play in the large garden which has a wonderful Herbie Tree. When they have used up enough energy they can lunch on meals specially planned and cooked for them by May Holdway, who with her husband, Tony, are the owners of this friendly place. Traditional bitter and 'Rough' Cider are popular and well kept by Tony who dispenses a pint with skill, and at the same time manages to make everyone welcome. It is simple and varied, from a dish of the day to a sandwich. The traditional roast lunch on Sundays is a favourite and you are requested to book.

USEFUL INFORMATION

OPEN: Mon-Fri: 11.30-3pm & 7-11pm
    Sat: 11-11pm
    Sun: 12-3pm & 7-10.30pm
CHILDREN: Welcome
CREDIT CARDS: None taken
LICENSED: Full Licence
ACCOMMODATION: Not applicable

RESTAURANT: Not applicable
BAR FOOD: Varied, home cooked
    menu & snacks
VEGETARIAN: On request
ACCESS FOR THE DISABLED:
    Yes, good
GARDEN: Large with seating &
    Herbie Tree

THE CORACLE
Restaurant

33A Upstairs
High Street,
Ironbridge, Shropshire

Tel: (0952) 433913

Iron Bridge Gorge is somewhere that most people want to visit for there is so much of historic and outstanding interest. Sightseeing is as tiring as it is exciting and for most people there is a longing for refreshment at some time. Catering for this need is the excellent restaurant The Coracle which is situated in the High Street in the upstairs part of a pretty Grade II listed building overlooking the Square.

Named after the small craft that has been used on the river for poaching and fishing for centuries - coracles are still made by Eustace Rogers who lives nearby - the restaurant is small and intimate seating just 24 people. It is most attractively furnished with pine tables and chairs whilst overhead are the original oak beams adding to the charm. The building dates from much the same time as The Iron Bridge; roundabout 1779 and started its life as a Bake House. Tony and Linda Prichard own and run the restaurant with the help of a friendly staff. The whole atmosphere of the Coracle is one of relaxation which is balm to the weary explorer. The food is cooked and prepared by Tony who uses nothing but fresh ingredients and local produce wherever possible. At lunchtime and in the evenings there is a varying menu which changes daily and includes Roast Duck with Orange Sauce, Sole Bonne Femme and a delectable Escalope of Pork with an Apple and Brandy Sauce. Snacks are available at lunchtime only.

USEFUL INFORMATION

OPEN: Tues-Sun: 11.30-3.30pm & 7-11pm
CHILDREN: Welcome. Childrens menu
CREDIT CARDS: Access/Visa/ Master/Euro
LICENSED: Wines, spirits, bottled beer
ACCOMMODATION: Not applicable

RESTAURANT: High quality. Wide range
BAR FOOD: Not applicable
VEGETARIAN: Normally 2-3 dishes daily
ACCESS FOR THE DISABLED: None
GARDEN: None

BENNETTS END INN
Inn & Restaurant

Knowbury,
Nr. Ludlow,
Shropshire.

Tel: (0584) 890220

If you sit in the secluded gardens of the unusually named Bennetts End Inn, you will be rewarded by the most superb panoramic views of the luscious Teme Valley. This is a truly rural and delightful 300 year old pub, situated at the bottom of the Clee Hills, and a wonderful place from which to ramble or walk. Inside, the oak-beamed lounge bar is well furnished and in winter especially welcoming with a log fire sending its warmth throughout the bar. In summer the bowling green outside offers much amusement and pleasure to the many regulars who visit the Bennetts End. It is reputed to be the only pub of this name in the whole of the country.

Not the easiest place to find yet it is only 5 miles from Ludlow or Tenbury Wells and one mile from the A4117. When you reach the centre of the village you will see a crossroad, turn left where it is signposted Hope Bagot and half a mile down this narrow lane you will come to the pub. It is somewhere that is more than worthwhile taking the trouble to find.

Roland and Ann Brown are the owners. Roland keeps an excellent cellar. Ann does all the cooking, a task she obviously enjoys, not only producing good home-cooked meals and a variety of snacks but also a selection of local jams and pickles which you may buy. Ann has a children's menu and she also caters for vegetarians. The portions are more than generous and booking is essential for her traditional Sunday roasts.

USEFUL INFORMATION

OPEN: Mon-Sat: 11.30-2.30pm & 7-11pm. Sun: 12-3pm & 7-10.30pm
CHILDREN: Welcome
CREDIT CARDS: None taken
LICENSED: Full Licence
ACCOMMODATION: Not applicable

RESTAURANT: Speciality home cooking
BAR FOOD: Extensive range
VEGETARIAN: 6 dishes daily
ACCESS FOR THE DISABLED: Level
GARDEN: Secluded, panoramic views

THE RED LION
Public House

Holly Road,
Little Dawley,
Telford, Shropshire.

Tel: (0952) 592294

This is a pub that manages to have the air of a country inn yet it is in the heart of Telford. The shopping centre is closeby as well as a pleasant park, pool and Telford's ice skating rink. To reach it you follow the signs from Ironbridge, only 4 miles away, towards Coalbrooke Dale and then the signs for Little Dawley.

The Red Lion has been an inn for almost three hundred years and at one time was a coaching inn seeing to the needs of weary travellers. Travelling is easier today but the same hospitality reaches out to every one who comes through the welcoming doors into an interior which has not changed all that much. The original oak beams are still insitu and the decor enhances the age of the pub. Fay and Nick Greenway took over The Red Lion in 1990 and have made many changes to improve the facilities but they have always dealt sympathetically with it and never lost sight of the age of the building. There are two comfortably furnished bars in which you can have tea and coffee all day long as well as alchoholic drinks. Cream teas are available in the afternoons. Fay and Nick's daughter Micheala is the chef, and her forte is producing good, fresh pub food at sensible prices. Breakfast is served from 10am, there are daily specials and Sunday roasts for which booking is necessary.

USEFUL INFORMATION

OPEN: All day
   Sun: 12-3pm & 7-10.30pm
CHILDREN: Welcome
CREDIT CARDS: Access/Visa
LICENSED: Full Licence
ACCOMMODATION: Not applicable

RESTAURANT: Not applicable
BAR FOOD: Home made specials
VEGETARIAN: At least 2 daily
ACCESS FOR THE DISABLED:
   Limited
GARDEN: Large childrens area

THE GREEN DRAGON
Inn

Ludlow Road,
Little Stretton,
Shropshire.

Tel: (0694) 722925

Shropshire has some beautiful villages and Little Stretton must be high on the list. It is a pretty place just off the main A49 between Church Stretton and Craven Arms, only 10 miles from Ludlow and 17 miles from Shrewsbury, two historic places which just beg to be explored.

In the middle of Little Stretton is the 250 year old village inn, The Green Dragon, owned and run by two friendly and hospitable publicans, Jim and Michelle Greenough. It is one of those blissful pubs that has no juke box and no gaming machines and devotes itself to being a real village inn. There is one en-suite twin bedded room if you would like to stay here - you certainly will not regret it. The village has one local shop which boasts that you can buy anything from a pack of bacon to a Ford Escort 24 hours a day!. The Green Dragon is a popular haunt of walkers on the Long Mynd Hills and Ashers Hollow, as well as people who just drive out from the nearby towns for the pleasure of having a drink or a meal in this welcoming pub. The food is all freshly prepared and home-cooked by Michelle - try her famous steak and kidney pie. Daily specials offer a wide choice and there is always fresh fish as well as steaks and other dishes. Simpler food is available too, including some very good toasted sandwiches and excellent Ploughman's lunches with a variety of cheeses. The portions are generous and the price is right.

USEFUL INFORMATION

OPEN: 11-3pm & 6-11pm
  Sun: usual hours
CHILDREN: Welcome
CREDIT CARDS: Access/Visa
LICENSED: Full Licence
ACCOMMODATION: 1 twin en-suite

RESTAURANT: Freshly prepared, home-cooked
BAR FOOD: Wide range meals & snacks
VEGETARIAN: Choice of 3/4
ACCESS FOR THE D ISABLED: Yes
GARDEN: Beer garden

CHARLTON ARMS HOTEL

Hotel

Ludford Bridge,
Ludlow
Shropshire.

Tel: (0584) 872813

Ludford Bridge is a fine and early medieval packhorse bridge just outside Ludlow alongside the river Teme and within a mile or ten minutes walk of Ludlow Castle. What better place could you wish to find for a meal, a drink or to stay than the Charlton Arms Hotel which is over 300 years old and quite delightful. The bedrooms are comfortable and it is wonderful to wake up in the morning to hear the sound of the river flowing almost beneath your bedroom window.

Inside, the old world charm still exists in the two bars where open fires add to the pleasure in the winter months. You can play Darts, Pool, Dominoes or Quoits or sit on the riverside patio or in the garden soaking up the sun and the extraordinarily relaxed air. Maybe you will want to plan a walk through Mortimer forest where you will normally see herds of deer. Canoeing on the river is also a popular pastime round here. Arthur and Thelma Keeley are the hospitable and welcoming hosts who will make sure your stay is enjoyable whether it is just for a drink, a meal or a night or two. Thelma runs the kitchen and serves some excellent meals, all of which are home-cooked. Enormous Mixed Grills are popular with the men and so too is the super Fisherman's Pie. Steak and Kidney Pie and a very good Beef and Ale which tempt many customers. It is a wide ranging menu and very good value.

USEFUL INFORMATION

OPEN: 12-3pm & 7-11pm
  Normal Sun. hours
CHILDREN: Well behaved welcome
CREDIT CARDS: Not at present
LICENSED: Full Licence
ACCOMMODATION: Single, twin,
  double

RESTAURANT: Not applicable
BAR FOOD: Wide range,
  home-cooked
VEGETARIAN: At least 2 daily
ACCESS FOR THE DISABLED:
  Limited but welcome
GARDEN: Large riverside, ample
  seating. Excellent parking

WINGFIELD ARMS

Public House & Restaurant

Montford Bridge,
Shrewsbury,
Shropshire

Tel: (0743) 850750

The Wingfield Arms is on the main A5, 4 miles west of Shrewsbury making it a popular stopping place for those travelling between the Midlands and Wales. The pub is over 300 years old and has that pleasant well loved and well lived in air about it. It has a wealth of old beams and splendid open fireplaces which hold roaring fires in the cold winter months.

At the rear are 6 acres of caravan parking, running right down to the water's edge from which there is some very good fishing. Inside there is a separate dining area, a restaurant, a function room, welcoming bars, children's play area outside and a large car park. Barrie Warner-Smith and his wife Margaret have been at The Wingfield since 1988 and have made many improvements but have never allowed modernity to take the place of tradition and the olde worlde charm. Barrie is the chef and contrives to produce an interesting English, Continental and Eastern menu, most of which is home - made as well as an extensive menu in the bar. The choice of starters whets ones appetite with dishes such as Cream of Pheasant Soup served with bread sticks or a refreshing Prawn, Cucumber and Yogurt Salad. You can follow this with something from the Healthy Eating Char Grill or a Wingfield Special, Duckling Bigarade, Beef Curry Meera or Steak and Guinness Pie. There are light meals as well and some tempting desserts including a rich Chocolate and Almond Torte.

USEFUL INFORMATION

OPEN: 11-3pm 6.30-11pm
  Sun: Normal hours
  Restaurant: 12-2pm & 7-10pm
CHILDREN: Welcome
CREDIT CARDS: None taken
LICENSED: Full Licence
ACCOMMODATION: Not applicable

RESTAURANT: English,
  Continental, Eastern
BAR FOOD: Extensive hot & cold
  menu
VEGETARIAN: Always 2 dishes
  available
ACCESS FOR THE DISABLED: Yes
GARDEN: Large area. Childrens
  amusements

THE PHEASANT INN

Inn

68 High Street,
Upper Bar,
Newport, Shropshire.

Tel: (0952) 811961

In the High Street, Upper Bar, is the 250 year old building, The Pheasant. The outside of the building might mislead you into thinking it was small, however once inside it has plenty of room, which includes a comfortable, friendly bar, a relaxing lounge as well as a games room, in which the pool table takes pride of place.

The Pheasant offers pleasant bed and breakfast accommodation for anyone who has business in the town or, as a base from which to explore the local countryside, including Ironbridge, which is only 10 miles away. Telford, a town which grows continuously, is just 6 miles from here. Philip and Lyn Collins are the proprietors who, in the three years they have been here, have made themselves very popular with locals and visitors. They have a nice brand of humour and a great understanding of people's needs. Breakfast is served all day. Home-made pies come high on the list of favourite dishes as well as a very good Fish Pie, amongst many other equally tasty meals. You can have anything from a succulent steak to a simple, freshly cut sandwich. Special pensioner's meals are available daily which include a sweet in the price. This is a value for money pub.

USEFUL INFORMATION

OPEN: 11-11pm daily except Tues/Sun
   Tues: 11-3pm & 5.30-11pm
   Sun: usual hours
CHILDREN: For food only
CREDIT CARDS: None taken
LICENSED: Full Licence
ACCOMMODATION: 3 doubles

RESTAURANT: Not applicable
BAR FOOD: Traditional &
   Original English
VEGETARIAN: Various
ACCESS FOR THE DISABLED:
   Easy access
GARDEN: No garden. Easy
   parking

THE MINERS ARMS
Public House

Priest Weston,
Chirbury, Shropshire.

Tel: (0938) 72352

This is a wonderful place. A 16th-century pub that is completely unspoilt and was saved from total neglect by Eddie and Glenda Edwards in 1987. These two people saw the Miners Arms, recognised that under the dust of years there was something special. They set about restoring it with patient and loving care and a determination that it would emerge an example of what a pub of this age should be. They could see the old oak beams had been covered in and the stone walls lost under plaster but their patience was rewarded and now you can have the pleasure of walking into this welcoming hostelry and enjoy the wonderful atmosphere which is enhanced by open fires which give out a tremendous heat and one of which sits in a unique inglenook. There is even a flood lit indoor well to add to the enchantment.

It is a busy pub today with a camping and caravan site on the pub's land which is very popular. At Easter and the first week in September there is a folk festival in the Miners with Morris dancing and live entertainment. The old church of Middleton just 1½ miles away has some wonderful carvings and Chirbury itself is set within the hills of South Shropshire amidst some superb walking country. Shrewsbury lies 16 miles to the west and Welshpool 8 miles. The food is all home-cooked by Glenda and her Sunday lunches are so popular it is essential to book. Her fare is wholesome, tasty and excellent value.

USEFUL INFORMATION

OPEN: 12-3pm & 7-11pm
Normal Sundays
CHILDREN: Welcome
CREDIT CARDS: None taken
LICENSED: Full Licence
ACCOMMODATION: Not applicable

RESTAURANT: Not applicable
BAR FOOD: Wholesome, tasty, good value
VEGETARIAN: Always a choice
ACCESS FOR THE DISABLED: Yes. Welcome
GARDEN: Large with tables & chairs

LION INN

Public House

Shifnal Road,
Priorslee,
Telford, Shropshire.

Tel: (0952) 290797

Less than five minutes from Junction 4 or 5 off the M54 is the very pretty village of Priorslee, the focal point of which is the delightful 16th-century coaching inn, the Lion Inn. It is a pub that has everything you would wish with oak beams, lots of glistening brass everywhere and in the winter, a flame effect fire roars out from the old Inglenook fireplace. It is charming and the tenants, Janet and Eddie Hickinbottom, who have been here since 1978, make sure that you are immediately put at your ease.

What is so useful about the Lion is that having eaten lunch you can set forth to so many different places of interest within easy reach. Ironbridge which has fascinated visitors for years is 10 minutes away, Cosford Aerospace Museum only 15 minutes. For railway buffs, the Severn Valley Railway is a mere 30 minutes by car. Golfers will find 5 good courses at hand and for those who prefer exploring places, the old market town of Shrewsbury is 16 miles away. For those who do not want to go anywhere but the Lion, perhaps you would like to challenge one of the keen local team players to a game of darts or dominoes. The food is good, simple pub fare, most of it home-cooked. Janet is well known for the light touch she has with pastry which makes her Steak and Kidney Pie a particular favourite. The menu is not vast but there is something for everyone.

USEFUL INFORMATION

OPEN: Normal pub hours
  Food: Mon-Fri: 11-2pm
CHILDREN: To eat or in the games
  room
CREDIT CARDS: None taken
LICENSED: Full Licence
ACCOMMODATION: Not applicable

RESTAURANT: Not applicable
BAR FOOD: Good variety.
  Home-cooked
VEGETARIAN: On request
ACCESS FOR THE DISABLED: No
GARDEN: Beer garden

THE NELL GWYNN

11a Park Street,
Shifnal,
Shropshire

Public House & Restaurant

Tel: (0952) 460063

The Nell Gwynn is one of the loveliest timbered buildings in Shropshire. Dating from the 1500s it takes you into the past the moment you see it and to step inside its welcoming doors is to fill you with a sense of history. It is still largely original with superb oak beams and very cosy, yet has ample space. A place to savour both the atmosphere and the excellence of the food, drink and hospitality.

You will see an equally old pub, The Charles II next door and this historic building is also part of the Nell Gwynn. Shifnal is lucky to have two such exciting places. The town is less than one mile from Telford Shopping Centre , 3 miles from the M54 and close to the beautiful and historic Shrewsbury. An ideal spot to visit. It is a good fishing area for those who enjoy it and a pleasant town to explore especially on Wednesday when it becomes alive with the bustle of Market Day. People come in from miles around to enjoy what must be one of England's most ancient attractions. The Nell Gwynn has an attractive restaurant which seats 63. It is also capable of catering for private parties and frequently for conferences. On Mondays and Fridays there is live entertainment. Friday evening you can dine to the accompaniment of the soft strains of guitar music. The food is wide ranging and Sundays is traditional English, Mexican and Italian. Good value for money.

USEFUL INFORMATION

OPEN: 11.30-2.30pm & 6-11pm
CHIILDREN: Welcome
CREDIT CARDS: All major cards
LICENSED: Full Licence
ACCOMMODATION: Not applicable
GARDEN: Beer garden. Large
 car park

RESTAURANT: English,
 Continental. Good value
BAR FOOD: Traditional,
 home-cooked
VEGETARIAN: 12+ dishes daily
ACCESS FOR THE DISABLED:
 Easy access

THE CORN HOUSE RESTAURANT

Restaurant & Wine Bar

59a Wyle Cop,
Shrewsbury,
Shropshire.

Tel: (0743) 231991

Shrewsbury is a magical place full of lovely old buildings and held within the gentle arms of the River Severn. Wyle Cop is a street that is full of history. Its buildings are some of the most historic in the town and its individal shops the most fascinating. In amongst them is The Cornhouse, which was built as a corn warehouse in 1780, and has been home to many crafts until it was converted into a restaurant and wine bar in 1980.

Pat Pennington and her son Grant own and run the business which is a mecca for many people who live in and around Shrewsbury and is certainly a place that a visitor should not miss. It has immense character and food and wine to match. It is also a starting or stoppping point when visiting the many super places around it. Just across the road is Tanners Wine Market and Museum, a firm that has been trading in wine since 1842 and is considered to be one of the country's top wine merchants. Then there is Clive House Museum in College Hill and Rowleys House in Barker Street. The wine bar on the ground floor of the Cornhouse is a popular meeting place. The atmosphere is informal and you are welcome for a drink or to choose from the daily changing blackboard menu of home-made dishes. It is open 7 days a week. Reservations are preferred for the first floor restaurant where you can enjoy a varied, seasonal menu of English and Continental cuisine. All meals are freshly cooked on the premises.

USEFUL INFORMATION

OPEN: 7 days 12-2.30pm & 6.30-10.30pm
CHILDREN: Yes. Highchairs
CREDIT CARDS: Access/Visa/Amex
LICENSED: Full & Supper Licence
ACCOMMODATION: Not applicable

RESTAURANT: Fresh, home-cooked, mixed
BAR FOOD: Mixed nationality. Wide range
VEGETARIAN: 4 dishes
ACCESS FOR THE DISABLED: Yes
GARDEN: None

CAROLS
Restaurant & Cafe

Meeting Point House,
Southwater Square,
Telford Town Centre,
Shropshire.

Tel: (0952) 290359

This is one of the most interesting places in Telford. In the heart of the town, next to the Town Centre Complex overlooking Southwater lake, Carols is part of an inter-denominational Charity building, which is used by most religious bodies in the town,and is the base for voluntary agencies in this area of Telford. It is a bright modern building and the restaurant is equally bright, fresh and very clean.

Carol Dixon owns the restaurant and operates it with her son, Gary. It has a pleasant outlook onto the lake where swans and ducks live in harmony, and look down with disdain on humans who venture onto the lake in paddle boats. The lake borders Telford's award winning gardens and nearby there are 450 acres of parkland with one of the largest free children's play areas in the country. Gary and Carol are busy people looking after both the restaurant and the function rooms on the upper level. There are many outdoor events in the parkland during the summer months. It is here you will see the musical fountain, and sometimes Morris Dancers or Marching Bands. Close by is an ice rink. Carol offers excellent food, all home-cooked but do not expect to find chips on the menu! There is an extensive vegetarian menu, super salads, pastas, pies, Chilli Con Carne and a tempting array of sweets.

USEFUL INFORMATION

OPEN: Mon-Fri: 10-5.30pm
  Sat: 10-5pm
  May to Sept: Sun: 2-5.30pm
CHILDREN: Very welcome. Highchairs
CREDIT CARDS: None taken
LICENSED: Table Licence
ACCOMMODATION: Not applicable

RESTAURANT: Extensive
home-cooked menu. Reasonably
priced
BAR FOOD: Not applicable
VEGETARIAN: Wide choice
ACCESS FOR THE DISABLED: Yes
GARDEN: Outside seating

THE SUTHERLAND ARMS

Public House

Tibberton,
Newport,
Shropshire

Tel: (0952) 550533

Tibberton was once part of the land belonging to the Duke of Sutherland hence the name of the village pub, The Sutherland Arms. What a pretty rural village this is and yet it is no distance from the shopping centres of Telford and Shrewsbury, Weston Park or Hodnet Hall and Gardens, the Ironbridge Museum, The Wrekin, the 'House that Jack Built' at Cherrington and a host of other places. This makes the village and especially the Sutherland a good place to visit before or after exploring some of these interesting places.

Jonathan Morris and his wife Sheila who run The Sutherland are an unusual pair. For years Jonathan was the lock-keeper on the Shropshire Union Canal and at one time, with Sheila, he ran the horse drawn trip boat, Iona, at Norbury Junction. Their joint experiences make them very good with people and you can see this for yourselves in the friendly, lively and happy atmosphere of the Sutherland. Currently various alterations are being done to enable food to be served in the evenings and make a better entrance for wheelchairs. In the meantime Sheila cooks delectable dishes every lunchtime as well as producing a good cold table. There are always sandwiches, freshly cut, a Vegetarian selection and Burgers and Bangers for the children. You can play darts, dominoes and pool and the playing fields nearby allow enough room for everyone to let off steam. This is a true pub and one you will want to return to.

USEFUL INFORMATION

OPEN: 12-2.30pm & 6-11pm
   Sat: 12-4pm & 7-11pm
   Sun: 12-3pm & 7-10.30pm
CHILDREN: Welcome
CREDIT CARDS: None taken
LICENSED: Full on and off Licence
ACCOMMODATION: Not applicable

RESTAURANT: Excellent pub grub
BAR FOOD: Good value pub fare
VEGETARIAN: 4-5 dishes daily
ACCESS FOR THE DISABLED:
   Garden only
GARDEN: Award winning with
   tables & benches

THE PLOUGH
Public House & Restaurant

Wall under Heywood,
Church Stretton,
Shropshire.

Tel: (0694) 771221

Wall under Heywood, situated in beautiful Ape Dale, is one of those places that are easily reached from Church Stretton 4 miles away, Much Wenlock 6 miles and Shrewsbury which is just 15 miles from the village. There are several interesting places to visit nearby such as Wenlock Abbey, once a Monastery and the Wenlock Edge walking trail which gives hours of delight to lovers of the countryside. Fishing is a popular pastime too. One of the most visited places is Acton Scott working farm museum, and another the old Roman village of Rushbury.

In the midst of Wall under Haywood is The Plough which is not only the village pub but also a good restaurant, renowned locally for the standard of its home cooking and the traditional Sunday lunch. The latter is so well attended that it is essential to book. The Dining Room which is separate from the bars, is somewhere in which smoking is banned. This attracts many people to The Plough although it is the overall friendliness and hospitality of Lloyd and Ann Nutting, the proprietors which makes the pub just that extra bit special. The garden is an attractive spot in summer with its lawned areas and colourful flower beds. All the year it is interesting however because of the display Aviaries. Whether you have a full meal or just a bar snack you will find the food tempting and excellent value for money.

USEFUL INFORMATION

OPEN: Weekdays: 12-2.30pm & 7-11pm
    Sundays: 12-3pm & 7-10.30pm
CHILDREN: Yes to eat
CREDIT CARDS: Access/Visa
LICENSED: Full Licence.
    Good wine list
ACCOMMODATION: Not applicable

RESTAURANT: Traditional.
    Home-cooked
BAR FOOD: Extensive hot & cold menu
VEGETARIAN: 3 dishes usually available
ACCESS FOR THE DISABLED: Easy access
GARDEN: Lawned areas. Aviaries

Whittington Castle, Oswestry

INCLUDES:

The Old Jack Inn	*Calverhall*	p. 282
Plas 'Y' Waun Inn	*Chirk*	p. 283
The New Inn	*Gledrid*	p. 284
The Hanmer Arms	*Hanmer*	p. 285
The Sun Hotel	*Llansantffraid -Ym- Mechain*	p. 286
The Green Inn	*Llangedwyn*	p. 287
The Clive and Coffyne	*Market Drayton*	p. 288
The Hinds Head Inn	*Norton in Hales*	p. 289
The Grape Escape	*Oswestry*	p. 290
The Cross Guns	*Pant*	p. 291
The Cherry Tree Hotel	*Whitchurch*	p. 292
Debbie's Restaurant	*Whitchurch*	p. 293
The Narrow Boat	*Whittington*	p. 294
Penrhos Arms	*Whittington*	p. 295

'If there's an end
On which I'd spend
My last remaining cash.
It's sausage, friend,
It's sausage, friend,
It's sausage, friend, and mash.'
A. P. Herbert

NORTH SHROPSHIRE

There are people who may tell you that North Shropshire is dull. That is absolutely untrue; it may be flatter than the south but within it you will discover it has miles of gentle green countryside, reed fringed meres, the excitement of the Shropshire Union and Llangollen Canals, red sandstone hills, a wealth of small villages and five historic market towns, **Oswestry, Ellesmere, Whitchurch, Wem and Market Drayton.**

Moreton Corbet Castle

On my way to Oswestry I made a detour from the A5 Shrewsbury to Oswestry road and drove towards **Pant** *along the B4396 stopping at the oddly named village of* **Knockin,** *where there are some pretty black and white cottages and an old Norman church hidden by trees. Knockin Castle was famous when John Le Strange set out from here to fight for King John in France and brought home as his bride the widowed Queen of Cyprus. Two centuries later it hit the headlines, metaphorically of course, when the heiress Joan, Baroness Strange married a nephew of Warwick the Kingmaker. You will see* *no sign of the castle today because it was pulled down four centuries later and its stones used to build the churchyard wall and a small bridge crossing the stream.*

*Whilst it is definitely out of your way to drive along the little lanes from Knockin to **Melverley**, you will be well rewarded when you see ST PETER'S CHURCH founded in 1406 and the oldest church in Shropshire. It was perched precariously on the banks of the RIVER VYRNWY, a picturesque timber framed building which has survived many floods. It is peaceful, serene and has a sense of belonging that is hard to compare. There is a quaint entry into the register which goes back to 1766 and tells of the marriage of Matthew Dodd and Elinor Foster. It must have been written by the Parish Clerk, one John Lewis:*

> *This morning I have put a Tye*
> *No man could put it faster*
> *Tween, Matthew Dodd, the man of God,*
> *And modest Nelly Foster*

I stopped in the village afterwwards and found quite a fascinating Pastoral Crafts centre and a very good tearoom in which I had a true country tea.

Melverley church is open during daylight hours.

***Pant** is a small village with a good, solid pub, THE CROSS GUNS right on the Welsh/Shropshire Border. The pub is an 18th-century coaching house which has had only slight modernisation to bring it up to todays standards. It has wonderful coal fires in winter, and landlords who are homely, welcoming people. The ale is well kept, the food home-cooked and the locals friendly. An ideal stopping off place for many super places such as POWYS CASTLE.*

*POWYS CASTLE you will find south of **Welshpool** on the A483. What an atmosphere it has, that has been steadily increasing since it was built around 1200AD by Welsh Princes. The Castle contained the finest country house collection in Wales. The 17th-century terraced gardens are wonderful and both historically and horticulturally important. So much history has gone into the centuries since the Castle was built and it has many associations. It houses the CLIVE OF INDIA MUSEUM.*

Powys Castle - Welshpool

The Castle is open in July and August from 12 noon until 5pm. Closed Mondays. April until June plus September, 12 noon to 5pm. Closed Monday and Tuesday. Open Bank Holidays except Christmas.

Close by the MONTGOMERY CANAL *in* **Llanymnech** *village on the A483 just south of Pant, is an old lime processing works which is now an informal heritage area. You can see the old bottle lime kilns and a rare Hoffman Rotary kiln. Close by is the canal wharf where the processed lime was transported out. The limestone was quarried from Llanymnech Hill which is connected to the kiln site by an incline tramway. You can also visit the quarry area which has marked footpaths. Part of the quarry has been designated a nature reserve and there is much bird life. On top of Llanymnech Hill, the ramparts of an old hill fort are still visible. Offa's Dyke also traverses the hill and there are old Roman mine workings in the Ogof Cave. For golfers there is an excellent golf course on the hilltop which is open to day visitors.*

Taking the B4390 from Pant across the border into Powys you will come to **Llansantffraid-Ym-Mechain,** *in a truly beautiful part of mid-rural Wales. In it is an old 17th-century coaching inn, THE SUN HOTEL, surrounded by Archaeological Excavations which has much to do with Caractacus's last stand against the Romans. The* hotel is noted for its one hundred hanging baskets of Fuchsias which make a glorious display, and have won many prizes. Here you can stay a while in the comfortable bedrooms, or pitch your tent and caravan overnight. There is trout and coarse fishing closeby. The food is excellent and Theo Jones and his family will make you very welcome.

Oswestry is in Shropshire but it has very strong ties with Wales. Apart from being a delightful market town to explore it is equally splendid to wander the hilly, sparsely populated border country. This is a town that has so much to do and see that you could well stay here for a month and still not have seen everything.

Market days are full of life with one of the busiest street markets in the county. Over 120 traders set up their stalls with every imaginable kind of product and produce. The Market days are all the year round on Wednesdays with an additional Market on Saturdays in the summer. There is ample car parking near the town centre.

One of the best ways to discover the secrets of this historic town is to use the Town Trail which wends its way through medieval streets, past ancient buildings like the FOX INN in Church Street, an old timber building which once had a gable projecting over the street. It had to be removed after a passer by damaged his silk top hat on it. Church Street has many fine buildings of historic and architectural merit such as the impressive WYNSSTAY HOTEL, with its grand entrance. You can just imagine it in the days when it was a coaching house, and to its rear the old stables and coach houses which can still be seen. They would have been alive with the clatter and rattle of horses hooves and coach wheels on the cobbles and the call of the coachman's horn as mail passengers began their perilous journey to Chester or Shrewsbury,

The trail starts at CASTLE BANK, the highest point in Oswestry and also finishes there. It is a trail of total fascination.

When you have followed it you will be more than ready for some refreshments and in English Walls, you will find THE GRAPE ESCAPE, a Wine Bar and Bistro that offers something splendid from 10.30am until well after midnight. It is a popular meeting place for those who live in Oswestry and one, that a visitor having once tried, will want to go back.

In Oswald Road is THE CAMBRIAN MUSEUM OF TRANSPORT which opens daily from 10-4pm. Oswestry was once the headquarters of the old Cambrian Railway and was at the centre of the railway network serving North and Mid Wales. One of the old engine sheds now houses a small museum which chronicles Oswestry's railway history. The Museum is operated by the Cambrian Railway Society, which regularly 'steams up' one of its locomotives. Apart from engines there is a collection of railway memorabilia and artefacts and another very interesting one of vintage bicycles, depicting the development of the machine. There is ample car parking space.

In addition to the bicycle display in the Cambrian Museum there is also the delightful small OSWESTRY BICYCLE MUSEUM in Arthur Street where you can see every imaginable kind of bicycle, together with the 'Old Bicycle Shop' in which you can trace the development of the bicycle from the penny farthing through to today's highly technical bikes.

The Museum opens daily except Thursday and Saturday, from 9.30am-4pm.

ST OSWOLD'S CHURCH is a striking building, mostly of the 17th century standing on more ancient foundations. The lower part of the massive tower is 750 years old and stands partly within the church. The interior is especially impressive with no less than 30 arches.

I have always found military museums very interesting and I was more than willing to visit THE OSWESTRY MILITARY MUSEUM in West Felton. It is full of weapons, uniforms, equipment and militaria covering all ages of history but focusing on the twentieth century. National Servicemen will remember the former 'Park Hall Camp' which has its own exhibit. At the end of a fascinating afternoon I was more than ready to enjoy the Edwardian Tea Room which provided me with a piping hot, and very welcome, pot of tea.

You will find the Museum open daily from 10am-8pm.

If you can spare the time it is worth exploring the old village which has an ancient castle mound and earthworks.

*One mile north of the town, signposted from Gobowen Road there is one of the best examples of an iron age hillfort to be found in the country. **Old Oswestry** is on a huge scale with its massive earthwork ramparts and salients. Excavations on the hillfort have failed to unearth its mysteries - no pun intended. It is an intriguing place and has an atmosphere unique to itself. The views from the top over the roofs of the town and the Shropshire Plain are nothing short of spectacular. You can visit there at any time of the year.*

One of the best ways to see much of this fine countryside is astride a horse and with 10 Riding Stables within easy reach of Oswestry you will not find it difficult to take day or hourly rides. Many of the stables can arrange trekking weekends or short breaks. Two stables that I am happy to recommend in the immediate vicinity are PEN-Y-COED RIDING STABLES at Llynclys Hill where Pam Hanson is in charge. She can cater for all ages and has the ability to give tuition from 5 years upwards. Caravan accommodation is available at the Centre or can be arranged in local guest or farm houses. The Stable organises holidays for children from 7 upwards - a great time for them and a blissful rest for their parents! Tel: (0691) 830608.

The second stable is Mrs Gilchrist's RHYDYCROESAU RIDING CENTRE which offers riding along Offa's Dyke or deep in the Borderland's countryside. Horse and Pony Trekking is available from 6 year old upwards. There is no accommodation but Mrs Gilchrist is happy to arrange it for you at local guest houses or country pubs. Tel: (0691) 653826.

*You really must make the effort whilst you are hereabouts to seek out **Llangedwyn**, a peaceful oasis on the B4396 between **Llynclys** and **Bala**. It has a first class Inn, THE GREEN INN, in which Gary and Robin Greenham wait to welcome you, whether to stay in one of their comfortable rooms, or to enjoy the food and drink. From here you can enjoy fly fishing, or go into Oswestry on Market Days, see POWYS CASTLE and LLANFYLLIN BIRD AND BUTTERFLY WORLD.*

Canals are very important to the way of life in this part of Shropshire and provide so much more than just water transport. Following the canal or 'the cut' is a wonderful way of exploring North Shropshire whether you have a boat or not. The towpath is a splendid traffic free footpath, on the level for miles and miles albeit in some places it is distinctly rough going and very muddy. You are rewarded though by the wildlife that abounds on the water, in the bankside vegetation, and along the hedges. You can learn so much from the canal which tells its own story of our industrial and architectural heritage.

At **Whittington** *you will meet with the LLANGOLLEN CANAL, which wends its way across the county right up into Cheshire where it joins the main SHROPSHIRE UNION CANAL close to* **Nantwich.** *Whittington is a very large village in the centre of which is the remains of WHITTINGTON CASTLE. All that you can see today of this important border castle is the magnificent gatehouse and the moat. It is a delightful place to visit, with a childrens play area, ducks to feed and a tearoom in which to relax. The village is reputed to have been the birthplace of Dick Whittington, the famous Lord Mayor of London and cat owner!*

I found a very good hostelry in Station Road, THE PENRHOS ARMS where the owners, Alan and Shirley Ball made me very welcome. It is quite close to the castle and with its large car park I had no difficulty in leaving my car. Inside it is oak beamed and has open fires but it was the warmth of the welcome that made it special. It is quite easy to reach Oswestry just three miles away and is only 4 miles from the lakeland area around Ellesmere.

For nearly two centuries Bridge No. 5 of the Canal was virtually on its own, only a small cottage with a large orchard kept it company. Now the cottage has grown and become a pub, THE NARROWBOAT INN and instead of the clucking chickens in the orchard there are ducks swimming in the canal lay-by, dug out to accommodate the 24 hire base known as MAESTERMYN (Hire Cruisers) Ltd, which has a gift shop, an off licence and chandlery. It has taken 15 years of devoted and dedicated work by Colin and Elaine Hill. It is an exciting venture and in a marvellous spot. In spring the high grassy banks are full of cowslips and primroses and even in the very height of the season there is something peaceful and reassuring about this little piece of an English Canal.

From here I went north a little until I came to **Chirk** *where it is the only way to cruise from England into Wales over the aqueduct on the Llangollen Canal, one of the seven wonders of Wales. This is quite* a place with a lot of history, right on the border of Shropshire and Clwyd; it has withstood the slings and arrows of outrageous fortune. CHIRK CASTLE, which belongs to the National Trust, is a place you must visit and you should make sure you get to LLANRHAEADR FALLS, another of the seven wonders of Wales. They are stunning.

In Chapel Lane, a short distance from the centre of Chirk and just a few moments away from THE CEIRIOG VALLEY and VALE OF LLANGOLLEN, there is THE PLAS-Y-WAUN INN. It is an establishment that was converted from a private house - previously the estate office for Chirk Castle - hence the name Plas-Y-Waun. It is a super place producing good food and a friendly atmosphere.

Just off the A5 Chirk by-pass is the small village of **Gledrid** and there is THE NEW INN backing on to the Llangollen Canal quite near the aqueduct. The pub has mooring rights on the canal and fishing rights on the Rivers Dee and Ceirog, very closeby. There is Salmon and Trout fishing for which boats come from all over the country. The pub was there in the 17th century before the canal was built and has been dispensing hospitality ever since. This is a super place to stay, and if you have a young family there are willing babysitters. At the weekends there is live entertainment. 50 acres of ground provide a site for caravans and campers with the use of facilities. What better way to spend either a lunchtime or an evening sipping a drink whilst you watch the boats on the canal, with the appetising smell of sausages and chops barbecuing not far away.

The Shropshire Union Canal, a popular waterway for pleasure craft, has played a great part in the history of **Ellesmere** and the OLD WHARF with its warehouse and crane is a reminder of a prosperous period for the development of the town when it was a centre of plans for a link to the River Mersey (at what was to become Ellesmere Port). This was nearly 200 years ago when some of Britain's leading industrialists first met to discuss the project, Thomas Telford included. Circumstances caused them to build instead a most attractive canal from Llangollen's Horseshoe Falls to Hurleston Junction near Nantwich.

If you can spare the time you will find the towpath a place of fascination. A short distance from the wharf is the old canal headquarters. Beech House stands opposite the spur to Ellesmere, while next door is the Ellesmere Works of British Waterways. Much of its equipment has been removed to museums but it is still an important maintenance depot. If you look closely at the east end of White Bridge you will see the outline of an old dry dock among the bushes.

The second place to join the canal is by the junction of the Whitchurch to Shrewsbury roads east of Ellesmere. The junction stands above one of the earliest tunnels to carry a towpath through it. To the east of this is Blakemere, a lake left by glaciers some 12,000 years ago. In Autumn the trees of the opposite bank attract innumerable artists trying to capture their elusive beauty,

From here you can continue to the bridge by the west end of **Colemere** or, alternatively you can reach this point by following the path from the picnic site at the south east end of Colemere. You are asked not to park your cars in Mill Lane.

There is much more to interest you especially if you are a canal archaeologist. I just loved the magnificent scenery and the peace. I noticed old lime kilns which I am told served the area as well as devices to control the water in this section. From the bridge in the woods it is only a short walk across the fields to bring you back to the picnic site.

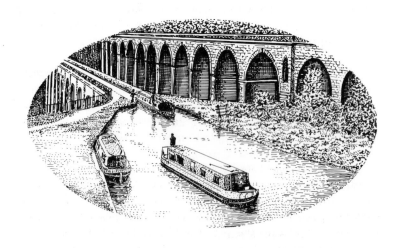

The Canals - North Shropshire

Whilst the town is not blessed with any major historical buildings, it is none the less full of interesting and attractive ones. There is a fine old Town Hall which dominates The Square. It was presented to the town by the Countess of Bridgwater in 1833. You will find underneath fine brick vaulted cellars which have been transformed into a restaurant. Then there are the Georgian Sheraton House, the Victorian Market hall and the impressive Victorian Railway Station, which sadly, is no longer in use. If you enjoy churches you will probably appreciate the mixture of styles, from the Norman Perpendicular and Tudor days in the parish church which stands overlooking the Mere. When its peal of eight bells ring out you will certainly not fail to notice this building.

There are several good places to eat and drink and you will find that most of the public houses have a story to tell. THE WHITE HART is believed to be the oldest public house in the county. THE BRIDGEWATER ARMS HOTEL commemorates the connection of Ellesmere with the Duke of Bridgewater to whom it owes its canal. THE RED LION is an old coaching inn from which horse-drawn coaches ran daily to Wrexham and Chester in the last century. Choose any of these and you will be well fed and watered.

Known as the capital of Shropshire's Lake Country, Ellesmere stands on the biggest of ten wonderful meres, the most important of which are BLAKE MERE, KETTLE MERE, NEWTON MERE, COLE MERE, WHITE MERE, CROSE MERE, and the biggest of all called simply, THE MERE. The very nature of these lakes makes them unique in Britain and indeed a rarity in global terms.

The word 'mere' is an old Anglo Saxon word for lake although unlike lakes they do not have streams flowing in or out. They receive their water from the slow drainage of the surrounding soils, and this nutrient rich water encourages the great variety of animal and plant life.

Naturalists have long been interested in these meres because of the phenomenon which occurs occasionally after a period of warm, calm weather; millions of tiny water plants, that we call algae, suddenly appear on the surface, so that the mere becomes thick like soup. This indicates the abundance and importance of this tiny plant life as the basis of food chains supporting the wildlife of the mere.

271

Fringed by trees and rushes, THE MERE covers 116 acres. It is home to swans and abundant wildlife, a place of beauty and peace. It offers boating and fishing and is an ideal place for bird watching, most especially in the Winter Migration season when many rare birds are seen here. On the shores of the Mere are the CREMORNE GARDENS, given by Lord Brownlow for the use of the people of Ellesmere. This lovely waterside park is a place beloved by the people of the town. It is a sheer delight to walk amongst its well kept lawns and avenues of trees always with The Mere and its wildlife in sight. Children use the playground and the paddling pool whilst their elders play tennis, from time to time the sound of music emanates from the band stand, and there are many other things which give pleasure to the whole family.

The Mere - Ellesmere

Quite by chance I discovered ELLESMERE RESTAURANT BOAT on which you can enjoy the luxury of dining on board as you glide along the Llangollen Canal through Shropshire's wonderful meres. It is something very different. The trips are available at the weekends for the general public but during the week the boat can be booked for private parties with a minimum of 20 people and a maximum of 52. There are all sorts of different occasions catered for including Buffets, Theme Evenings, Educational Trips, Afternoon Teas and Roast Meals. It is extremely good value. You do need to book by telephone. The number is (0691) 75322.

When you ring this number you may want to inquire about other outings that can be arranged. One is fascinating. You meet and then set forth for **Welsh Frankton** *where you are taken to visit Alf Strange who is both a Blacksmith and Author. He demonstrates his craft and tells you tales of his life. It is quite riveting, as indeed are his books. From there you go on to The Narrowboat Inn at Bridge 5 - somewhere I wrote about earlier in this chapter - and then to Llangollen over the Aqueduct. The whole trip is called 'A Step Back in Time' and I am quite sure you will enjoy every minute of it.*

Welsh Frankton is a site of special pilgrimage to canal buffs. Here the line of canal to **Newtown** *branches off. Now referred to as THE MONTGOMERY CANAL, this is one of the great restoration projects of the new canal revival for leisure use. I was told that before too many years you will be able to turn a boat off here and head for* **Welshpool,** *then up to Severn Valley to Newtown. Until the remaining restoration is put in hand, the journey is only for the walker.*

The most helpful and efficient way to learn more about the Meres is to visit THE MERES VISITOR CENTRE which has recently undergone considerable alteration. There is a Tourist Information point and a well stocked shop selling local craft products as well as interpretive environmental material. It certainly helped me to appreciate how the Meres were formed and what wildlife was to be found both aquatic and ornithological.

Adjacent is the country's first WATCH CENTRE which is specifically aimed at children though I enjoyed it thoroughly. There are various live animal displays including small mammals; amphibians and pond life also have live microscopic displays. The Watch centre is often used by schools and other organisations and on Sundays during the summer there is a knowledgeable person on hand to answer questions, and advise visitors on aspects of local wildlife.

The Centre is open every afternoon from Easter until the end of October. If you would like more information please telephone Ellesmere 622981.

Llangollen *is enchanting and I will give it full coverage in 'Inviation to Lunch, Dine, Stay and visit in Wales' which is due out in the Spring of 1993. The name comes from St Collen, who would* have been proud of the lasting International friendships which are made during the International Musical Eisteddfod which has been held here since 1946. High above the town is the famous Horseshoe Pass which is named after its enormous bend from where splendid views of Eglwyseg Mountains can be seen. The old bridge was built in 1131 and the view towards Barbers Hill is magnificent.

Hanmer to the north east of Ellesmere also has its own Mere. Strictly speaking, this lovely typically English village is in Clwyd, Wales but geographically it is considered to be part of the 'Shropshire Lake District'. It is one of the most peaceful places you could possibly find, indeed sometimes the only sound is the soft noise of the wind stirring the water as it laps the shore of the lake.

In the midst of the attractive cottages that are so much part of this village, is THE HANMER ARMS, a very special place where tradition is paramount. It has not forgotten its role as the village pub, but discreetly and very comfortably, 20 en-suite rooms have been added. A wonderful place for a break or for business people wanting a Seminar in quiet surroundings.

That most unpleasant of men, the hanging judge, Judge Jefferies, took the title Baron Jefferies of **Wem**. This was not popular with the people who lived here. He resided at Lowe Hall and I doubt if anyone had a good word for this lewd, hard drinking man who sought Court favour to become a judge.

This is a town that still manages to preserve more of the old market town atmosphere than most others. It is delightful and dates back before the Conquest in 1066. In fact it is the only town mentioned in the Domesday Book which can trace descendants from before and after the Conquest.

The fire of 1677 destroyed many of the ancient houses and it suffered for its staunch support of the Protestant cause in the Civil War, being the first town to declare for Parliament and hence became a prime target for the Royalists of Whitchurch and Shrewsbury who laid siege to it for a long period without success. The Church dates from the 14th century and has an uncommon doorway of that period, and a Perpendicular style upper tower.

It is always the odd findings that make travelling so rewarding. Just to the west of Wem, is **Loppington** where the traffic passes over *a ring fastened to the ground in front of an inn; the only relic of a Bull ring remaining in the county. The oldest possession of the village is the Norman arch in the church tower, though most of the tower is 16th century and the church of the 14th. If you take a look towards the heavens you will see there are black and white roofs with grotesque carved faces looking down at you from the ends of the beams.*

*There is a small, winding road leading to the west from Loppington which leads to **English Frankton**. I had convinced myself that there I would find another character like Al Strange, the Blacksmith from Welsh Frankton - I was sadly mistaken but never mind, the countryside was beautiful and I enjoyed the drive which ended up at the unlikely named **Cockshutt!** What an extraordinary name.*

*This diversion took me away from my intended route which was up the B5478 to **Whitchurch**. This is the most ancient of the market towns dating from 60AD when it was founded as a garrison for the Roman legions marching between Chester (Deva) and Uriconium (Wroxeter, near Shrewsbury). They called it Mediolanum which is the same Roman name as Milan, because it was the 'mid-place of the plain' standing on a strategic hill commanding the surrounding countryside. Many Roman artefacts and buildings have been found in the town centre notably in 1967 and 1977, and the High Street, Pepper Street and Bluegates occupy the same situation as the Roman streets.*

I always remember the town because it is here that the quiet,unassuming, musical genius Mr E. G. Jones was born. Jones, who on earth was he, I can hear you asking. The world knows him by the name his initials stand for, Edward German. Today perhaps his music is less well known but choirs throughout the country still perform his well beloved 'Merrie England'. During the war years when I thought myself as something of a singer - an impertinence no doubt - I had an examination to pass and the test piece was none other than 'O Peaceful England, wherefore art thou sleeping.' The day and time of the examination coincided with an Air Raid. The bombs came down, I continued singing and I doubt if the examiner even noticed the duff notes that came from my voice box. I passed with flying colours! Edward German will never be forgotten by me nor will he by the people of Whitchurch. He died at the age of 74, never seeking fame, known and admired among a circle of fellow musicians, yet the British public loved him.

He is not the only famous son of Whitchurch, John Talbot, first Earl of Shrewsbury, is buried here. He was virtually the hero of the first part of Shakespeare's Henry VIth. He was born towards the end of the 14th century, fought against Owen Glendower and twice governed Ireland. A great leader and a courageous fighter, he became famous for his deeds in France. He sometimes displayed the courage of a madman and it was this rashness that brought about his death. At Castillon, accompanied by his gallant son, he beat off besiegers but without waiting for artillery, made a reckless assault on the enemy's camp. Seeing death was inevitable for himself, he pleaded with his son to flee.

That wish was refused and the son was mortally wounded before his father's eyes. Father and son died together and were mourned by England. His body was recovered and it lies in a tomb in the handsome Georgian church of ST ALKMUND which in 1713 replaced one which collapsed after an Evensong service in 1712. It is as lovely outside as in. The porch is semicircular, there are pretty balustrades and pinnacles, the Earl of Bridgewater's arms and a fine clock on the tower's South side. Inside the magnificent, classical columns give the whole an appearance of nobility. John Talbot, first Earl of Shrewsbury's body is inside but his heart is buried in the porch.

The church is open from 7.30am-7pm Tuesday to Sunday and from 9am on Mondays.

Whitchurch is a busy market town though its old Market Hall is now Barclays Bank. Until 1939 the great Cheese Fairs were held here and even today it is still regarded as the centre of THE CHESHIRE CHEESE INDUSTRY. Many local farmhouses still produce this famous cheese which you are welcome, and encouraged, to sample when they are brought to market on Fridays.

You will find much to see here with a fine variety of architecture including a 15th-century old cooperage shop in the High Street which is now a bakers. Almost in the Town Centre you will find a pleasant wooded park which has had a recent addition in the shape of the well-designed HARRY RICHARDS MEMORIAL GARDEN. There is a modern indoor swimming pool, the championship Golf Course and Country Club at Hill Valley and a variety of good hotels, pleasant inns, restaurants and eating houses.

I can recommend DEBBIE'S RESTAURANT in the High Street in a 19th-century building which has been many things, including a coaching inn, a butchers and a bakehouse. Today it has charm, a lot of character and good food.

Looking for somewhere to stay it was suggested to me that I would be more than welcome and very comfortable in THE CHERRY TREE HOTEL at **Prees Heath.** The recommendation was a good one. It is a happy place to visit. There is one thing you should watch for here though because the owners are in a bit of a quandary. Whilst the hotel is currently called The Cherry Tree the locals insist on calling it The Witchball. The decision has been reached that as soon as the local history has been traced, it will revert to this name so it may be you will be visiting The Witchball rather than The Cherry Tree. Whatever the name this is a charming spot.

Coming in from the east, the Llangollen Canal climbs the triple staircase of locks at **Grindley Brook** on the A41 north of the town. A mile further on, where the canal takes a loop under the new by-pass at curiously named **Chemistry,** a branch leads into the centre of Whitchurch. Derelict for many years, this branch is now being restored so that boaters at least will no longer have an excuse for by-passing this pleasant town.

The rural peace of the little village of **Calverhall,** two miles off the A41 between **Market Drayton** and Whitchurch, within easy reach of either, and also the Potteries and Shrewsbury, tempted me to stay at THE OLD JACK INN which dates from 1811 and has been the centre of village life ever since. The pub lived up to my expectations, the bedrooms were simply furnished and comfortable. Rosemary and Geoffrey Hancock, the owners could not have been more helpful or welcoming. Whether you stay there or merely pop in for a meal or a drink, it is somewhere to enjoy.

A famous drinking vessel was kept for hundreds of years in the village and housed in The Old Jack Inn. Known as 'The Jack of Corra' it was made of leather, lined with horn, and silver mounted. On the upper band was a couplet:

'Jack of Corra is my name,
Don't abuse me then for shame.'

The vessel was used at rent dinners and similar village feasts, and it was the custom to challenge any of the guests to drain the Jack at a single draught. This was difficult owing to the thickness of the rim, which allowed only a very thin stream of liquor to enter the mouth. The cup, which was kept at The Old Jack Inn, disappeared about 1860 and its present whereabouts are unknown.

Calverhall does not live in the past, it is a village with good amenities including tennis courts, a children's playground, football and cricket pitches and a bowling green. Its church is modern and joined to a group of 18th-century almshouses. The church has some fine panelling round the walls and a beautiful Morris window of Simeon chanting the Nunc Dimittis as he holds the Child Jesus in his arms.

From here some winding and very pretty lanes, revealing the beautiful countryside, lead a little further to the East, crossing the busy Nantwich-Market Drayton A529 and then to **Norton-in-Hales,** Shropshire's best kept village. Only 3½ miles north of Market Drayton, it is completely rural. A delightful place with the BRIDGEMERE and STAPELEY WATER GARDENS nearby, making the ideal place to visit after sampling the generous hospitality of THE HINDS HEAD, a 300 year old coaching inn. The inn is a pretty place and especially so in summer when the colourful hanging baskets outside add to the charm.

Joan and Colin Leighton are mine hosts, a couple entirely suited to this way of life. Their food is excellent and I loved their description of a Prawn Cocktail which they say is 'Pink and Plump just like the owners!'

In the middle of the village green is a curiosity, the Bradling Stone, on which they bumped anyone found working after mid-day on Shrove Tuesday. Closeby is the old church which has a chancel of the 13th century, a tower of the 15th, and an unsual octagonal baptistry.

My final destination in this unexpectedly interesting and beautiful county was **Market Drayton.** This attractive market town has retained its medieval street plan. The lovely red local sandstone and the mellow hand-made bricks of the 18th and 19th-century houses give the town its charm and warmth. Black and white half-timbered buildings including several of the eighteen pubs, are interspersed amongst the red brick.

Market in name and market by nature, ideally you should come here on a Wednesday and join in the bustling bargain hunting tradition that has been going on for over 750 years. Since the Norman Conquest this seemingly sleepily and isolated town has been the scene of revolt, riot, murder, adventure and trade; its links have extended worldwide.

It was the prospect of trade which encouraged the Cistercian Monks of Combermere, near Whitchurch, to seek a market charter from Henry II in 1245 for the town. It was trade, the East India Company and the fabulous Spice Trade, which took young Robert Clive, the town's most famous son, to India at the age of seventeen. As a boy he spiced up the lives of the townspeople with such escapades as sitting on a gargoyle of the church tower which overlooks the Old Grammar School that he attended, and building a dam which flooded the shops. His birthplace was STYCHE HALL where his family had lived for 300 years, and which he rebuilt from his Indian fortune, at the same time paying his improverished father's debts. After his memorable, if sometimes controversial career as builder of the Indian Empire he was finally laid to rest in the church at **Moreton Say** close to Styche Hall.

Clive will never be forgotten in Market Drayton for many reasons and not the least for THE CLIVE AND COFFYNE, a splendid inn made famous by its co-tenant, Paul Roberts who makes Clive pies from a recipe that Clive gave in 1768 to the French town of Pezanas. The recipe has been adapted and Clive's petits Pates, have brought his home town much fame recently. Paul won the Guinness Best Food Pub award with his Clive Pie. This fine timber-framed inn is to be found in Shropshire Street. If you are worried about the second part of its name, don't be - a coffyne is the local name for a pie crust.

You will find much to enjoy in Market Drayton, including the celebrated product of the local bakers' shops - Gingerbread Men, which come in a range of novelty shapes and packages, all faithful to recipes over 200 years old. A true taste of history.

You must find time to travel 6 miles down the A53 to **Hodnet** *where THE HODNET HALL GARDENS covering 60 acres are unrivalled for their beauty and natural valley setting. The magnificent trees, lawns and lakes provide a background to an ever changing seasonal colour and interest. Between April and July the rhododendrons are fantastic. The gardens are nationally famous and have been the subject of several TV and radio programmes. If you would like to add to your own collection of plants, you may purchase some from the kitchen garden. A cup of tea is enjoyable in the tearooms in which you are gazed upon by a remarkable collection of Big Game trophies. The Hall itself is not open to the public.*

Hodnet Hall and Gardens

The Gardens are open from early April until late September daily including Bank Holidays from 2pm until 5pm (gardens cleared at 6.30pm). Sundays and Bank Holidays from 12-5.30pm (gardens cleared at 8pm).

This was a visit to remember among the many very happy recollections I have of this county.

Whittington Castle, Oswestry

THE OLD JACK INN
Inn & Restaurant

Calverhall,
Nr. Whitchurch,
Shropshire.

Tel: (094876) 235

In the north of Shropshire, 2 miles off the A41 between Market Drayton and Whitchurch is The Old Jack Inn at Calverhall. It is a different and delightful place as many people have found out over the years. Whether you just call in, dine or stay you will be welcomed by the hospitable owners, Rosemary and Geoffrey Hancock. It is the sort of place that people use for wedding receptions and family gatherings as well as business meetings. That does not mean that the individual is not well cared for; the Hancocks make everyone feel special.

The pub has been the centre of village life since it first opened its doors in 1811 and part of its history is the story of The Jack of Corra. This was a famous drinking vessel kept for hundreds of years in the village of Calverhall or Corra. It was made of leather, lined with horn, and silver mounted. The upper band bore the couplet:

'Jack of Corra is my name,
Don't abuse me then for shame'

At rent dinners and similar village feasts, it was the custom to challenge any guest to drain the Jack at a single draught. It was difficult, the thickness of the rim only allowed a thin stream of liquor to enter the mouth. The cup, which was kept at the inn, disappeared about 1860, and its present whereabouts is unknown. The food here matches the excellence of the inn whether it is A La Carte, Sunday Lunch or the wide choice of home-made meals and Daily Specials, all using fresh produce.

USEFUL INFORMATION

OPEN: 12-2.30pm & 7-11pm
Supper hour extension
CHILDREN: Yes but no special
facilities
CREDIT CARDS: Access/Visa
LICENSED: Full on Licence.
Good wines
ACCOMMODATION: 3 doubles.
H&C, tea etc

RESTAURANT: A La Carte.
Special evenings
BAR FOOD: Wide choice,
home-made meals
VEGETARIAN: Yes on request
ACCESS FOR THE DISABLED: Yes
GARDEN: Patio. Occasional BBQ

THE PLAS-Y-WAUN INN
Public House

Chapel Lane,
Chirk,
Clwyd

Tel: (0691) 773278

The Plas-Y-Waun was once the Estate Office for Chirk Castle, hence its name. It is wonderfully situated just moments away from the Ceiriog Valley and Vale of Llangollen with Oswestry not too far off. As you approach it you will see it is surrounded by tall trees masking the large garden which includes a playground for the children. There is also a large car park.

In the twenty years it has been a pub, it has shed the estate office image and yet managed to keep its association with the Castle. A large tapestry loaned by the Castle hangs on a wall in the lounge. It is a comfortable pub with a large slate fireplace and the lounge has a nice olde worlde feel about it. Beams and brasses complete the picture. The Public Bar has a pool table, darts and tables for cards and dominoes. There is live entertainment every Thursday and Saturday evenings with an occasional Friday evening as well. It is a busy, friendly place enjoyed by locals and visitors alike.

The 22 cover restaurant, which is incorporated into the lounge, has a Food Carvery used for Buffets and each Sunday there is a traditional lunch carved to order. A three course lunch is served from Monday to Saturday and a Childrens menu is available. In addition there are any number of A la Carte choices including chicken, steaks and fish. The authentic Indian curry is particularly good. Bar snacks are available as well. It is a value for money pub and a happy one.

USEFUL INFORMATION

OPEN: Sat: 11-11pm
  Sun: 12-3pm & 7-10.30pm
CHILDREN: Play area. Allowed in
  Dining room
CREDIT CARDS: Access/Visa/
  Euro/Master
LICENSED: Full Licence
ACCOMMODATION: Not applicable

RESTAURANT: Wide selection for
  all tastes
BAR FOOD: Prepared as ordered.
  Good value
VEGETARIAN: Always 9 dishes
ACCESS FOR THE DISABLED:
  Small step
GARDEN: Large. Tables. Play area

THE NEW INN

Inn

Gledrid, Chirk,
Wrexham,
Clwyd.

Tel: (0691) 773250

Long before the Llangollen canal was built in 1703, The New Inn offered hospitality to travellers but the advent of the canal at the back of the pub gave it a new dimension and a changing clientele. It is situated in a delightful spot, surrounded by wonderful countryside on the Shropshire-Welsh border. With mooring rights on the canal, and fishing on the River Dee which can be arranged, it is popular with a vast number of people who visit The New Inn regularly.

You do not need to be boating people or fishermen to enjoy the hospitality of the pub. There is so much else that you can see and do around here. Chirk Castle, for example, is a fascinating place to visit and just 6 miles away is the famous Llangollen Horse Shoe Pass.

There are three double bedrooms for people wanting to stay with the added benefit of Baby sitting. Peter and Linda Whiteley and Peter and Janet Castle, the owners, have young families and have children's interests very much at heart. There is a 5 acre site for caravans and campers who are welcome to use the facilities of the inn. Friday and Saturday is the time for live entertainment and on Sundays there is Karaoke and a disco. The food is excellent and imaginative, with regular theme evenings being the speciality of the house. Italian, Greek and Chinese cuisine is on offer. The New Inn is an enjoyable experience.

USEFUL INFORMATION

OPEN: Bar: Mon 7-11pm
 Tue/Sat: 11-11pm
 Sun: 11-3pm & 7-11pm. All day food
CHILDREN: Welcome
CREDIT CARDS: Access/Visa/
 Diners/Amex
LICENSED: Full Licence. Fine wines
ACCOMMODATION: 3 doubles

RESTAURANT: Delicious quality
BAR FOOD: Bar menu & daily
 specials
VEGETARIAN: Several dishes
ACCESS FOR THE DISABLED:
 From car park & canal
GARDEN: Extensive overlooking
 canal. BBQ

THE HANMER ARMS
Hotel

Hanmer,
Nr. Whitchurch,
Shropshire

Tel: (094874) 532/640

Strictly speaking this lovely, typically English village is in Clwyd, Wales but geographically it is considered to be part of the Shropshire 'Lake District' centred on Ellesmere. It is one of the most peaceful places you could possibly find, indeed sometimes the only sound is the soft noise of the wind stirring the water as it laps the shore of the lake.

In the midst of the attractive cottages is The Hanmer Arms which has never forgotten its role as the village inn but has added to it 20 apartments, traditionally designed most of which have been converted from the original farm buildings. The rooms nestle round a cobbled courtyard and offer every possible modern comfort. They are en suite and have colour Satellite T.V., Direct Dial Telephones and Tea and Coffee making facilities.The staff are both courteous and a mine of information, willing to provide a comprehensive list of places to see.

In the village bar on the ground floor you can sample a full range of hand drawn traditional beers, enjoy Morning Coffee, Lunch, Afternoon Tea and Light Snacks. The Restaurant and Bar on the first floor have superb views of the Berwyn Mountain Range to the west and the Cheshire Plains to the north. The accomplished chef produces excellent traditional fare. It is a super place to visit and you will find it exceptional value.

USEFUL INFORMATION

OPEN: All day every day
CHILDREN: Welcome
CREDIT CARDS: Access/Visa/Amex
LICENSED: Full Licence.
    Traditional ales
ACCOMMODATION: 20 en-suite
    rooms

RESTAURANT: Traditional.
    A La Carte
BAR FOOD: Varied & high quality
VEGETARIAN: Always 6 dishes
ACCESS FOR THE DISABLED:
    Yes. 2 rooms all facilities
GARDEN: Courtyard garden.
    Childrens area

THE SUN HOTEL
Hotel & Restaurant

Llansantffraid-Ym-Mechain
Powys

Tel: (0691) 828214

For those of us who do not speak Welsh, half the charm of visiting some of the towns and villages in Wales is the struggle one has to correctly pronounce the names. The Sun Hotel is the only simple part of the difficult pronunciation required for this delightful venue, in a lovely village in the heart of mid-rural Wales. You will find it on the Mid-Wales-Shropshire border, just three miles from Ian Woosnam's home Golf Course and ten miles from the famous Distyl Rhaeadr Falls in the village of Llanrhaeadr-Ym-Mochnant.

The Sun is an old coaching inn dating back to the 17th century which just oozes history. If you are a reader of the Sunday Times you may remember reading about the Archaelogical Excavations here last year, which revealed the last stand of Caractacus against the Romans. For those whose interests are rather more horticultural than historical, the 100 hanging baskets of Fuschia adorning the outside of the pub will make you green with envy. The colour is fantastic and the many awards the display has won have been richly deserved. The Sun is a small family run hotel in which you are more than welcome to stay in the four letting rooms, or use the overnight Caravan and Camping Facilities. Fishermen enjoy the Trout and Coarse fishing close by, and for those who are thinking more of the inner man, both the Beer and the food are excellent. The Menu is extensive, with new dishes daily. Trout and Almonds is the House speciality. The Sun is a thoroughly happy establishment.

USEFUL INFORMATION

OPEN: All day except Sundays
Close 3pm
CHILDREN: Welcome
CREDIT CARDS: None taken
LICENSED: Full Licence
ACCOMMODATION: 4 rooms inc.
1 family

RESTAURANT: Extensive
A La Carte
BAR FOOD: Wide range.
Home-cooked
VEGETARIAN: 3-4 daily
ACCESS FOR THE DISABLED:
Restaurant & Bar
GARDEN: No garden

THE GREEN INN

Inn & Restaurant

Llangedwyn,
Nr. Oswestry
Shropshire

Tel: (0691) 828234

You have to seek out Llangedwyn which is a turn off from the B4396 between Llynclys and Bala. This charming place is a peaceful oasis and in it is the 16th-century Green Inn, owned and run by Gary and Robin Greenham. The Greenhams love their pub and have carefully continued the restoration which has gone on over many years, making sure that it remains largely unspoilt. Inside it is a cosy place full of character with large open fires in the bars.

People have been coming to eat and drink here for years and more recently to stay in the 2 family rooms. It is a wonderful spot from which to enjoy the fly fishing ½ a mile away, or to set out to enjoy all the fun of Market Day in Oswestry on Wednesdays, and Welshpool on Mondays. Whilst you are in Welshpool you can visit Powys Castle and Llanfyllin Bird and Butterfly World. At another time go and see the waterfalls and Dolwen Gardens at Llanrhaeadr or sail on Bala Lakes.

The excellent food is available in the bar or the restaurant offering a choice that will please everyone. The Green Inn prides itself on using all fresh produce in its home-cooked dishes. Sunday Lunch with traditional roast meats has a great following and it is advisable to book. Christmas Day lunches are also very popular and you need to reserve a table early.

USEFUL INFORMATION

OPEN: 11-3pm & 6-11pm
  Normal Sundays
CHILDREN: Welcome
CREDIT CARDS: Access/Visa/
  Diners
LICENSED: Full Licence. 32 wines
ACCOMMODATION: 2 family rooms

RESTAURANT: A La Carte.
  Fresh produce
BAR FOOD: All home-made.
  Wide selection
VEGETARIAN: Always 6 dishes
ACCESS FOR THE DISABLED: Yes
GARDEN: Large with a brook.
  Car park

THE CLIVE AND COFFYNE

Inn

6, Shropshire Street,
Market Drayton,
Shropshire.

Tel: (0630) 653263

This unusually named pub was once the mundane Elephant and Castle, but 2 years ago it was rechristened The Clive and Coffyne, in honour of Clive of India who lived at nearby Styche Hall, and Coffyne because that is an old English word meaning pie casing. The importance of the word Coffyne becomes apparent when I tell you that it was a traditional 'Clive Pie' of minced lamb and fruit that won the pub the Guinness Top Pub Food Award for 1991.

Built in 1665 it looks quite small from outside, but once through the welcoming doors you enter a spacious interior with a tremendous atmopshpere. There are oak beams, roaring log fires and everywhere Clive memorabilia. It really is a super place. Market Drayton is delightful to explore and on Wednesdays the activity is heightened by the weekly market. Parking is not a problem because there is a public car park in Buttercross which backs onto the rear entrance of The Clive. The pub offers excellent food of all kinds but it does specialise in traditional pies, all of which are home made and served with fresh vegetables. The receipe for the prize winning pie goes back to 1768 and because the pub has been unable to find pie moulds of the right size and shape, resembling a large cotton-reel, Clive's pies are baked in straight-sided coffee mugs. The Clive is a great experience.

USEFUL INFORMATION

OPEN: Food: 12-2.30pm Mon-Sat
CHILDREN: Garden only
CREDIT CARDS: None taken
LICENSED: Full Licence
ACCOMMODATION: Not applicable

RESTAURANT: Not applicable
BAR FOOD: Traditional & original home-made pies
VEGETARIAN: At least 3 daily
ACCESS FOR THE DISABLED: Difficult
GARDEN: Beer garden

THE HINDS HEAD INN

Inn & Restaurant

Main Road,
Norton in Hales,
Shropshire.

Tel: (0630) 653014

Joan and Colin Leighton moved into the 300 year old coaching inn, The Hinds Head in 1991 and very rapidly created the warmth about them that has made this such a popular venue in Shropshire's best kept village, Norton in Hales. The inn is a pretty place and especially so in summer when the colourful hanging baskets add to the charm.

The village is only 3½ miles north of Market Drayton but it is completely rural. A delightful place, with the Bridgmere Garden Centre and Stapeley Water Gardens nearby, making ideal places to visit after sampling the generous hospitality of The Hinds Head. There is a separate restaurant which is attractively furnished and very comfortable. Many customers prefer to use this for food rather than the bar because it is quieter and no one is in a rush. It is a pleasant place to enjoy a good meal and sample some wine from the well chosen wine list. The menu is based on traditional fare and mainly home-cooked using fresh produce. As a result there are super pies with pastry that melts in the mouth, fish cooked in a variety of ways and succulent steaks cooked to order. For starters you would do well to choose the Prawn Cocktail which is described as 'Pink and Plump just like the owners'! Children have their own menu and the bar food includes a wide range of excellent dishes.

USEFUL INFORMATION

OPEN: Food 11.30-2pm & 6-10pm
CHILDREN: To eat only
CREDIT CARDS: Access/Visa/
Eurocard
LICENSED: Full Licence
ACCOMMODATION: Not applicable

RESTAURANT: Home-cooked, fresh produce
BAR FOOD: Varied, generous portions
VEGETARIAN: At least 6 daily
ACCESS FOR THE DISABLED: Easy access
GARDEN: Enclosed patio

THE GRAPE ESCAPE
Wine Bar & Bistro

English Walls,
Oswestry,
Shropshire

Tel: (0691) 655251

This is much more than a Wine Bar and Bistro. It is a popular meeting place for local people in Oswestry and has built up a reputation both for its wines and food. Opening as it does at 10.30am and staying open until midnight it has several different types of clientele. There are those who enjoy popping in for coffee in the mornings whilst they are shopping, or sometimes escaping from offices for a quick brew. The lunchtime crowd brings a mixture of business people who either want to relax or talk over some knotty problem whilst enjoying a meal and a glass of wine, or the visitors to this interesting old market town which holds so much to charm the explorer.

Later in the day there is a change of emphasis again but always you will find that people enjoy the happy and relaxed atmosphere of The Grape Escape. Joan Jones is the owner of this delightful establishment and it seems to be run almost entirely by females. Hazel, the chef is well known in the area for the work she does in Outside Catering, in a business called 'Ravishing Bites' but this does not detract from the high standard of superb food that she produces for The Grape Escape. Every dish is home produced using fresh and organic vegetables. The menu offers a remarkable choice from an imaginative range of starters to steaks, pasta and a large selection of puddings which would tempt the most iron willed of dieters. The Grape Escape is a must for anyone visiting or living in Oswestry.

USEFUL INFORMATION

OPEN: 10.30am-midnight
CHILDREN: Welcome
CREDIT CARDS: None
LICENSED: Large range wines.
    Lager
ACCOMMODATION: Not applicable

RESTAURANT: No additives.
    No frozen food
BAR FOOD: Delicious & tempting
VEGETARIAN: 4-5 dishes
ACCESS FOR THE DISABLED: Yes
GARDEN: Small patio

THE CROSS GUNS
Public House

Pant,
Nr. Oswestry,
Shropshire.

Tel: (0691) 830821

Pant has all the feel of a Welsh village but is in fact just on the Welsh / Shropshire border surrounded by the beauty of the Shropshire countryside. In its centre is the small country pub, The Cross Guns, well known locally for its charm and for the warmth of its hospitality.

The Cross Guns is an 18th-century coaching house which has been lovingly cared for throughout the centuries and although it has been modernised to bring it up to the standards required today, essentially it remains the same, with a traditional coal fire to warm the cockles of your heart in the winter. Because of its situation this family run pub is an ideal stopping place for people wanting to visit Powis Castle just ten miles away. Shrewsbury, always an enchanting place to visit, is less than half an hour away and so is Llangollen. If you enjoy the bustle of markets then you will find Oswestry is a busy market town on Wednesday and Saturday.

Food is simple at the Cross Guns but it is all home-cooked and offers a good choice of dishes from succulent steaks to vegetarian dishes. If you have a sweet tooth you will relish the pies, especially apple. On Sunday for less than five pounds you can enjoy a traditional roast with all the trimmings. Good value for money.

USEFUL INFORMATION

OPEN: 12-3pm & 7-11pm
  Food: 12-3pm & 7-10pm
CHILDREN: Welcome. Play area
CREDIT CARDS: None taken
LICENSED: Full Licence
ACCOMMODATION: Not applicable

RESTAURANT: Not applicable
BAR FOOD: Inexpensive.
  Home-cooked
VEGETARIAN: Always dishes
  available
ACCESS FOR THE DISABLED: Yes
GARDEN: With tables & play
  area

THE CHERRY TREE HOTEL

Hotel

Prees Heath,
Whitchurch,
Shropshire.

Tel: (0948) 3234

Terry and Chris Rooney and Bill and Val Dunn find themselves in a quandary over the name of this pleasant hotel. It is currently called The Cherry Tree but the locals insist on calling it by its old name The Witchball. A decision has been reached that as soon as they have been able to trace the local history they will give in gracefully to local opinion and revert to The Witchball. So, if you are looking for The Cherry Tree on Prees Heath, Whitchurch bear this in mind.   It is a charming spot and was once three cottages which have been joined together over the years and had various additions as well.

There are five en-suite letting rooms, complimented by a good restaurant seating 26, a comfortable lounge bar, friendly public bar, a function room for 200 in which there is a portable skittle alley. Senior citizens enjoy the singalong evenings with a live organist and those who have a feel for country and western music will revel in the meetings once a month. There are singles nights and Karaokes and with such a large car park and function room it is ideal for wedding receptions and business meetings. It is Terry and his wife Chris who look after the catering and with a wealth of experience between them you can rely on good food. The steaks, cooked to perfection, are some of the best you will ever taste. It's a happy place to visit.

USEFUL INFORMATION

OPEN: 11am onwards
CHILDREN: Families welcome
CREDIT CARDS: Access/Visa
LICENSED: Full & Entertainments
Licence
ACCOMMODATION: 5 en-suite
rooms

RESTAURANT: Variety & quality
at pub prices
BAR FOOD: All home cooked.
Childrens menu
VEGETARIAN: Various dishes
available
ACCESS FOR THE DISABLED:
Level & toilets
GARDEN: Yes. Patio. Play area.
BBQ. Marque

DEBBIE'S RESTAURANT

Restaurant

39, High Street,
Whitchurch,
Shropshire.

Tel: (0948) 6356

Whitchurch is one of those interesting old market towns where it is nice to linger awhile and explore the many listed buildings. It is also only ten minutes drive from two famous castles which are well worth visiting, Cholmondley and Beeston.

Having spent time looking around you will be in need of food and drink and what better place can you choose than Debbie's Restaurant in the High Street. Built in the early 19th century it has been many things, a coaching inn, butchers and bakehouse. It still contains the old fireplace where bread was baked. It is a restaurant with a lot of character and charm enhanced no doubt by the original oak beams and the skilful decor. It is certainly relaxing and the hospitable owner Debbie Chapman, with her staff, make sure you are welcome. She is a remarkable lady who started here as a waitress and through hard work and determination became the owner within two years. The restaurant is open 7 days a week from 9am until 3pm then from 7pm until last orders at 10pm. In the morning Debbie's serves a full breakfast - the smell of bacon and freshly ground coffee gets all the taste buds working. Lunch is a varied menu with specials of the day and in the evening the A La Carte menu offers a wide choice. On Sundays there is a traditional roast lunch with all the trimmings.

USEFUL INFORMATION

OPEN: 9am-3pm & 7-10pm
CHILDREN: Welcome
CREDIT CARDS: None taken
LICENSED: Restaurant Licence
ACCOMMODATION: Not applicable

RESTAURANT: English, A La Carte
BAR FOOD: Not applicable
VEGETARIAN: 6 dishes available
daily
ACCESS FOR THE DISABLED:
Level entrance
GARDEN: No

THE NARROWBOAT

Public House & Restaurant

Ellesmere Road,
Whittington,
Nr. Oswestry, Shropshire

Tel: (0691) 661051

For almost two hundred years only a cottage and an orchard marked Bridge No 5 on the Llangollen Canal, the official address of which is Ellesmere Road, Whittington. Fifteen years ago the enterprising and multi talented Hill family changed all that. Colin Hill built what he calls the largest 'Narrowboat' of them all, which is now the pub of that name. It is a delightful place just outside Welsh Frankton, surrounded by farmland and next to a boatyard also owned by the Hills. Here 24 narrowboats tie up ready for hiring and it buzzes with activity.

The extension to the old cottage is long and narrow to fit into the space between the road and the canal. It is certainly different and the very genuine welcome you get from Colin, his wife Elaine and son Martin makes visiting the pub a truly memorable experience. They will tell you that the motto of The Narrowboat is 'Eat, Drink and be Nautical.'

The Hills work tremendously hard. On a Sunday morning you will see Elaine, cleaning the pub, Martin restocking the shelves and Colin organising the kitchen in which he will personally cook the succulent roast beef and Yorkshire Pudding which has become traditional. All the food is delicious and the prices are quite ridiculously inexpensive. Book for Sunday lunch to save disappointment.

USEFUL INFORMATION

OPEN: Mon-Sat: 11-3pm & 7-11pm
Sun: 12-3pm & 7-10.30pm
CHILDREN: Accompanied by adults
CREDIT CARDS: None taken
LICENSED: Full Licence
ACCOMMODATION: Not applicable

RESTAURANT: Wide variety, wholesome food
BAR FOOD: Wide variety
Excellent value
VEGETARIAN: Always 3 dishes
ACCESS FOR THE DISABLED: No
GARDEN: Beer garden with bench seating

THE PENRHOS ARMS
Public House & Restaurant

Station Road,
Whittington,
Shropshire.

Tel: (0691) 662456

It was quite a challenge for Alan and Shirley Ball when they came to the Penrhos Arms in 1991 directly from running a very successful establishment in Manchester. The Penrhos was something totally different, another type of clientele, a rural area and a very large garden which they have made good use of for children and also for the now welcome barbecues.

The Penrhos has something about it, almost an intangible air of well being that has been developed by the Balls who mix true professionalism with a relaxed friendly attitude towards their customers. The pub has oak beams and open fires which always help but without good management both behind the bars and in the kitchen they would amount to very little.

Whittington is on the Whitchurch to Oswestry road just off the main A5 and close to Whittington Castle. The lakeland area of Ellesmere is only 4 miles away and between Oswestry and Whitchurch, there is also a Marina at Ellesmere, so there is plenty to see and do after or before you have enjoyed a drink and a good meal here. Shirley is the chef and she specialises in fish dishes and home-cooked traditional fare using local produce whenever it is possible. She considers it important to produce food that children will enjoy and is very conscious of the needs of vegetarians for whom there are always six dishes available. A pub to savour.

USEFUL INFORMATION

OPEN: 11.30-2.30pm & 5.30-10pm
CHILDREN: To eat
CREDIT CARDS: Access/Visa/ Mastercard
LICENSED: Full. Draught Guinness
ACCOMMODATION: Not applicable

RESTAURANT: Traditional home-cooked
BAR FOOD: Choice of 30 dishes
VEGETARIAN: 6 dishes daily
ACCESS FOR THE DISABLED: Limited but welcome
GARDEN: Very large. Childrens area

Hadrians Arch, Staffordshire County Museum

INCLUDES:

The George	*Alstonfield*	p. 324
The Shoulder of Mutton	*Barton under Needwood*	p. 325
The Black Lion	*Butterton*	p. 326
The Red Lion	*Cheddleton*	p. 327
The Country Kitchen	*Eccleshall*	p. 328
St George Hotel	*Eccleshall*	p. 329
Il Mago Restaurant	*Hanley*	p. 330
The Quiet Woman	*Leek*	p. 331
Parrotts	*Longnor*	p. 332
The Lord Nelson	*Oakamoor*	p. 333
The Wheatsheaf	*Oulton*	p. 334
The Horse and Jockey	*Penkridge*	p. 335
The Ash Tree	*Rugeley*	p. 336
The Wharf Inn	*Shebdon*	p. 337
Granvilles	*Stone*	p. 338
The Hare and Hounds	*Stramshall*	p. 339
The Red Lion	*Thorncliffe*	p. 340
The Roebuck Inn	*Uttoxeter*	p. 341
The Greyhound Inn	*Warslow*	p. 342

'Die I must, but let me die drinking in an Inn!
Hold the wine cup to my lips sparkling from the bin!
So when angels flutter down to take me from my sin,
'Ah, God have mercy on this sot,' the Cherubs will begin.'
Walter de Map

STAFFORDSHIRE & THE POTTERIES

'The calm and characteristic stream of Middle England.'
Arnold Bennett

For a county that has so many familiar landmarks it is strangely unknown; visitors rush in to see and sample the sights and delights - Lichfield, Alton Towers, the Potteries and Cannock Chase - yet they rarely stay to investigate this most versatile and handsome of counties.

The Romans found a sparsely-occupied but heavily forested country and things cannot have changed greatly during the following centuries, for the Norman clerks compiling the Domesday Book classified much of the land as 'wasta est' - two words for the bleak phrase 'it is wasted'. The beasts of the forest, the deer, the wild boar and the wolves, greatly outnumbered any human population; Staffordshire was rated one of the poorest counties in the Domesday survey - yet within two centuries all began to change, and by the 19th century the county was one of the richest in England. Its natural resources of wood, iron ore, coal and limestone were feverishly exploited while the moorlands of the north became prime sheep-pastures, contributing to a flourishing woollen trade. The power of the rivers was harnessed to production and advantage taken of the clear fresh waters that welled up from under the deep limestone to brew ales that were in demand all over the country. The very soils and the skills of the people combined to produce pottery for export all over the world. The wealth of Staffordshire gave it a pride and an individuality that was reflected in the character of its people.

Access by rail and road is extremely good with the M5 running north to south through the western half of the county. The southern half of the region, including the county town of Stafford, is mainly low-lying agricultural land riven with canals, rivers and streams. The principal exception to this is the higher heath and woodland of Cannock Chase which divides the region, running in from the south and the industrial conurbations of the West Midlands.

Much of the wealth generated by the industries of the Black Country and its neighbours found its way into this half of

Staffordshire; note the many fine churches and estates which have influenced the landscape.

Penkridge is a pleasant town, where the waters of the River Penk and the Staffordshire and Worcestershire canal wind through green meadows, and was known to the Romans as Pennocrucium. and Penkridge is still one of the few market towns for the region. The old turnpike road between Wolverhampton and Stafford was good for business and trade further increased when the canal came - the town expanding eastwards to meet it. The 20th century saw the old road turned into a dual carriageway and the town endured thirty years of thundering heavy lorries until the motorway brought relief. The canal, which had suffered severely from the competition of both railway and road, now contributed fresh business to the town with boatyards and moorings catering to the leisure industry. There are several boat-hire operators in the town including BIJOU LINE and the TEDDESLEY BOAT COMPANY, and exploring by water, as in so many other parts of the Heart of England, is nothing but pure delight.

The handsome CHURCH OF ST MICHAEL, built of the local reddish sandstone, was one of the six collegiate (teaching centres) churches in the county until the Reformation and contains a number of memorials to the Littleton family, including a very grand affair to a father and son who bore the same Christian name. Their tomb bears the following inscription:-

> Reader, 'twas thought enough upon ye tombe
> Of that great captain th' enemy of Rome
> To write no more of HERE LIES HANNIBAL.
> Let this suffice thee then of all
> Here lie two knights ye father and ye sonne
> Sir Edward and Sir Edward Littleton.

There are a number of attractive buildings in the town, including the Old Deanery, of stone and timber construction, several fine Georgian facades and not a few pubs. I particularly liked the 16th-century HORSE AND JOCKEY in Market Street where I had a thoroughly enjoyable meal and enjoyed listening to the knowledgeable sporting conversation at the bar (the landlord is an ex-professional footballer).

To the south-west, the country roads wander through an area of small farms and rural communities with the odd dormitory village providing a taste of country life for the commuters of the West Midlands. Another canal runs through the area and has quite different characteristics from James Brindley's 'Staffs and Worcs'. Whereas Brindley elected, as far as possible, to follow the natural lie of the land along stream and river valleys, Thomas Telford's Shropshire Union was designed to compete with the railways and hence goes in almost straight lines, cutting through or climbing over the obstacles in its path. The canal's cuttings, locks, tunnels, embankments and bridges are now well-established landscape features in their own right.

Thr Littleton Monument, Penkridge

Brewood (pronounced "Brood') is a most attractive place, founded in the 12th century, and with narrow streets lined with pleasant houses. My favourite is the grandly-named SPEEDWELL CASTLE, which stands in the Market place. Not of course a castle but a tall 18th-century Gothic house, built on the proceeds of a bet - the successful horse being 'Speedwell'. It was in this area that Charles II hid from searching Parliamentarian forces, after his grievous defeat at Worcester in 1651. At the time, the staggering sum of £1000 was offered for his capture, but he was not betrayed and after forty-four days on the run he reached the safety of France. Two of his most loyal subjects are remembered in the parish church, a dignified edifice with a tall and elegant spire. The Royalists are Walter Giffard and Colonel Carless, and a plaque to the latter reads:-

'He not only assisted Charles I of ever blessed memory, but was also the chief preserver of his son King Charles II in the Royal Oak at Boscobel.'

We shall come across **Boscobel** later, but Giffard is interesting because he was descended from Henry VIII's standard-bearer, Sir John Giffard and was a member of a family who had lived at nearby **Chillington** since 1178. They are still there today, in the big Georgian CHILLINGTON HALL, designed by Sir John Soane in 1786 and incorporating an earlier Tudor house. The grounds were laid out by Capability Brown and provide a beautiful setting for the Hall, and it was on this land (well before Brown's days) that the strange incident occurred that gave rise to the family's unusual motto. Sir John Giffard had a collection of wild animals and his favourite was a ferocious panther. One day it escaped and Sir John, his son and almost the entire household turned out to look for it. The animal had naturally travelled a considerable distance before it was sighted in the act of preparing to attack a young woman and her child. Although some way off, Sir John, although no longer in the first flush of youth, raised his cross-bow. His son, seeing how exhausted his father was from the chase, and apprehensive that he might miss, called out, Prenez haleine, tirez fort!' The old knight took note of his son's advice and loosed the bolt just as the panther sprang. It was a brilliant shot; the projectile took the panther through the head, killing it instantly and saving the woman and child. In gratitude, Sir John erected a cross to mark the spot and adopted his son's words as the family motto - 'Take breath, pull strong'. The old marksman now lies, with many others of his family, in Brewood Church.

North-west, on the Shropshire border is the former hunting lodge of the Chillington Estate, BOSCOBEL HOUSE, and it was here, from the 4th-7th September 1651, that Charles II took refuge - 'by the advice of Mr Giffard', as the King later noted. As the search intensified, Charles and his companion Carless hid in the massive branches of a nearby oak. The present 'Royal Oak' is thought to be descended from an acorn of that original Royal refuge.

Not much more than a mile away lies another great house, WESTON HALL, home of the enterprising Earl of Bradford. A *handsome and well-proportioned house of mellow red brick, it is complemented by its grounds - once again the creation of the industrious and more-than-capable Mr Brown. Built in 1671, the Hall is particularly noteworthy for the fact that it was designed by the enterprising and talented heiress to the estate, Lady Elizabeth Wilbraham.*

Apart from magnificent tapestries, furniture, and pictures, the present owner encourages numerous events in the grounds and has also provided numerous outdoor attractions. The neighbouring village rejoices in the wonderful name of Weston-under-Lizard; the Lizard being a local hill.

The rolling wooded countryside is ideal for walking, and both Chillington and Weston have well laid-out trails.

*Thomas Telford's sixty-six mile canal was built to link the industrial city of Birmingham with the great port of Liverpool and was originally named the Birmingham and Liverpool Junction Canal. Looking at the peaceful waters running straight through the lovely countryside, it is difficult to see them as the 17th and 18th equivalent of our motorways - yet that is what they were. Quiet tree-fringed stretches where the tranquillity is only disturbed by quacking of mallard and the puttering of an occasional leisure boat, were once bustling highways where entire generations of families lived their lives afloat. Goods of every conceivable kind were carried by boat, together with passengers and even livestock, and a community such as **Gnosall,** situated beside both canal and major road, would have been an important distribution centre. The popularity of the canals can be understood when one realises the appalling state of the majority of roads which were virtually impassable except by pack-horse. Almost overnight, the waterways enabled vast quantities of raw materials and finished goods to be moved quickly and economically - thus contributing enormously to the prosperity of the nation as a whole.*

It is easy to forget the logistics involved in such a venture as our own century places an enormous reliance on powerful and sophisticaated machinery to construct the roads and motorways - today's equivalent of the canal systems. Labour in enormous numbers had to be accommodated, fed and paid during the building of such projects; to drive the great waterways through the heart of our country relied chiefly upon the speed and expertise of men aided with little more than picks, shovels and wheelbarrows. The problems were not over once the canal was built, for there was the continual problem of maintenance - reinforcing banks, clearing weed, surfacing towpaths, breaking ice in winter and all the more skilled work involving the locks, their gates and associated machinery. Failure in any of these departments could lead to blockage of the canal, or worse still, to loss of water, leaving boats and their cargoes stranded for days even weeks. Gangs of men were allocated a length of canal to maintain, and many spent their lives working to keep the waterway running. Close to the aqueduct carrying the 'Shroppy' across the attractive countryside at **Shebdon,** is THE WHARF INN, once headquarters for a maintenance gang of 'lengthman'. These gangs were noted for the prodigious amounts of food and drink they could consume - the Wharf obviously did a good job in these departments and carries on the tradition by catering to today's visitor with the same cheerful generosity.

Shebdon is close to the Shropshire border, a mile or so to the north of the A519 which runs through **Eccleshall.** The beauty of the surrounding undulating and wooded countryside, together with the architecture and charm of this small town make it one of the most attractive communities in Staffordshire. Pronounced 'Eccle-shawl', it has a long history dating back to a Roman settlement and over the centuries became an important strategic, eccelesiastic and market centre. Soldiers, bishops and traders have all gone but their legacy remains in the buildings they left behind. ECCLESHALL CASTLE was the principal residence of the Bishops of Lichfield for 600 years. Bishop Muschamp was granted a licence to fortify his house in 1200 and this led to the construction of the castle. Interesting to note that bureaucracy ruled even then, and one wonders whether there is still a department deep in the bowels of Whitehall dealing with requests of this nature . . .

In its heyday, the castle would have been square in shape with a tower at each corner, the whole surrounded by a moat. Damage and subsequent demolition during the Civil War siege in 1643 led to the remains being converted into a large house, with only one of the polygonal flanking towers standing as a reminder of the fortifications.

Naturally, as an important ecclesiastical centre, the town required a church of considerable stature and THE CHURCH OF

HOLY TRINITY has been described as one of the finest 13th-century churches in the country. Restored in 1868, it is a tall, light and lofty building of considerable grace and contains the tombs of five of the Bishops of Lichfield.

The roads from Newcastle, Stone, Stafford, Newport and Market Drayton all meet here and the town and its inns did a roaring trade in the great coaching days. THE ST GEORGE HOTEL was one of those hostelries - and is still going strong, offering accommodation and hospitality to the weary traveller. A most attractive interior and the charming GEORGE'S BISTRO ensure its continuing popularity. The wealth of good Georgian and Victorian architecture gives the town a comfortably old-fashioned and prosperous air and it comes as no surprise to find, in the High Street, a proper old-fashioned cafe, THE COUNTRY KITCHEN. Beginning with breakfast, the establishment serves meals throughout the day and places a strong emphasis on the freshest of ingredients together with home-cooking and baking.

'I am, Sir, a Brother of the Angle.'

This was how the 17th-century writer and sometime linen-draper, Izaak Walton, modestly described himself. An enthusiastic and expert fisherman, he wrote a gently humorous anthology that is still published to this day - 'The Compleat Angler'. He died at the age of 90 in 1683 and left his estate at **Shallowford** *to the town and corporation of Stafford, where he was born. THE IZAAK WALTON COTTAGE on the estate has been restored to display the working and living arrangements of Walton's day and also contains a collection of fishing equipment used over the past three centuries. Outside, there is a delightful period herb garden and the sharp-eyed will notice that the attractive little half-timbered cottage has been recently thatched; this is because the original thatching had been replaced by tiles for many years, because of fire damage from the steam trains that used to run nearby.*

Sited alongside the Stafford to Crewe railway lane in **Meece Brook** *Valley about three miles north of Eccleshall is MILL REECE PUMPING STATION. If you like things mechanical then this is a splendid attraction; two enormous steam-powered pumps and their accompanying boiler house contained in handsome turn of the century buildings with numerous displays and exhibits. Water was* *pumped up from over 1000 feet below the limestone to supply the populations of* **Stoke-on-Trent** *and* **Newcastle-under-Lyme.**

Isaak Waltons Cottage

East of Mill Meece and across the M5, lies **Stone,** *a thriving and good-looking town. Two local stories account for the name; some say it comes from a cairn of stones that marked the graves of two Christian Mercian princes murdered by their pagan   father, while others maintain it derives from a mineral-rich local stream that petrifies plant life. Whatever the truth, the area has been inhabited for a long time - as shown by the number of fine stone axe-heads found locally.*

A market town which did well out of the Canal Era (the River Trent and the Trent and Mersey Canal run parallel south of the town), Stone produced two notable figures; Admiral John Jervis, later Earl St Vincent (1735-1823) and the water-colourist Peter de Wint (1784-1849). The neat 18th-century Gothic CHURCH OF ST MICHAEL with its galleries and box pews contains a memorial to the Admiral who lies with other members of his family in a small Palladian-style Mausoleum. St Vincent was a remarkable man, to whom the Royal Navy owes much. His abilities of leadership and unrivalled judgment led to numerous victories, including the crushing defeat of the Spaniards at Cape St Vincent, whilst his humanity and breadth of vision contributed to major reforms in conditions afloat and the health of seamen in general. He was also an unrivalled judge of character, and amongst his many proteges was a young man called Horâtio Nelson. In his old age, St Vincent faced ceaseless appeals from poverty-stricken old shipmates and their families, and more than lived up to his quiet statement 'I never yet have forsaken any man who served well under me'.

Stone has a number of notable buildings including the church (which is sited by the ruins of a mediaeval priory); Henry Holland, architect to the Prince Regent, designed the CROWN HOTEL and there is a fine gabled brick RAILWAY STATION of 1848. GRANVILLES in Granville Square is set in a row of attractive small houses, and was once the Corn Exchange. Now it is a successful and attractive restaurant and wine bar, complete with a charming, and award-winning, garden.

A. W. Pugin (1812-1852) was a talented young architect who designed and modelled much of the decorations and sculpture for the Houses of Parliament. Converted to Catholicism, he worked largely within that faith and designed the chapel of ST MARY'S ABBEY at **Oulton,** *a Benedictine convent originally founded in the 17th century in Ghent, Belgium, and which moved to England in 1794.*

Oulton is just to the north of Stone, and at DOWNS BANK the National Trust owns and manages an area of beautiful undulating moorland, presented to the Trust in 1946 as a war memorial. There's nothing like fresh air to wet the appetite, and at THE WHEATSHEAF in Oulton, the attractive pub has a first class restaurant in addition to a welcoming and friendly bar.

South down the A34 brings us to the county town of **Stafford,** *the city constructed on the site of a hermitage built by St Bertelin some 1200 years ago. Commercial development has left the town surprisingly untouched - apart from the jutting intrusion of a few tower blocks. Stafford still wears the bucolic air of a country town even though it has been an important manufacturing centre for centuries; manufacturing internal combustion engines and electrical equipment since the beginning of the present century. Nevertheless its ancient heritage is on proud display for all to admire.*

STAFFORD CASTLE sited on a hill outside the town and built in 1070, is an impressive example of an early Norman fortress, constructed of earth and timber, with a second stone structure built on the site in the early 1300's. Most of this was destroyed in the Civil War when Parliamentarian forces captured the Castle - the defending forces were led by the Dowager Lady Stafford. In the last century, an eccentric heir to the ruins attempted to rebuild but the scheme was never completed and the building abandoned. However, thanks to intervention by Stafford Borough Council, the site has been brought alive through thorough archeological investigation and there is now a purpose-built Visitor Centre with video displays, models and a fully reconstructed guardroom of the original timber fortress.

The central building in Stafford is the late Georgian SHIRE HALL, a most handsome building that fits the part well, while not far away is a positive triumph of the timber house-builders art, THE HIGH HOUSE. Built in 1595 for a wool merchant, John Dorrington, it is the largest timber-framed town house in the country. In 1642, both King Charles I and Prince Rupert stayed here, and the fortunes of war are reflected in the fact that in the following year the house was used as a prison for captured Royalist officers and as a garrison for the Parliamentarians. It has over 8000 square feet of floor space, excluding the cellars, and has been lovingly restored to act as a heritage and exhibition centre.

Stafford High House

Further evidence of Stafford's past can be inspected in the 18th-century surrounds of the WILLIAM SALT LIBRARY, in Eastgate Street, where a comprehensive and valuable collection of books, drawings, documents and engravings are displayed.

Another fine old building but with a very modern use is the GATEHOUSE THEATRE COMPLEX, a clever conversion housing an extremely well-equipped arts and entertainment centre which bills itself as 'Stafford's most flexible venue' - being able to host conferences, stage plays and concerts, produce and edit in video and sound, show films and offer facilities for receptions. There is even a pub, THE GLOBE TAVERN.

CHETWYND HOUSE, a handsome Georgian building that is now the Post Office, was once the home of William Horton, a leading shoe manufacturer. Here the ebullient playwright, theatre-manager and MP for Stafford, Richard Brinsley Sheridan, would stay on visits to his constituency. Records show that being a politician in those days must have required all his considerable charm and theatrical talents - not to mention money. The accounts for the 1780 election show that it cost him the huge sum of £1000; this included large numbers of bribes accounted for in the form of vouchers for 'Dinner and six quarts of ale', 2 guineas each to clergymen's widows and a 5 guinea subscription to the Infirmary. This may have been a reference to SIR MARTIN HOEL'S ALMSHOUSES, in Mill Street, founded by an earlier MP in 1660. The Almshouses have been extensively modernised and are still in use today.

Due west of Stafford, on the very tip of Cannock Chase, is SHUGBOROUGH ESTATE, ancestral home of the camera-wielding Earl of Lichfield. A beautiful mansion, dating back to 1693, and set within a magnificent 900-acre estate, Shugborough contains fine collections of 18th-century ceramics, silver, paintings and French furniture. The house was remodelled in 1794 by Samuel Wyatt for George Anson, first Viscount Lichfield, but the house had been given its most radical rebuild in the 1760's when Thomas Anson was left a fortune by his younger brother, George. It is a strange coincidence that two of the most influential and important naval commanders of the 18th century, St Vincent and Anson, should both have come from this land-locked county. Admiral Lord Anson, circumnavigator and First Lord of the Admiralty was responsible for the great revival of the Royal Navy in the mid-18th century and died childless in 1762. His fortune came from prize-money (the monies made from capture of enemy ships and their cargo; on his voyage around the world he had captured a Spanish treasure ship of which the cargo was valued at £500,000 in 1743, and which was paraded in triumph through the City of London in thirty-two wagons). Such triumph had its price - of the men who set out on the voyage, only four died as a result of enemy action, but over 1300 died from disease.

THE STAFFORDSHIRE COUNTY MUSEUM is housed in the old servants quarters and there are splendid recreations of life 'behind the green baize door'. SHUGBOROUGH PARK FARM is a working agricultural museum where rare breeds are kept, horse-drawn machinery used and an old mill grinds corn. The wonderful gardens and parkland feature a series of eight monuments of architectural importance, reflecting the influence of classical Greek and Oriental architecture and decoration on the period.

Rugeley is another old market town, and ideally situated to explore CANNOCK CHASE. An attractive and friendly community with a faintly Victorian air, Rugeley was, in the 16th century, the northernmost outpost of that vast community of smiths who worked the iron ingots produced by the Black Country; metal craftsmen who made agricultural implements, bits, spurs, locks and nails in small coal-fied forges, often in their own homes. Further prosperity came to the town with the arrival of the Trent and Mersey Canal. The hustle and bustle of those days have long gone, but the canal now provides the ideal setting for THE ASH TREE, a splendid water-side pub with its own moorings and an attractive and ornate interior.

Whether you arrive by canal or by car, CANNOCK CHASE remains the greatest attraction of the region. As its name implies, it was once a Royal hunting-ground, but Richard I sold it to the Bishops of Lichfield (apparently he needed the money to go crusading). In those times, it was a much larger area, extending from the River Penk in the west to the Trent in the east, with Stafford to the north and including Wolverhampton and Walsall to the south. Now it is around 26 square miles of forest and heath land that have been declared an 'area of outstanding natural beauty'. Mediaeval industrial activities meant the loss of much of the native oakwoods while the southern part was given over to coalpits, but these activities have long ceased and the deer and wildlife have returned to their natural habitat. The highest point is at CASTLE RING with wonderful views over the *countryside and the site of an Iron-Age hill fort, dating from around 500BC. Information on the history and wildlife of the Chase can be found in the FOREST AND DEER MUSEUMS, Birches Valley, near Rugeley. Picnic spots, trails and walks abound.*

Deer at Cannock Chase

Close to the eastern side of Cannock Chase lies the ancient city of Lichfield with its unique CATHEDRAL OF ST MARY AND ST CHAD, a magnificent red sandstone structure with three spires, known as 'the Ladies of the Vale'. The Cathedral is considered the Mother Church of the Midlands and is the third building on the site since the first was consecrated in 700AD by St Chad. The present structure is a magnificent example of Early English and Decorated work, a triumph of the mediaeval craftsman's skill. It is staggering to think all this was created with only the simplest of tools and assembled with the most elementary of mechanical aids, such as crude timber scaffolding and blocks and tackles. Construction began in 1195 and ended thirty years later, although the ornate west front was built in the amazingly short period of five years. The interior does not disappoint, being equally ornate but delicately graceful with the Lady Chapel being the piece de resistance, with seven of the nine great windows filtering light through glorious 16th-century glass brought over from Herkenrode Abbey, near Liege. The indefagitable Gilbert Scott undertook the restoration of the Cathedral during the last century, although extensive works were required in 1662 after the great building had been savaged in the Civil War. The results say much for the skill and sympathy of all those concerned with such works. Numerous memorials and tombs are to be found, including busts of Samuel Johnson and David Garrick.

The surrounds of the Cathedral are equally beautiful with attractive houses of the 14th and 15th centuries surrounding the green lawns of VICAR'S CLOSE. We have to be thankful that so much of the glories of Lichfield still miraculously survive, for the fighting during the Civil War was particularly fierce in this area.

Samuel Johnson (1709-1784) best described as critic, poet, journalist, dictionary writer, biographer and wit, was Lichfield's most famous son and in Breadmarket Street is THE SAMUEL JOHNSON BIRTHPLACE MUSEUM. In the cobbled square outside stands his statue, facing across to that of his one-time pupil, the famous actor-manager, David Garrick. Further literary connections are to be found in the GEORGE INN, in Bird Street, where the playwright George Farquhar stayed in 1704, immortalising the ball-room in his comedy 'The Beaux Stratagem'. Around the corner is 18th-century DONEGAL HOUSE, containing the 'Lichfield Sketchbook' Exhibition, presenting Lichfield by means of graphics, historical characters and period settings and music. Further information on the past can be found at the LICHFIELD HERITAGE EXHIBITION in Market Square.

To the south-east of the town there is the MUSEUM OF THE STAFFORDSHIRE REGIMENT at Whittington Barracks, with eight of the thirteen VC's won by the Regiment on display, while 2 miles to the south-west there is the WALL ROMAN SITE, where soldiers of an earlier period once lived.

The A38 leads north-east from Lichfield, passing by the neat little village of **Barton under Needwood** (a reference to the other great Royal hunting-grounds of the Needwood Forest). In the nave of the church is a coat of arms with an unusual device; that of a shield with three babes' heads. The church was the gift of a Dr John Taylor in 1533. He was one of triplets, born to a country tailor and his wife, an event so unusual that the children were presented to Henry VII. The King was so taken with this exemplary example of fertility, that he paid for their education, and John Taylor took full advantage of the *opportunity and rose to become Archdeacon of Derby and Buckingham and Master of the Rolls. Just opposite the church is THE SHOULDER OF MUTTON, a fine country pub only a century younger than the church and everything a good local should be.*

Pubs mean beer and beer means **Burton-upon-Trent.** *The brewing capital of England has been about its convivial business for a very long time; monks from the vanished Abbey brewed ale noted for its excellence in mediaeval times. With the Dissolution, private enterprise moved in to exploit the high quality of the local well water, and small breweries were established. Although the product was considered second to none, prohibitively high transport costs made it difficult to enlarge the market until the Trent was made navigable. Export began to boom, with demand for Burton's ales coming from the most unlikely places - the Empress Catherine the Great of Russia was said to have been 'immoderately fond' of the beverage, and the opening of the Trent and Mersey Canal made it possible to satisfy the demands of Empire, with 'India Pale Ale' being specially formulated to survive the long journey from Liverpool to the 'Jewel in the Crown'. The demand for the products of Messrs Allsop, Bass and Worthington was so great that the major London breweries, such as Inde Coope, Truman and Charrington, were forced to move up to Burton in order to exploit the gypsum-rich waters themselves.*

The town is surprisingly attractive for what is, in effect, a major industrial centre and one that has been in an almost continual state of development over the centuries. Compact, with a number of good Georgian and Victorian buildings, the centre of the city has two fine statues; one of a cooper making a barrel and the other of Michael Arthur Bass, first Lord Burton. The major brewing families all contributed handsomely to the town that made them wealthy, but the Bass family outdid them all - streets of houses, the splendid Victorian Gothic Town Hall and no less than four dignified and handsome churches.

THE BASS MUSEUM, VISITOR CENTRE AND SHIRE HORSE STABLES in Horninglow Street is a fine way to get to know the town and its industry, and so is the HERITAGE BREWERY MUSEUM, in Anglesey Road. Both museums have exhibitions and displays devoted to the gentle art of making beer and naturally sampling is encouraged!

An old custom, whose origins are lost in the proverbial mists of time, is to be found at **Abbots Bromley,** *a small and ancient market town which lies due west of Burton-upon-Trent. In the church are to be found several sets of reindeer antlers. Once a year, on the first Sunday after the 4th September, the famous HORN DANCE is enacted. Six men wearing the antlers, accompanied by a Maid, a Jester, a Hobby Horse and two boys, one carrying a crossbow and the other a triangle, set out from the church porch on a 20-mile circuit of the local farms, performing the dance wherever they stop. No-one really knows the origin of this strange ritual, but it was recorded in Norman times and is thought to be far older than that - and why reindeer antlers? Whatever the answer, Abbots Bromley is worth visiting whether the dance is being performed or not; an extremely attractive village with some fine half-timbered houses, it is set in the beautiful countryside of the* **Blythe Valley.** *Edinburgh House, in Bagot Street, contains THE PUPPET THEATRE MUSEUM, a fascinating collection of hundreds of puppets, costumes and equipment.*

Northwards is that mecca for Midlands racing fans, **Uttoxeter.** *The cheerful little market (every Wednesday since 1309) town has three different ways of pronouncing its name - 'Uxeter', 'Utcheter' or 'U-tox-eter' - and its name has been spelt in seventy-seven different ways since first recorded in the Domesday Book as Wotocheshede. The town evidently suffers no neuroses as a result of all this confusion, but sits four-square in the delightful countryside and goes about its quiet business, waking up for market days and race meetings at UTTOEXETER RACECOURSE, home of the Midlands Grand National. Racing fans are a convivial crowd and the handsome old ROEBUCK INN is ideally situated to offer hospitality to them and to any other passer-by, being a mere half-mile from the Racecourse and five minutes' walk from the Market Place. It was here, at the age of 70, that Dr Johnson stood bareheaded in the rain for several hours; a penance for the fact that, as a boy, he had steadfastly refused to help his father behind his bookstall that stood on the spot. Many displays of historical interest and a reconstruction of an Edwardian shop-window (complete with prices!) can be found in the excellent little UTTOXETER HERITAGE CENTRE, an award-winning conversion of 17th-century timber framed cottages in Carter Street.*

In the pretty little village of **Stramshall,** *just to the north of Uttoxeter, is the fine 400-year-old HARE AND HOUNDS INN.*

Once a coaching inn serving the busy routes to Derby, Stoke-on-Trent, and Stafford, it is now a quiet and peaceful place, providing good food and accommodation and rightly popular.

In the northern half of the county the hills become steeper and the rich pasture land is no longer in evidence. The north-eastern quadrant possesses countryside that is the equal of Wales or the Borders for a sense of wild remoteness, whilst the north-west is dominated by the industries of the Potteries and the high bleak moorland that divides Staffordshire from Cheshire. If the Cannock Chase acts as a 'playground' for the West Midlands, then the north-east of Staffordshire performs a similar function for the north-west, and, in one particular instance, for the entire country.

Set in the deep and craggily attractive Churnet Valley, ALTON TOWERS is unquestionably the UK's premier theme park with over two million visitors a year and contains more than 120 different rides and attractions spread over 200 acres of wonderful landscaped gardens. The story behind these amazing statistics is equally remarkable; the Talbots, Earls of Shrewsbury, acquired the estate by marriage in the 15th century, but never lived there until the 15th Earl, a shy and romantic man, moved there in the late 1790's, attracted by the grandeur of the countryside. By the time of his death in 1827, he had laid out the magnificent gardens with their walls, terraces, pools, lakes and staircases and had transformed the modest farmhouse into the great house he named Alton Abbey. His nephew, who inherited the title, carried on the works and was ably assisted by A. W. Pugin. The house was renamed Alton Towers. One Earl later, after a family wrangle involving the inheritance, the contents of the house were put up for sale in order to pay the legal fees. Some idea of the scale of the house's contents can be gauged by the fact that the auction, in 1857, took place over 29 days! Another four Earls were to inherit before the estate was finally sold to a group of local businessmen in 1924, who invested much time and money into improving the gardens and the grounds for public use. We tend to think of Alton Towers as a late 20th-century attraction, but it has been open to the public - with entertainments - since the days of the 18th Earl, in 1860. By the 1890's, Alton was attracting crowds of over 30,000 to watch acrobats, lion tamers, elephants, bands and firework displays. Alton Towers now belongs to a major public company who have invested millions in up-dating and renovating the whole truly incredible enterprise. The modern 'white-knuckle' rides *are the equal - if not better - than anywhere in the world and the latest in technology is employed in the various attractions such as Gloomy Wood, Fantasy World, and the Festival Park. A large proportion of the attractions are sensibly under cover and there are a variety of shops, restaurants, theatres and exhibits to choose from. The wonderful gardens and wooded estate continue to provide a marvellous setting.*

The Corkscrew, Alton Towers

The surrounding countryside is an attraction in its own right and the National Trust owns and manages land at **Hawksmoor** and **Toothill Wood. Oakamoor,** a delightful small community lying a mile or so to the north-west of Alton, is a popular spot with those touring and walking in the area as well as visitors to The Towers. THE LORD NELSON HOTEL is the village inn, and is a most cheerful, welcoming and friendly institution. As well as the one-eyed Admiral on the inn-sign, there is another tenuous connection with the sea - the first cross-channel telephone cable was made here at the Boulton Copper Works.

There is a tendency to think of the **Peak District** as belonging exclusively to Derbyshire, but natural physical features have a distressing habit of ignoring man-made boundaries, and there is more than a little truth in the local boast that 'the best parts of Derbyshire are in Staffordshire'. . . . This is fascinating countryside, almost cosy in scale one minute, then possessed of a wild grandeur the next. North-east of Oakmoor, through the hills and dales, lies one of the most beautiful valleys in the region, THE MANIFOLD VALLEY. The village of **Ilam,** standing at the southern end, makes a good starting point for exploring the area, and the old mansion,. ILAM HALL, is now a Youth Hostel. The Valley is relatively flat at this point but becomes increasingly deep and narrow as one journeys northwards. The RIVER MANIFOLD has a disconcerting habit of disappearing underground and at Ilam Hall, it re-emerges from its subterranean journey from **Darfur Crags.**

The rambling roads that wander, seemingly haphazardly, up the valley join the B5053 near **Butterton,** a stone-built village in stone-wall country and beautifully described as having 'the charm of the forgotten, the unsophisticated, and the remote'. Surrounding the Victorian church with its tall spire, the houses and farms spread out over the dramatic landscape, Butterton can be a popular spot and 'far from forgotten' when the weather is fine; but in winter, in common with the rest of the region, the setting is bold and dramatic.

Fine weather or foul, THE BLACK LION INN is everything you could wish for; food, accommodation, situation and hospitality ensure that this 18th-century establishment is rated highly by all those who make their way to the southern Peak District. The village is also home to another enterprise, THE MANIFOLD VALLEY ARTS AND CRAFTS CENTRE. Housed in an old school, the Centre displays superb selections of knitware, ceramics and original works of art.

The neat 'estate' village of **Warslow,** with its glorious views of the surrounding country, is a mile to the east of Butterton, and was once a coaching stop on the route from Buxton to Uttoxeter. It must have been a wonderful journey when the weather was fine and the roads dry, but one shudders to think what conditions must have been like in the depths of winter. Having arrived in the small village, passengers, coachmen (and horses!) must have blessed the cosy warmth of THE GREYHOUND INN. Still dispensing welcome hospitality two centuries later, the Greyhound (which was the name of the Stagecoach) is popular with both travellers and locals alike.

Obviously, this beautiful area has long been a favourite with those who love what is described in the glossy-brochure-trade as 'The

Great Outdoors' - even if writers of such hyperbole rarely get nearer to the fresh air than kicking the cat out last thing at night. Over three hundred years ago, two learned gentlemen, close friends and 'Brothers of the Angle' rambled the length and breadth of the glorious river valleys in pursuit of the shy brook trout. Izaak Walton and Charles Cotton could discuss the Classical poetry of Homer or the merits of a fishing lure with equal facility and enthusiasm, and had a particular fondness for the river that runs down the border between Staffordshire and Derbyshire, the Dove. Cotton, who was to contribute a chapter on the art of fly-fishing in Walton's 'Compleat Angler' was a poet and author in his own right who lived at Beresford Hall near **Alstonfield**. The Hall was pulled down in the 1800's but the fishing lodge by the river still survives, and the village church still contains the Cotton family pew.

Fishing is still a matter for much learned - not to mention heated - debate, best undertaken in the comfortable surrounds of a friendly hostelry; Alstonfield provides the venue in the shape of THE GEORGE, a local pub for over 250 years. Not only anglers, but walkers, climbers, naturalists and campers (the George has its own year-round camp site) enjoy the atmosphere of this well-run and most welcoming pub.

Longnor is a tiny market town in the farthermost corner of north-eastern Staffordshire on the same road that the intrepid Greyhound rattled its way across the rutted and pot-holed road over the moors. The road may have improved, but Longnor is little altered; good-looking 18th-century facades and a square with a small Market Hall dated 1873. Stone-lined streets and alleyways with determined little houses of the same material give a sense of dogged continuity, yet change - and welcome change at that - has taken place; tucked discreetly down narrow Chapel Street is PARROTTS BISTRO RESTAURANT. Authentic French cuisine is now dispensed with flair and imagination from attractive premises that not long ago were the semi-derelict remains of a 17th-century inn.

Wandering westwards one comes across the highest village in England, set close by the high road from Leek to Buxton. The oddly-named **Flash** claims the title at 1,158 feet above sea-level. A Nepalese would doubtless fall off his mountain laughing, but it is a respectable height for our 'sceptr'd isle' and probably just as cold in winter as the Himalayas.

The road heads south, through the popular climbing area of the Roaches and continues over undulating countryside covered with seemingly endless stone walls, testimony to the hill-farmer's dogged determination to wrest a living from the thick acid soil. One can only admire the effort and determination that went into their creation, and which still goes into their upkeep. **Thorncliffe,** to the east of the south-bound road is another community which has survived as testimony to this courageous obstinacy. A delightful and quiet backwater established within the wonderful scenery of the region, it has long forgotten the rumbustious days of mining and enclosure, the link between ancient and modern being continued in the handsome interior of THE RED LION INN. Good panelling, together with brass, copper and exposed beams, make this old pub a great favourite with those fortunates who visit the area. Incidentally, should you see a wallaby hop by - don't worry; unlikely as it seems, a colony has existed here for many years. The beer is good but not that good . . .

'The Metropolis of the Moorland' was how one writer described **Leek,** though Dr Johnson was not so charitable 'An old church but a poor town'. Nowadays, it is a neat mill town standing in magnificent countryside. Its origins are ancient if somewhat fragmentary; there are Saxon preaching crosses in the churchyard of the CHURCH OF ST EDWARD THE CONFESSOR (a 16th-century building with an extraordinary 18th-century tiered gallery) but Domesday makes no mention of a church on the site. William the Conqueror's nephew was the first Norman to own the domain. Known as Hugh the Fat, his greed was unlikely to have allowed any form of commerce to flourish; however, matters improved over the centuries and real prosperity arrived in the 18th century with the introduction of the silk, hosiery and dyeing industries. Mills and factories were built and the little community rapidly expanded to become a substantial yet good-looking industrial town. Like so many of its kind, Leek has a cheerful and generous nature and welcomes visitors; particularly on Wednesdays when the old cobbled market square is thronged with stalls and the air filled with cheerful banter. There are a surprisingly large number of antique shops and many of the mills have their own shops. On the whole, buildings are good-looking and substantial; the best to be seen in and around the area of St Edward Street. There are some pretty almshouses, founded in 1676, and a fine Dutch-influenced inn from the same period, THE QUIET WOMAN. Once upon a time, this was the meeting-place of a secret society which did not remain secret for long due to the indiscretion of an inquisitive and *gossipy barmaid. To discourage further revelations, the society took the somewhat drastic step of removing the poor girl's head from her body, resulting in the somewhat gruesome inn-sign and the name of the pub - or so the story goes. Customers and barmaids need have no such fears today, and The Quiet Woman is a popular pub offering good food at remarkably good prices.*

*The great canal-builder, Brindley, started his working life as a mill-wright and THE BRINDLEY MILL, in Mill Street, tells the story of his life and graphically demonstrates the many facets of this once important craft. One of his later works was the CALDON CANAL, which runs with the River Churnet in the valley alongside the hillside village of **Cheddleton**. CHEDDLETON FLINT MILL ground up flints from Kent and Sussex for use in the pottery industry, and the waterwheels and grinding equipment are on display, together with other items associated with the trade, including a restored canal barge. Today's canal boats and their crews, along with many other visitors to the area, make use of the hospitable facilities offered by THE RED LION, an attractive 18th-century establishment situated beside the canal on the Cheadle Road. The canal's successor, the railway, is also commemorated at the CHEDDLETON RAILWAY CENTRE, with displays, mementoes, engines and other paraphernalia set in and around the attractive Victorian station.*

*The two different forms of transport were obviously of major importance to the development of the industries of the north-western sector of the county. **Newcastle-under-Lyme** and **Stoke-on-Trent** lie side-by-side, geographically close yet separate in terms of history and character.*

*Coming from the east, the first is Stoke-on-Trent, a combination of the six communities of **Tunstall, Burslem, Hanley, Longton, Stoke** and **Fenton** - known the world over as THE POTTERIES. The companies based here, both large and small, have a world-wide market for their products and their heritage dates back many centuries. Wherever fine china-ware is used and appreciated, names such as Spode, Copeland, Minton, Coalport, Royal Doulton and Wedgewood are revered and respected. Although archeological excavations have shown that pottery was made in the area well before the Roman Occupation, the present industry owes much to the genius of Josiah Wedgewood (1730-1795), whose originality and drive turned a craft* *into an industry and who established the first proper factory in the region.*

Wedgewood Vase, Wedgewood Visitor Centre

The Potteries must have had much of the flavour of the Black Country in their heyday, with smoke belching from the bottle-shaped kilns; fire by night, smoke by day. However, unlike the Black Country, Stoke and its fellow towns (they still retain a strong individuality) continue in the same trade that first brought them to prominence. Newer and cleaner methods of powering kilns have been introduced, the smoke and industrial grime have been vanished away, but the product remains; dozens of concerns, large and small, turn out every conceivable form of pottery from lavatory pans to the most delicately-modelled porcelain figurines. Nearly all the major works have their museums, devoted to their own particular heritage and specialities, but perhaps the best perspective of the region's history can be gained in the STOKE-ON-TRENT CITY MUSEUM AND ART GALLERY. From here tours set out to cover the dozens of factories (and their shops) still in operation. It seems invidious to single out any in particular, but THE ETRURIA INDUSTRIAL MUSEUM is where Wedgewood first started mass-production, and THE GLADSTONE POTTERY MUSEUM, working 18th-century pottery with equipment and demonstrations should not be missed. Before the advent of gas and electricity, coal was the principal source of heat for the kilns and THE CHATTERLEY WHITFIELD MINING MUSEUM is fast becoming one of the major tourist attractions in the area, enabling visitors to be guided through the underground workings in the company of ex-miners and to inspect the machinery and equipment used through the ages.

The Potteries have the flavour of a rural area; a feeling of continuity and a sense of tradition. The same family names crop up time and again and, even in these difficult times, there is a pride in achievement and product. For all this, the city does not stay rooted in the past and has made enormous efforts to clean up the detritus of yesteryear and make Stoke an attractive place in which to work and live. TRENTHAM GARDENS cover over 800 acres of parklands, gardens and lakes with numerous sporting facilities. FESTIVAL PARK is an amazing 23-acre complex which includes a sub-tropical aquatic playground with flumes, water-slides and rapids.

The architecture is predominantly Victorian red-brick since the city was in a constant state of development, but there are exceptions; the Minton family brought over French artists to decorate their wares and built them ornate Italianate villas - their sense of geography being obviously inferior to their business acumen. However, both Italian and French influences of another kind can be sampled at IL MAGO, a stylish and totally delightful restaurant in Cobridge Road, Hanley.

Mow Cop, Newcastle-under-Lyme

321

Newcastle-under-Lyme is the oldest of the two cities, dating back to its incorporation as a borough in 1180, at a time when the neighbouring Potteries were hamlets or villages. Lyme was the name given to the ancient forest that once covered the region and the 'new' castle has long disappeared, along with the old - once a Roman fort. Although Stoke-on-Trent and Newcastle have grown into each other, they still retain their distinct identities; the delicate craft of the Potteries being complemented by the ruder skills of the iron workers and colliers of their older neighbour. Modern Newcastle is an attractive town with much good architecture and is host to KEELE UNIVERSITY. Markets and a fair date from mediaeval times and further entertainment is on offer at THE NEW VICTORIA THEATRE. THE BOROUGH MUSEUM AND ART GALLERY features collections of ceramics, textiles, weapons, clocks and toys, and for a view of the town's industrial past visit SPRINGWOOD BLAST FURNACES, off Audley Road.

Jambo the chimpanzee - Twycross Zoo

The surrounding countryside is immensely attractive with villages containing much good domestic architecture and a number of beautiful gardens (such as the DOROTHY CLIVE GARDENS at **Willoughbridge***) and country parks liked BATHPOOL PARK,* **Kidsgrove.** *and colliers of their older neighbour. Modern Newcastle is an attractive town with much good architecture and is host to*

KEELE UNIVERSITY. Markets and a fair date from mediaeval times and further entertainment is on offer at THE NEW VICTORIA THEATRE. THE BOROUGH MUSEUM AND ART GALLERY features collections of ceramics, textiles, weapons, clocks and toys, and for a view of the town's industrial past visit SPRINGWOOD BLAST FURNACES, off Audley Road.

The surrounding countryside is immensely attractive with villages containing much good domestic architecture and a number of beautiful gardens (such as the DOROTHY CLIVE GARDENS at Willoughbridge) and country parks liked BATHPOOL PARK, Kidsgrove.

Staffordshire is a little-known county of remarkable contrast, interest and beauty that will repay the curious a thousandfold.

THE GEORGE
Public House

Alstonfield,
Nr. Ashbourne,
Derbyshire.

Tel: (033527) 205

In lovely countryside six miles north of Ashbourne off the A515 is the little village of Alstonfield. Nothing disturbs its peace too much, apart from the visitors who come to enjoy the many wonderful walks and the scenery in what has become known as Isaak Walton country. In the midst of the village is its focal point, The George which has been caring for travellers and local people for over 250 years. It is a simple, happy and comfortable pub in which Richard and Sue Grandjean have been mine hosts for almost thirty years.

There is little the Grandjeans do not know about the area and they are happy to share their knowledge with their customers. There are all year round camping facilities attached to the pub which attract many families. They take themselves off during the day to explore and return in the evening to enjoy the hospitality and the fun in the bar. Chatsworth House and Haddon Hall are within striking distance and so are Alton Towers and Tittersworth Reservoir. For those who like golf, Buxton Golf Club welcomes visitors.

Whatever you choose to eat at The George will be home cooked using fresh produce. The order for all meals is taken at the Kitchen Door, which makes it homely and friendly. Brown Bread is used for the fresh and well filled sandwiches, a selection of home-made puddings is listed on the Kitchen Door every day. It is a delightful place and good value.

USEFUL INFORMATION

OPEN: 11-2.30pm & 6-11pm
Sun: All day
CHILDREN: Welcome
CREDIT CARDS: None taken
LICENSED: Full Licence
ACCOMMODATION: Not applicable

RESTAURANT: Not applicable
BAR FOOD: Good value.
Home-cooked
VEGETARIAN: Varied
ACCESS FOR THE DISABLED:
Easy access
GARDEN: Beer garden. Village
green & garden

THE SHOULDER OF MUTTON

16 Main Street,
Barton-Under-Needwood,
Staffordshire.

Public House

Tel: (0283) 712568

Barton-under-Needwood is a charming village in the heart of the Staffordshire countryside, just off the A38 and near the canal. In its midst is The Shoulder of Mutton, a much loved village inn, used regularly by the locals. Owned and run by Steve Jackson and Nicky Coombes, it is a welcoming place in which strangers are rapidly made to feel at home. The building is old, probably dating back as far as the 17th century and it is full of character. Oak beams, old pictures and memorabilia decorate the walls. It is comfortable and unpretentious; somewhere to relax, enjoy a pint, have some good conversation and tuck into a meal that will delight your taste buds and do no harm to your bank balance.

This is a pub to visit all the year round, but in summer you have the added bonus of being able to sit out in the garden, watching the children occupy themselves safely in the play area, whilst you relish a glass of chilled white wine.

The menu has many familiar dishes and you can eat here seven days a week either at lunchtime or in the evenings. The chef has a gift for making light pastry and his Pigeon Pie is probably the best you will ever taste. He is a stickler about the need to use fresh produce and every dish is prepared to order. Bar snacks are readily available and there are several dishes for vegetarians.

USEFUL INFORMATION

OPEN: Mon-Thurs: 11-2.30pm & 5-11pm
   Fri/Sat: 11-11pm
   Sun: 12-2.30pm & 7-10.30pm
CHILDREN: Yes. Play area with swings
CREDIT CARDS: None taken
LICENSED: Full Licence
   Selection of wines
ACCOMMODATION: Not applicable

RESTAURANT: Not applicable
BAR FOOD: Wide range. Daily
   specials
VEGETARIAN: Daily selection
ACCESS FOR THE DISABLED: Yes
GARDEN: Yes, with tables &
   benches

THE BLACK LION
Inn

Butterton, Nr. Leek,
Staffordshire

Tel: (0538) 304232

Mentioned in many of the best guides, newspapers and magazines, The Black Lion dates from 1782 and is built of mellow stone which has aged gracefully over the centuries. It is an old fashioned place with up-to-date facilities that have been added without in anyway harming the character or the fabric of the building. Inside there are lots of small rooms to explore. A noisy Parakeet overlooks the front bar, original low beamed ceilings, gleaming brass, interesting pictures and an abundance of plants; all adding up to a charming village inn.

The Black Lion is situated in the small Conservation village of Butterton in the Peak National Park and half a mile above the glorious Manifold Valley. You will find it opposite the church with a terraced beer garden overlooking the magnificent countryside. Staying here in one of the newly decorated en-suite bedrooms is very comfortable, and a wonderful base from which to explore the many fascinating places around. There is The Manifold Valley, Chatsworth House, Trentham Gardens, the Bass Museum, Alton Towers and many more including all the Pottery Factory Shops. The pub offers a full range of excellent bar meals - you should try the delectable steak and mushroom casserole. A Carvery Restaurant is open on Friday and Saturday evenings and for Sunday Lunch. The four bars are friendly, the ale well kept and you can revel in the very happy atmosphere.

USEFUL INFORMATION

OPEN: 12-3pm except Wed
Eve: 7-11pm
CHILDREN: Welcome
CREDIT CARDS: Amex
LICENSED: Full Licence
ACCOMMODATION: 3 en-suite rooms.
2 double family rooms

RESTAURANT: Carvery. Excellent
menu
BAR FOOD: Home-made, wide
range
VEGETARIAN: Vegetarian food
available
ACCESS FOR THE DISABLED:
Not level but wide
GARDEN: Terraced with tables &
chairs

THE RED LION

Public House

Cheadle Road,
Cheddleton,
Staffordshire

Tel: (0538) 360935

You will find the 18th-century listed building, The Red Lion, in the busy village of Cheddleton on the main road between Stone and Leek. It is an ideal stopping point for anyone who wants to enjoy the countryside and take advantage of the many nearby walking trails. Golfers too use this pub because it is in close proximity to the popular Leek Golf Club.

If you have a penchant for antiques you might well consider having lunch in The Red Lion and then spend the afternoon discovering the many antique shops in Leek, for which the town is famous. Inveterate Canal lovers will find that The Caulden Canal runs along the bottom of the Patio and Childrens Play area. It is a favourite haunt of those taking a holiday on the canal because temporary moorings are available and they enjoy stepping ashore to join in the fun and hospitality to be found at the bar of The Red Lion. Howard and Sue Foster, the proprietors have only been at the pub for just over a year but during that time they have done much to improve the facilities including a ramp for wheelchairs from the canal to the bar. They have also improved the food to such an extent that it is now advisable to book lunch on Sundays if you want to enjoy this traditional meal which is incredibly good value. All the dishes are sensibly priced and cooked to order. In addition to main meals there are a wide selection of snacks and sandwiches.

USEFUL INFORMATION

OPEN: 11-3pm & 6-11pm
   Sun: 12-3pm & 7-10.30pm
CHILDREN: Welcome
CREDIT CARDS: None taken
LICENSED: Full Licence
ACCOMMODATION: Not applicable

RESTAURANT: Not applicable
BAR FOOD: Wide range.
   Home-made specials
VEGETARIAN: Always 4 & specials
ACCESS FOR THE DISABLED:
   Yes. Ramp available
GARDEN: Large with meadow.
   Play area. Patio

THE COUNTRY KITCHEN
Cafe

29, High Street,
Eccleshall,
Staffordshire

Tel: (0785) 851162

It was in 1983 that Susan Sanders and Margaret Chell opened the doors of The Country Kitchen in the High Street, for the first time. This friendly pair had identified the need for the type of establishment that they wanted to run and almost from the first day it has grown in popularity both locally and with people who visit Eccleshall.

Eccleshall is one of the prettiest places in Staffordshire and has a lot to offer anyone who cares to stay awhile and seek out its treasures. The High Street was once a coaching route from London to Chester and it has retained the charm that many a small town has lost. Its buildings, dating mainly from the 18th and 19th centuries, are distinctive and lead to the medieval sandstone church standing on higher ground between a group of fine Georgian houses and rich farmland beyond. There are many attractions nearby including Izaak Walton's Cottage in the hamlet of Shallowford and the Mill Meece Pumping Station. You will find plenty to do here and at the end of your exploration or before you start The Country Kitchen will feed you on excellent food whether it is a gigantic English Breakfast, morning coffee with home made scones, lunches which include delicious specials of the day or afternoon teas with home-made cakes that tempt everyone. If you would prefer a snack to take away this too can be dealt with. The prices are right and no one ever goes away hungry.

USEFUL INFORMATION

OPEN: Mon-Sat: 9-4.30pm
    Wed: 9-2pm
CHILDREN: Welcome
CREDIT CARDS: None taken
LICENSED: No
ACCOMMODATION: Not applicable

RESTAURANT: Breakfast, snacks,
    lunches, teas
BAR FOOD: Not applicable
VEGETARIAN: On request
ACCESS FOR THE DISABLED: No
GARDEN: No

THE ST. GEORGE HOTEL
Inn & Bistro

Castle Street,
Eccleshall,
Staffordshire.

Tel: (0785) 850300

Eccleshall is one of the prettiest, small, market towns in Staffordshire, lying between Stafford and Stoke-on-Trent. Its most comfortable and prestigious hotel, is the old coaching inn, The St. George, built in 1818. This is a privately owned and run inn whose proprietors, Gerard and Moyra Slater work hard to ensure the inn upholds its old traditions, character and atmosphere whilst allowing for the comforts of the present day. They have succeeded admirably.

The ten en suite bedrooms are luxuriously furnished and encourage people to return to stay time and time again. There is one friendly bar, an intimate and beautifully furnished restaurant plus the lively and interesting Bistro. The large car park comes into its own offering simplicity to the motorist visiting the pub; Eccleshall is not the easiest place in which to park. One of the interesting places you can visit round here is Izaak Waltons cottage in the town, another is the superb Shugborough Hall not too far away or Stapley Water Gardens.

For hungry people or those who just want a small snack, food is available all day. The choice is far ranging with everything from Barbecue Buffalo Wings to Tagliatelle Carbonara. There are Chicken dishes, Fish dishes and superb Steaks. Vegetarians have several choices, and Children a menu of their own. The sandwiches are fresh with a variety of exciting fillings. Sunday lunch is traditional and there are Daily Specials. It is all reasonably priced and good value for money.

USEFUL INFORMATION

OPEN: All day: 11am-11pm
CHILDREN: Welcome
CREDIT CARDS: All cards accepted
LICENSED: Full Licence
ACCOMMODATION: 10 en-suite
rooms

RESTAURANT: Traditional.
Pastas, steaks etc
BAR FOOD: Home-made pastas,
pies. Good value
VEGETARIAN: Always 6 dishes
ACCESS FOR THE DISABLED: Yes
GARDEN No. Large car park

IL MAGO

Italian/French Restaurant

28 Cobridge Road,
Hanley,
Stoke-on-Trent, Staffordshire

Tel: (0782) 274644

Il Mago, an imaginative and delightful restaurant, is located in the heart of the Potteries at Hanley. It is readily found with easy access to the M6, on the A53 opposite the Festival Park. It would be an ideal venue for a meal before or after visiting one of the many fascinating places closeby. You are really spoilt for choice with The City of Stoke-on-Trent Museum in Broad Street which has a Spitfire display, The Wedgwood Pottery Museum and Visitors Centre at Barlaston, Royal Doulton and The Moorcroft Pottery at Burslem and Alton Towers is nearby.

Stoke-on-Trent was the birth place of a myriad of famous people, Reginald Mitchell the designer of the Spitfire, Captain Smith of the Titanic, that great footballer, Sir Stanley Matthews, Arnold Bennett and Sir Josiah Wedgwood.

Formerly a pub, Il Mago was transformed by the present owners into this exciting restaurant, six and a half years ago.

It has a wonderful, traditional Continental ambience which beguiles you into relaxation and a readiness for a super meal. A drink at the Reception Bar whilst you study the extensive menu gives you time to soak in the atmosphere. The choice is difficult because it is all so tempting. Only fresh produce is used. There is a large selection of fresh fish, prime meats, for example. The choice is yours.

USEFUL INFORMATION

OPEN: Mon-Sat: 12-2pm & 7-10.30pm
CHILDREN: Welcome
CREDIT CARDS: Visa/Access/
Master/Amex
LICENSED: Full Licence
ACCOMMODATION: Not applicable

RESTAURANT: Classic, Modern,
Italian, French
BAR FOOD: Not applicable
VEGETARIAN: Minimum 4 dishes
ACCESS FOR THE DISABLED:
Level. Step to toilet
GARDEN: Not applicable

THE QUIET WOMAN

Public House

St Edward Street,
Leek,
Staffordshire

Tel: (0538) 382544

Leek is one of those places that attracts many people for different reasons. One of them is the excellence of the Antique shops. Another should be to discover an interesting pub in St Edward Street, The Quiet Woman, one of only two pubs in the whole of the country to bear this name. In this one Denise and Michael Williams are mine hosts. In the short time they have been here they have made many friends, acquired a considerable following and spent both time and money on gently refurbishing this 17th century building to bring it up to their standards.

The Quiet Woman is definitely haunted and the spirit has made her presence felt on many occasions - she probably is interested in the changes that are taking place and maybe resents them. The name of the pub, which is unusual to say the least, is rumoured to have come about because of an indiscreet barmaid who relayed the secret conversations of Bulls who used the pub as a meeting place. Her reward was to lose her head. Perhaps it is she who haunts the pub.

The menu consisting of good pub grub is wide ranging and ridiculously low in price. You can get a three course Sunday lunch for less than a fiver! Open sandwiches are very popular and very generously filled. Vegetarians are catered for with a whole range of dishes. Quiz nights are held on Tuesdays and Sundays and in the summer you can enjoy a drink in the pretty courtyard. This is certainly a value for money pub.

USEFUL INFORMATION

OPEN: 11.30-2.30pm & 7-11pm
CHILDREN: Welcome
CREDIT CARDS: None taken
LICENSED: Full Licence
ACCOMMODATION: Not applicable

RESTAURANT: Not applicable
BAR FOOD: Varied, wholesome, good value
VEGETARIAN: Comprehensive menu
ACCESS FOR THE DISABLED: Easy access
GARDEN: Courtyard with seating

THE PARROTTS

Bistro Restaurant

5, Chapel Street,
Longnor, Buxton,
Derbyshire

Tel: (0298) 83521

Longnor is all that one would expect of a typical English village. Close to Buxton, it is picturesque enough to delight both professional and amateur photographers, and yet lively enough to support one of the most interesting eating places in Derbyshire. In a conservation area with a cobbled street and tucked away between the church and the market place is The Parrotts Bistro Restaurant, a venue that has endeared itself to locals as well as the many visitors who once having discovered it continue to beat a path to its doors.

Parrotts was once an old inn built somewhere about 1640. By 1989 it was just about derelict until it was given a new lease of life and was transformed into an authentic French restaurant which acquired a first-class reputation very quickly. Since then there have been more developments which have included the opening of the popular Bar-Bistro. Run by the husband and wife team, Paul and Audrey Jones it thrives and delights everyone.

Dining here is a gastronomic experience; imagine a starter of Prawn Oriental - prawns in mayonnaise with fresh ginger and orange juice followed by Chicken Veronique and rounded off with a hot chocolate fondue served with fresh fruit and marshmallows. More simply, until 6pm daily, you can enjoy snacks and sandwiches washed down by a pint of Real Ale or a glass of wine from the extensive list. Parrotts is not to be missed.

USEFUL INFORMATION

OPEN: 11am-11pm
CHILDREN: No
CREDIT CARDS: Visa / Access
LICENSED: Extensive wine list.
 Real Ale
ACCOMMODATION: Not applicable

RESTAURANT: Superb food
 prepared to order
BAR FOOD: Snacks, sandwiches
 until 6pm
VEGETARIAN: Several dishes
ACCESS FOR THE DISABLED: No
GARDEN: No. Tables on street

THE LORD NELSON
Public House & Hotel

Carr Bank,
Oakamoor, Nr Cheadle,
Staffordshire

Tel: (0538) 702242

In the heart of the small and picturesque village of Oakamoor, near Cheadle, you will find The Lord Nelson Hotel, the focal point. Local people congregate in the bars, people from surrounding areas come in for meals and regularly people come back here to stay in the comfortable rooms.

The Lord Nelson is a warm-hearted place where Glyn and Kathy Norcup are the Proprietors. This experienced, friendly couple have a vast knowledge of the area and together with their staff are more than ready to answer any questions. The pub is only one mile from Alton Towers and provides an oasis of tranquillity after a hectic day there. Several of the famous Pottery museums are close by, for example Wedgwood, Beswicks and the Gladstone Pottery. Trentham Gardens attracts a number of people. There is Croxden Abbey, lots of woodland walks, an Otter Sanctuary, Canal Boat Rides and a host of other ways to keep you occupied, all within easy distance.

The food on offer is good, traditional pub fare, well cooked and mainly home-made using local, fresh produce. There is nothing pretentious about it, the portions are generous and the price is extremely reasonable. Children enjoy the Pets Corner; the large Beer Garden is the venue for many a Barbecue on a summers day. Live entertainment every Saturday night gives great pleasure to a lot of people. It is a very happy place.

USEFUL INFORMATION

OPEN: 12-4pm & 7-11pm
CHILDREN: Welcome. Childrens menu
CREDIT CARDS: None taken
LICENSED: Full Licence
ACCOMMODATION: Double rooms
& family

RESTAURANT: Traditional,
home-cooked
BAR FOOD: Wide selection
VEGETARIAN: Always 4 dishes
ACCESS FOR THE DISABLED: Yes
GARDEN: Large beer garden

THE WHEATSHEAF
Public House & Restaurant

Kibbleston Road,
Oulton, Stone,
Staffordshire

Tel: (0785) 812767

The Manifold Valley is home to several pretty villages and one of these is Oulton, close to the busy little town of Stone. It is close to the Wedgwood Vistor Centre, the Potteries, Cannock Chase and Barlaston Downs. This makes it an ideal place to visit before setting out to see any of these places or simply to enjoy walking in the sumptuous countryside.

In Kibbleston Road is The Wheatsheaf built in the mid Victorian era. It is a pub that has seen many changes and has recently been extended to improve its facilities. Barry and Jean Holland are the cheerful and professional hosts whose own high standards are manifest in the efficient way in which this pub is run. They are ably assisted by a talented chef and a very good restaurant manager who, between them, make lunching or dining a pleasurable experience. The restaurant has been refurbished attractively and makes an ideal setting for wedding receptions or private parties. It is equally sufficiently intimate to make dining a deux a special occasion. You will find enjoyment too in the comfort of the bar, in which not only will you get a good pint, but an excellent bar snack. The Restaurant is closed on Mondays but at other times it offers a full International A la Carte menu as well as a Table d'Hote menu. The traditional Sunday lunch is a favourite and it is advisable to book.

USEFUL INFORMATION

OPEN: 11.30-2.30pm & 6.30-11pm
CHILDREN: Welcome
CREDIT CARDS: Access/Visa
LICENSED: Full Licence
ACCOMMODATION: Not applicable

RESTAURANT: Full A La Carte & Table d'Hote. Closed Monday & Sunday evening
BAR FOOD: Wide choice. Fresh. Good value
VEGETARIAN: Always 5 dishes
ACCESS FOR THE DISABLED: Slightly limited
GARDEN: Outside seating

THE HORSE AND JOCKEY
Public House

Market Street
Penkridge,
Staffordshire.

Tel: (0785) 712602

Penkridge is famous for its markets which transform this pleasant town on Wednesdays and Saturdays, when it bustles with people, colour and excitement. A good pub is an essential ingredient to the success of these days, and no one could find a more welcoming hostelry than The Horse and Jockey in Market Street. Bob and Julie Hutchinson are the lively, welcoming proprietors. He is an ex-professional footballer used to playing at the top of his form. His energy and a desire to please is what has made the pub so popular with the regulars and the many visitors who seldom just come once.

If the hospitality of the Hutchinsons was not sufficient in itself, then the 16th-century building would appeal to anyone with its low oak beams, old floors and bits and pieces that have been passed down through the centuries, adding character and interest everywhere. In the future it is hoped to add a restaurant but in the meantime you will be extremely well fed and very comfortable eating in the bars.

Home-cooked food is the hallmark of success here. The wide range of dishes are all freshly prepared. It is simple, wholesome pub food with many of one's favourite dishes appearing on the 'Daily Special' list. If you are a vegetarian you will particularly enjoy eating at The Horse and Jockey which has no less than 10 dishes to tempt you. This is essentially a good, honest pub offering value for money.

USEFUL INFORMATION

OPEN: 11-3.30pm & 7-11pm
  All day Saturday
  Sun: 12-3pm & 7-10.30pm
CHILDREN: Yes. Play area in garden
CREDIT CARDS: None taken
LICENSED: Full Licence
ACCOMMODATION: Not applicable

RESTAURANT: Not at the moment
BAR FOOD: Wide range.
  Home-cooked
VEGETARIAN: Always 10 dishes
ACCESS FOR THE DISABLED: Yes
GARDEN: Beer garden & play
  area

THE ASH TREE INN
Public House & Restaurant

Armitage Road,
Rugeley,
Staffordshire.

Tel: (0889) 578314

Canalside pubs always have great appeal and the Ash Tree Inn right beside Bridge No 62 of the Trent and Mersey Canal is everything this sort of establishment should be. It offers not only good car parking facilities but overnight moorings for waterborne visitors.

You will find The Ash Tree halfway between Rugeley and Armitage; a venue that is popular with people for miles around who come here regularly to enjoy the pleasant atmosphere of this up to date, stylish and comfortable inn. It has undergone many changes since the days it was just a General Store. It was acquired by Banks Brewery in December 1989 and they spent a lot of time and money to produce the pub it is today.

As you would expect, Banks traditional beers and lagers are very well kept. One large bar has darts, traditional pub games and there is a Boules sand pit. From May to October the large Patio area is the venue for Sunday Barbecues, rain or shine.

Banks have a good reputation for food and The Ash Tree is a fine example. The grills are excellent, especially The Ash Tree Mighty Mixed Grill, which is renowned. There are many home-cooked dishes to suit all tastes including Vegetarians. On Sunday in addition to the Barbecue there is a traditional Sunday lunch. Food is not served on Sunday evenings. You will find it exceptional quality and very good value for money.

USEFUL INFORMATION

OPEN: Apr-Oct: 12-11pm
   Nov-Mar: 12-3pm & 5.30-11pm
CHILDREN: Yes, large play area
CREDIT CARDS: No credit cards
LICENSED: Banks beers. Full Licence
ACCOMMODATION: Not applicable

RESTAURANT: Grills,
   home-cooked foods
BAR FOOD: Good pub fare
VEGETARIAN: At least 5 dishes
ACCESS FOR THE DISABLED:
   Level entrance
GARDEN: Patio, benches, tables &
   large BBQ

THE WHARF INN
Public House

Adbaston Road,
Shebdon,
Stafford

Tel: (0785) 280541

From the pub garden of The Wharf Inn you can see the old Aqueduct which carries Thomas Telford's Shropshire Union Canal. It is a tranquil place built originally to provide lodgings for the workmen who toiled for years to create the Telford dream.

Since Richard and Sue Busby took over the Wharf in 1990 they have worked painstakingly to redecorate and refurbish this attractive pub. Their aim has always been to acquire a reputation as good innkeepers who specialise in the excellence of their traditional ales, new varieties of which are always being added to the already popular range. This Freehouse has so much going for it. It is welcoming, serves good food as well as its ales and from The Wharf you can set off for any number of delightful walks or a trip to the stately Weston Park just 8 miles away. Good fishing is to be found along the canal and from time to time there are Steam Traction Rallies at Mill Meece closeby. Just being at The Wharf is pleasure enough.

You can eat in the bar or in the separate dining area and in summer sit outside to enjoy a drink and the scenery. Your children will be more than content with the safe playground that has been provided for them. If you are very hungry The Wharf Mixed Grill is for you. It is vast, and includes steak, chop, gammon, jumbo sausage, eggs, chips and a side salad. There are many tempting home-made dishes on the menu and traditional puddings. There is a Children's Menu as well.

USEFUL INFORMATION

OPEN: Mon-Fri: 6-11pm
   Sat: 12-3pm & 6-11pm
   Sun: 12-3pm & 6-11pm & 7-10.30pm
CHILDREN: Welcome
CREDIT CARDS: None taken
LICENSED: Freehouse. Real Ales
ACCOMMODATION: Not applicable

RESTAURANT: Full menu.
   Excellent
BAR FOOD: Huge portions. Wide
   choice
VEGETARIAN: Always 3 dishes
ACCESS FOR THE DISABLED:
   Yes. No problem
GARDEN: Ideal for children

GRANVILLES
Restaurant & Wine Bar

Granville Square,
Stone, Staffordshire.

Tel: (0785) 816658

Stone is a tranquil, picturesque canal town and in it, at the top of the High Street, shaded by the most northerly Plane tree in the country, is Granvilles, a restaurant and wine bar. What a delightful place it is, set in a row of Georgian properties. It was once the Corn Exchange and when Adam Jones bought the building 9 years ago, all sorts of old items were found in the attic, including an old ledger, which provided fascinating reading on the prices existent at that time.

In the last nine years the place has been transformed from a small cafe into this exciting business. Everything about it has a great deal of charm including the garden which was just an overgrown jungle. Hard work and green fingers produced this wonderful walled oasis, which won 'The Stone in Bloom' competition for small businesses last year. Granvilles is a favourite haunt of many people who have discovered its delights and passed on the news to their friends. Famous names including Cliff Richard and Paul Jones and other actors have visited the restaurant. Granvilles has long been established and is well known for the excellence of its food. This can be proved by the number of satisfied regular customers. The Wine Bar has only been open for two years but is proving equally successful, with classic bistro food, good wine and live music, mostly Jazz, from internationally famous acts, including George Melly, Aker Bilk, Humphrey Lyttleton, to less well known local groups. Do go there. It is super.

USEFUL INFORMATION

OPEN: Rest: Tues-Sat: 7-10pm
　　Wine Bar: Mon-Sat: 12-2pm & 7-10pm
CHILDREN: Permitted
CREDIT CARDS: Access/Visa/Amex
LICENSED: Wines. Draught beers.
　　Continental bottled beers
ACCOMMODATION: Not applicable

RESTAURANT: French, English,
　　all fresh
BAR FOOD: Classic Bistro.
　　Continental
VEGETARIAN: 4 Rest. 3 Bistro &
　　specials
ACCESS FOR THE DISABLED:
　　One shallow step
GARDEN: Walled patio garden

THE HARE AND HOUNDS
Inn

Stramshall,
Uttoxeter,
Staffordshire

Tel: (0889) 566778

Stramshall is a pretty village made even lovelier by the 400 year old Hare and Hounds where Linda and Bryan Moore welcome their customers. It has taken a while for them to create exactly the atmosphere that they wanted in this old coaching inn which still has an original postbox from that period. The transformation is a huge success and an ever increasing number of people come here to enjoy the food, the wines, and the beer, of course. The bar is known as 'Cobblers', an odd choice you might think but it acquired its name because the room was used as a cobblers shop until the 1950s.

One of the virtues of The Hare and Hounds is a separate dining room for non-smokers. There is also a function room used for private parties and if you wish to stay a night or two whilst you explore the nearby Wedgwood Museum or enjoy the beauty of Trentham Gardens, there are two well furnished double rooms with adjoining bathing facilities.

Linda is the house chef and prides herself on producing home-cooked fresh meals. The range is quite extensive and always includes daily specials. No one could possibly be hungry after a meal here; the portions are more than generous and extremely good value. Sunday lunches are strictly traditional with all the trimmings although Vegetarians will always find dishes to suit them.

USEFUL INFORMATION

OPEN: 12-3pm & 7-11pm
  Closed Tuesday lunchtime
CHILDREN: Welcome
CREDIT CARDS: None taken
LICENSED: Full Licence
ACCOMMODATION: 2 double rooms

RESTAURANT: Extensive
  home-cooked menu
BAR FOOD: Daily specials & bar
  meals
VEGETARIAN: At least 4 dishes
  daily
ACCESS FOR THE DISABLED: Yes
GARDEN: Small pretty garden.
  Large car park

THE RED LION

Public House & Restaurant

Thorncliffe,
Nr. Leek,
Staffordshire

Tel: (0538) 300325

Thorncliffe is only two miles out of Leek, you take the A53 Buxton road and turn right on to the Thorncliffe road about a half a mile out of the town. In the heart of the village is The Red Lion which has served the locals since 1787. Since that date it has been much extended but each time the old world atmosphere has been retained. Ron and Sheila Mitchell have owned the pub since 1984 and run it with their daughter and son-in-law who do the catering. This warm family atmosphere pervades the whole pub and makes it a very friendly place to visit.

The Red Lion has comfortable bars and a separate restaurant. It is also able to provide Conference facilities. It is a welcome stopping place for coach parties - the coach driver is always given a courtesy meal. The large car park saves drivers the worry of looking for a place to leave their car. In the garden there is a safe place for children to play complete with special equipment. Ideal in fact for families.

The food on offer is traditional, home cooked and whenever possible fresh local produce is used. Juicy steaks are cooked to perfection, and for people who enjoy fish there are several dishes. The Red Lion is Vegetarian recommended so there are always at least eight dishes from which to choose. Salads accompanied by Home-cooked Roast Beef, Chicken, Prawns or Cheese tempt many people. There is a Childrens Menu and a good range of freshly cut sandwiches. Try the Sunday lunch.

USEFUL INFORMATION

OPEN: Mon-Fri: 7-11pm
 Sat: 12-3pm & 6-11pm
 Sun: 12-3pm & 7-10.30pm
CHILDREN: With diners
CREDIT CARDS: Access/Visa
LICENSED: Full Licence
ACCOMMODATION: Not applicable

RESTAURANT: Traditional
 home-cooked
BAR FOOD: Wide range
VEGETARIAN: Always 8 dishes
ACCESS FOR THE DISABLED:
 Yes. Ramps & toilets
GARDEN: Yes. Childrens play
 area. Car park

THE ROEBUCK
Inn

Dovebank,
Uttoxeter,
Staffordshire.

Tel: (0889) 565563

Half a mile from Uttoxeter's pretty racecourse and just 5 minutes walk from the Town Centre, you will find The Roebuck Inn. It is so conveniently sited on the main route for Alton Towers, Tutbury Castle, The Potteries and many other places.

The age of the pub is uncertain. Certainly it goes back to the beginning of the 1600s and probably earlier. It is constructed of brick-quarry tile, has wonderful oak beams, inglenooks and a fine open log fire place. David Lankester and John Smith, the Proprietors and their wives have developed The Roebuck into one of the most popular pubs in the area. With 2 comfortable bedrooms available, it is an ideal place in which to stay either on business or as a base from which to explore the area as well as the Peak District National Park. There is excellent fishing, game and coarse, locally, and shooting facilities in the immediate area. The large beer garden is an attractive area in which to relax on a sunny day.

Freshly cooked specialities and country fare are the backbone of the food served in The Roebuck. All meals are cooked to order so please be a little patient. One of the house specialities is 'Chicken Roebuck Style' - a large boneless breast of chicken, stuffed with ham, cheese and herbs and gently cooked with white wine, garlic, mushrooms and fresh cream. Absolutely delicious and comes to the table with an assortment of fresh vegetables.

USEFUL INFORMATION

OPEN: Weekdays: 11-11pm
Sun: 12-3pm & 7-10.30pm
CHILDREN: Yes. Ante room & beer garden
CREDIT CARDS: None taken
LICENSED: Full Licence. Real Ales
ACCOMMODATION: 2 double

RESTAURANT: Freshly cooked fare. Set 3 course Sunday lunch
BAR FOOD: Fresh cut & carved to order
VEGETARIAN: Available
ACCESS FOR THE DISABLED: Yes
GARDEN: Beer garden, tables & benches

THE GREYHOUND INN

Inn

Warslow
Nr. Buxton,
Derbyshire.

Tel: (0298) 84249

Anyone wanting a run out from Leek or from Buxton would be well advised to turn their cars in the direction of the village of Warslow which stands 1000ft above sea level towards the southern end of the Peak District. The local scenery is both beautiful and dramatic. It is adjacent to many walks including the Manifold Valley - an old railway line, the Tissington Trail and the mountainous peaks of The Roaches.

In the heart of the village is The Greyhound Inn owned and run by two friendly people, David and Dale Mullarkey. The pub takes its name from the Buxton to Uttoxeter coach, which used to stop at the inn to rest its horses, and allow the passengers a chance to get refreshment. It also used to be half farm and half inn with cattle sales taking place at the rear of the pub. The Greyhound is said to be haunted although no sitings have been witnessed recently. You can well imagine it though, and understand any ghost wanting to remain in this attractive and comfortable pub, with its long beamed bar and cushioned antique settles. There is a large log fire in the lounge and an open fire in the tap room. In summer there are rustic seats with tables under Ash trees in the Beer Garden. The food is good home-made fare with a special mention for the crisp, home-made chips. Accommodation is available too, not en-suite but comfortable, clean and decorated in a cosy cottage style.

USEFUL INFORMATION

OPEN: 12-2pm & 7-11pm
CHILDREN: Until 9pm in Tap & Garden
CREDIT CARDS: None taken
LICENSED: Full Licence
ACCOMMODATION: 4 rooms. Not en-suite

RESTAURANT: Not applicable
BAR FOOD: Good selection, many home-cooked
VEGETARIAN: At least 2 daily + salads etc
ACCESS FOR THE DISABLED: Level at front
GARDEN: Beer garden. Ample parking

Gothic Gazebo at Tong

INDEX TO PLACES AND VENUES

A

Abbots Bromley 313
Alcester 26
Allesley 71 *The Rainbow Inn* 71, 77
Alstonfield 317 *The George* 317, 314
Archenfield 158-160
Arlescote 12
Arle 61 *The New Inn* 61, 78
Atherstone 73-74 *The Gate Inn* 74, 7 *The White Lion* 74, 80

B

Badger 227
Bala 267
Barton under Needwoo 311-31 *The Shoulder of Mutton* 312, 325
Bascote 34
Bearley Cross 29 *Golden Cross Inn* 29
Bedworth 73 *The Mount Pleasant Inn* 73, 81
Berrow 113 *The Duke of York* 113, 121
Bewdley 60 *The Great Western* 82
Bickenhill 71
Birdsgreen 227
Birmingham 10, 68-71
Birtsmorten 11Bishops Frome 144-145, 156 *The Green Dragon* 145, 176
Boscobel 211-212
Bournville 69
Bradnor Hill 170
Brampton Bryan 170-171
Bredwardine 165
Bretforton 107 *Fleece Inn* 107
Brewood 300
Bridgnorth 225-7 *The Carpenters Arms* 226, 235 *The Falcon Hotel* 225, 236
Brierley Hill 65
Broadheath 104
Brockhampton 145
Brockton 224-5 *The Feathers* 237
Bromsgrove 58
Bromyard 145 *The Falcon* 145
Broseley 222-223 *The Forester Arms* 223, 238
Brownhills 68 *The Terrace Restaurant* 68, 83
Burslem 319
Burton Dasset 14-15
Burton upon Trent 312
Butterton 316 *The Black Lion* 316, 326

C

Callow End 118 *The Old Bush* 122
Calverhall 277-8 *The Old Jack Inn* 277, 282
Cannock Chase 68
Carey 157 *The Cottage of Content* 157, 177
Castle Pulverbach 234 *The Woodcock Inn* 234, 239
Castlemorton 113
Chaddesley Corbett 59
Cheddleton 319 *The Red Lion* 319, 327

Chemistry 277
Chesterton 34
Chillington 301
Chirk 268-9 *Plas Y Waun Inn* 269, 283
Church Lench 106
Church Stretton 231-2 *Acorn Wholefood Restaurant* 232, 240
Claverley 227, *The Plough Inn* 227, 235
Clunton 230-31 *The Crown Inn* 230, 242
Coalbrookdale 216-217
Coalport 220
Cookley 62 *The Eagle and Spur* 62, 84
Corley Moor 71 *The Red Lion* 85
Cosford 207-209
Coventry 10, 72-73 *The Prince William Henry* 86
Croswall 164
Craven Arms 229-30 *Stokesay Castle Hotel* 229, 243
Crowle 105-106

D

Darfur Crags 316
Dinmore 149-150
Donnington 207 *The Champion Jockey* 207, 244
Dormston 106
Dorridge 71 *The Forest Hotel* 71, 87
Dorstone 166
Droitwich 56 *The Eagle and Sun* 88
Dudley 65

E

Eardisland 168-169
Eardisley 166 *The New Inn* 166, 178
Earl's Croome 111 *The Yorkshire Grey* 111, 123
Eastnor 112
Eccleshall 303-4 *The Country Kitchen* 304, 328 *St George Hotel* 304, 329
Edgehill 11-12
Ellesmere 262, 269-273
English Frankton 275
Escley Brook 164
Evesham 107

F

Farnborough 14
Fazeley 74
Fenton 319
Fladbury 109
Flash 317
Franton *The Friendly Inn* 40

G

Garway 160
Gaydon 15 *The Gaydon Inn* 15, 41
Gledrid 269 *The New Inn* 269, 284
Gnosall 312
Golden Valley 161
Goodrich 141 *The Crosskeys Inn* 141, 179

Great Malvern 113
Grimley 119
Grindley Brook 277

H

Halesowen 65 *The Why Not Inn* 65, 89
Hampton-in-Aden 71
Hampton Lucy 26 *The Boars Head* 26, 42
Hanley, Staffs 319-321 *Il Mago Restaurant* 321, 330
Hanley, Worcs 112
Hanmer 274 *The Hanmer Arms* 285
Hanbury 34 *The Gamecock* 43
Harewood End 158 *Harewood End Inn* 158, 180
Hawksmoor 315
Hay Bluff 164
Hay on Wye 164-165
Henley-in-Arden 29
Hereford 151-155 *Gilbies* 153, 181
Highley 228 *Bache Arms* 228, 245
Hoarwithy 157
Hockley 69
Hodnet 280
Honington 17

I

Ilam 316
Inkberrow 106 *The Bulls Head Hotel* 124
Ironbridge 214-223 *The Coracle* 215, 246 *The Library House* 214

J

Jackfield 221

K

Kempsey 118-119 *The Huntsman Inn* 119, 125 *The Walter De Cantelupe inn* 118, 126
Kentchurch 161-162 *The Bridge inn* 161, 182
Kidderminster 58 *The Little Tumbling Sailor* 90
Kidsgrove 322
Kilpeck 159-160
Kingswinford 64
Kington 106 *The Red Hart Inn* 106, 127
Kington (Herefordshire) 169-170 *The Queens Head* 170, 183 *The White Pheasant* 169, 184
Kinver 62 *The Whittington Inn* 62, 91
Kinwarton 27
Knighton 170 *The Geoge and Dragon* 170, 185
Knockin 262
Knowbury 229 *The Bennetts End Inn* 229, 247
Knowle 71
Kyre Park 145

L

Leamington Spa 32-33
Ledbury 112, 142-144 *Feathers Inn* 143 *The Talbot* 143
Leek 318 *The Quiet Woman* 318, 331
Leominster 146-149 *Barons Cross Inn* 149, 186 *The Black Horse Coach House* 149, 187 *The White Lion* 147, 188

Letton 171 *The Swan Inn* 171, 189
Lichfield 310-311
Lilleshall 205
Little Dawley 214 *The Red Lion* 248
Little Malvern 113
Little Stretton 231 *The Green Dragon* 231, 149
Llangedwyn 267 *The Green Inn* 287
Llangollen 273
Llansantffraid-Ym-Mechain 264 *The Sun Hotel* 264, 286
Llanymnech 264
Llynclys 267
Long Itchington 33 *The Two Boats* 44
Long Lawford *The Sheaf and Sickle* 45
Longnor 317 *Parrotts* 317, 333
Longton 319
Loppington 274-5
Lower Broadheath 119
Lower Moor 109 *The Old Chestnut Tree* 128
Lower Wick 105
Lower Quinton 18 *The College Arms* 46
Ludford Bridge 228 *Charlton Arms Hotel* 250
Ludlow 228

M

Madeley 213-214
Madley 167 *The Red Lion* 167
Madresfield 118
Malvern 113-117 *Malvern Link* 113
Malvern Wells 113 *Cottage in the Woods Hotel* 113, 129
Market Drayton 262, 277-9 *The Clive and Coffyne* 279, 288
Martley 119-120
Meece Brook 304
Melverley 263
Merbach Hill 166
Meon Hill 18
Meriden 71
Michaelchurch Escley 163-164 *The Bridge Inn* 164, 191
Middle Littleton 107
Moccas 167
Mordiford 155
Montford Bridge 234 *Wingfield Arms Hotel* 234, 251
Moreton Say 279
Mortimer's Cross 171-172
Much Marcle 142
Much Wenlock 223-224

N

Nantwich 268
Newcastle under Lyme 305, 319, 322
Newport 206 *Pheasant Inn* 206, 252
Newtown 273
Norton-in-Hales 278-9 *The Hinds Head Inn* 289
Nuneaton 73 *Badgers Wine Bar* 73, 92

O

Oakamoor 315 *The Lord Nelson* 315, 333

Offchurch 33
Old Oswestry 267
Oswestry 262, 265-7 *The Grape Escape* 265, 290
Oulton 306 *The Wheatsheaf* 306, 334
P
Pant 263 *The Cross Guns* 263, 291
Penkridge 299 *The Horse and Jockey* 335
Pershore 109-110 *The Imperial Restaurant* 110, 130
Pontrilas 162-163
Pound Green 61
Powick 118
Priors Frome 156 *The Yew Tree Inn* 156, 192
Priest Weston 232 *The Miners Arms* 232, 253
Priors Marston 38 *The Hollybush Inn* 38, 47
Priorslee 207 *The Lion Inn* 207, 254

Q
Quatt 227

R
Radway 11 *The Castle Inn* 12
Ratcliffe Culey 74 *The Gate Inn* 79
Ratley 15
Redditch 57 *The Hotel Montville* 57, 93
Ross on Wye 137-139 *Cloisters Wine Bar* 139, 193
Fresh Grounds 139, 194 *Pheasant's Restaurant* 138, 195 *Rosswyn Hotel* 139, 196
Royal Leamington Spa 32-33 *Jephson's Restaurant* 48 *The Leamington Rendezvous* 49
Rugby 34-36
Rugeley 309 *The Ash Tree* 309, 336
Ryton-on-Dunsmore 36

S
Sellack 158 *The Lough Pool Inn* 158, 197
Shallowford 304
Shatterford 61 *The Red Lion* 61, 94
Shebdon 303 *The Wharf Inn* 303, 337
Shifnal 209 *The Nell Gwyn* 209, 255
Shottery 25
Shrewsbury 232-234 *The Cornhouse Restaurant* 234, 256
Shuckburgh 37-38
Southam 34
St Johns (Worcester) 105 *The Crown Inn* 131
Stafford 306-309
Stoke on trent 305, 319
Stoke Prior 57, 149 *The Lamb Inn* 149, 198
Stone 305 *Granvilles* 305, 338
Stonleigh 36
Stourbridge 64
Stourport-on-Severn 60 *The Black Star* 60, 95
Stramshall 313 *The Hare and Hounds* 313, 339
Stratford-upon-Avon 10-11, 19-25 *The Oddfellows Arms* 50 *Sorrento Restaurant* 51 *Black Swan* 23
Symonds Yat 140

T
Tamworth 74-75 *The White Lion* 76

Telford 204-205 *Carols* 205, 257
Temple Balsall 71
Tenbury Wells 146 *Cadmore Lodge Hotel* 146, 199 *Royal Oak Hotel* 146, 200
Tewkesbury 100
Thorncliffe 318 *The Red Lion* 318, 340
Thorngrove 119
Tibberton 207 *The Sutherland Arms* 207, 258
Tong 212-213
Toothill Wood 315
Tunstall 319
Tysoe 15

U
Upper Quinton 18
Upton upon Severn 110-111 *The White Lion* 111
Uttoxeter 313 *The Roebuck Inn* 313, 341

W
Wall under Heywood 232 *The Plough* 232, 259
Walsall 67 *The Oak Inn* 67, 96
Warmington 12-13
Warslow 316 *The Greyhound inn* 316, 342
Warwick 30-32 *The Cape of Good Hope* 31, 52
Welford-on-Avon 19
Welsh Frankton 273
Welsh Newton 158-159
Welshpool 263-264, 273
Wem 262, 274
Weobley 167-168 *Ye Olde Salutation Inn* 168, 201
West Felton 266
West Malvern 113
Weston-on-Avon 19
Weston under Lizard 210, 301-2
Whitchurch 262, 275-7 *The cherry tree Hotel* 277, 292 *Debbie's Restaurant* 277, 293
Whittington 268 *The Narrow Boat* 268, 292 *Penrhos Arms* 268, 295
Wichenford 119
Willoughbridge 322-3
Wilmcote 25
Woodgate 59 *The Gate Hangs Well* 97
Wooten Wawen 28 *The Golden Cross Inn* 53
Worcester 100-105 *Coppertops* 132 *The Real Sandwich Shop* 133

Leisure in Print Publications

24-26 George Place, Stonehouse, Plymouth Devon PL1 3NY
Tel: (0752) 265956/7   Fax. (0752) 603588

Dear Reader

I hope you have enjoyed the selection of places in which you can lunch, dine, stay or visit. I have enjoyed researching and writing this book.

It would make the next edition more exciting if you would contribute by suggesting places that could be included and your comments on any establishment you have visited would be much appreciated. In return, I will be very happy to send you a complimentary copy of one of the other books in this series or an 'Invitation' 'T' shirt. The choice is yours.

I enjoy corresponding with my readers and look forward to hearing from you.

Bon appetit!

Yours sincerely,

Joy David

AN INVITATION
TO
LUNCH, DINE, STAY & VISIT

The following titles are currently available in this series:

To order please tick as appropriate:

Devon & Cornwall	☐	£6.20 inc p&p
Somerset, Avon & Glos	☐	£6.20 inc p&p
East Anglia	☐	£7.20 inc p&p
Mid-Shires	☐	£7.20 inc p&p

To follow in Spring 1993

Wales	☐	£7.20 inc p&p
Yorkshire	☐	£7.20 inc p&p
North East Counties	☐	£7.20 inc p&p
North West Counties	☐	£7.20 inc p&p
Southern England	☐	£7.20 inc p&p
Thames & Chilterns	☐	£7.20 inc p&p

NAME ....

ADDRESS ....

....

....

Tel: No (daytime)

Please make cheques payable to Leisure in Print
**Leisure in Print, 24-26 George Place, Stonehouse,
Plymouth PL1 2NY. Tel: (0752) 265956**

READER'S COMMENTS

Please use this page to tell us about Pubs, Hotels and places of interest that have appealed to you especially.

We will pass on your approval where it is merited and equally report back to the venue any **complaints.** We hope the latter will be few and far between.

Please post to: Joy David, Leisure in Print, 24-26 George Place, Stonehouse, Plymouth PL1 3NY and expect to receive a book or 'T' shirt as a token of our appreciation.

Name and Address of Establishment	Your recommendation or complaint

Your Name (Block Capitals Please) ....

Address ....

....

....

READER'S COMMENTS

Please use this page to tell us about Pubs, Hotels and places of interest that have appealed to you especially.

We will pass on your approval where it is merited and equally report back to the venue any **complaints.** We hope the latter will be few and far between.

Please post to: Joy David, Leisure in Print, 24-26 George Place, Stonehouse, Plymouth PL1 3NY and expect to receive a book or 'T' shirt as a token of our appreciation.

Name and Address of Establishment	Your recommendation or complaint

Your Name (Block Capitals Please) ....

Address ....

....

....

READER'S COMMENTS

Please use this page to tell us about Pubs, Hotels and places of interest that have appealed to you especially.

We will pass on your approval where it is merited and equally report back to the venue any **complaints.** We hope the latter will be few and far between.

Please post to: Joy David, Leisure in Print, 24-26 George Place, Stonehouse, Plymouth PL1 3NY and expect to receive a book or 'T' shirt as a token of our appreciation.

Name and Address of Establishment	Your recommendation or complaint

Your Name (Block Capitals Please) ....

Address ....

....

....

READER'S COMMENTS

Please use this page to tell us about Pubs, Hotels and places of interest that have appealed to you especially.

We will pass on your approval where it is merited and equally report back to the venue any **complaints.** We hope the latter will be few and far between.

Please post to: Joy David, Leisure in Print, 24-26 George Place, Stonehouse, Plymouth PL1 3NY and expect to receive a book or 'T' shirt as a token of our appreciation.

Name and Address of Establishment	Your recommendation or complaint

Your Name (Block Capitals Please) ....

Address ....

....

....